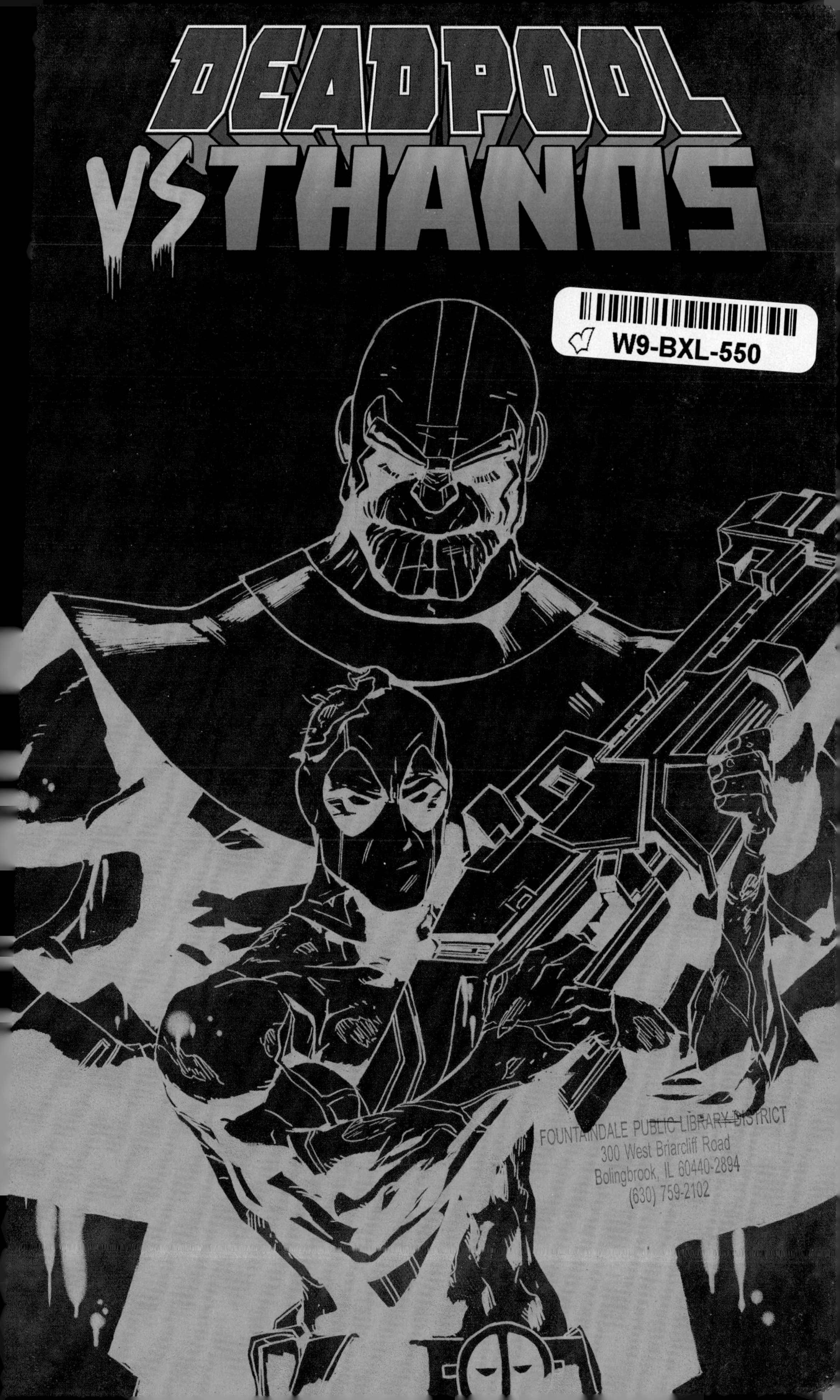
DEADPOOL
VS THANOS

COLLECTION EDITOR ALEX STARBUCK

ASSISTANT EDITOR SARAH BRUNSTAD

EDITORS, SPECIAL PROJECTS JENNIFER GRÜNWALD & MARK D. BEAZLEY

SENIOR EDITOR, SPECIAL PROJECTS JEFF YOUNGQUIST

SVP PRINT, SALES & MARKETING DAVID GABRIEL

BOOK DESIGNER ADAM DEL RE

EDITOR IN CHIEF AXEL ALONSO

CHIEF CREATIVE OFFICER JOE QUESADA

PUBLISHER DAN BUCKLEY

EXECUTIVE PRODUCER ALAN FINE

DEADPOOL VS. THANOS. Contains material originally published in magazine form as DEADPOOL VS. THANOS #1-4. First printing 2015. ISBN# 978-0-7851-9845-1. Published by MARVEL WORLDWIDE, INC., a subsidiary of MARVEL ENTERTAINMENT, LLC. OFFICE OF PUBLICATION: 135 West 50th Street, New York, NY 10020. Copyright © 2015 MARVEL. No similarity between any of the names, characters, persons, and/or institutions in this magazine with those of any living or dead person or institution is intended, and any such similarity which may exist is purely coincidental. Printed in Canada. ALAN FINE, President, Marvel Entertainment; DAN BUCKLEY, President, TV, Publishing and Brand Management; JOE QUESADA, Chief Creative Officer; TOM BREVOORT, SVP of Publishing; DAVID BOGART, SVP of Operations & Procurement, Publishing; C.B. CEBULSKI, VP of International Development & Brand Management; DAVID GABRIEL, SVP Print, Sales & Marketing; JIM O'KEEFE, VP of Operations & Logistics; DAN CARR, Executive Director of Publishing Technology; SUSAN CRESPI, Editorial Operations Manager; ALEX MORALES, Publishing Operations Manager; STAN LEE, Chairman Emeritus. For information regarding advertising in Marvel Comics or on Marvel.com, please contact Jonathan Rheingold, VP of Custom Solutions & Ad Sales, at jrheingold@marvel.com. For Marvel subscription inquiries, please call 800-217-9158. Manufactured between 10/2/2015 and 11/9/2015 by SOLISCO PRINTERS, SCOTT, QC, CANADA.

10 9 8 7 6 5 4 3 2 1

DEADPOOL VS THANOS

WRITER
TIM SEELEY

ARTIST
ELMO BONDOC

COLORIST
RUTH REDMOND

LETTERER
VC's JOE SABINO

COVER ART
TRADD MOORE & MATT WILSON

ASSISTANT EDITOR
HEATHER ANTOS

EDITOR
JORDAN D. WHITE

DEADPOOL CREATED BY ROB LIEFELD & FABIAN NICIEZA

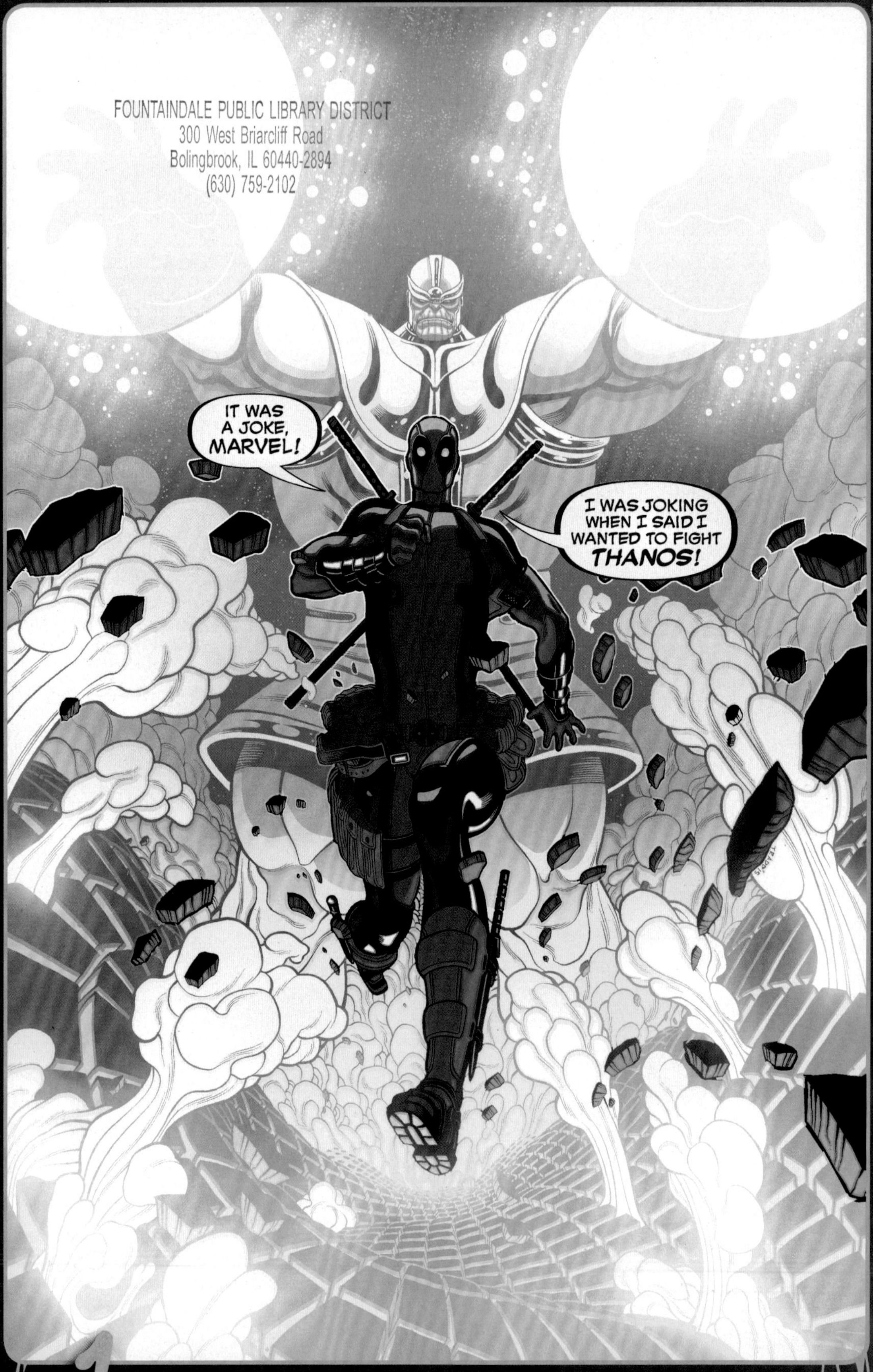
IT WAS A JOKE, MARVEL!
I WAS JOKING WHEN I SAID I WANTED TO FIGHT THANOS!

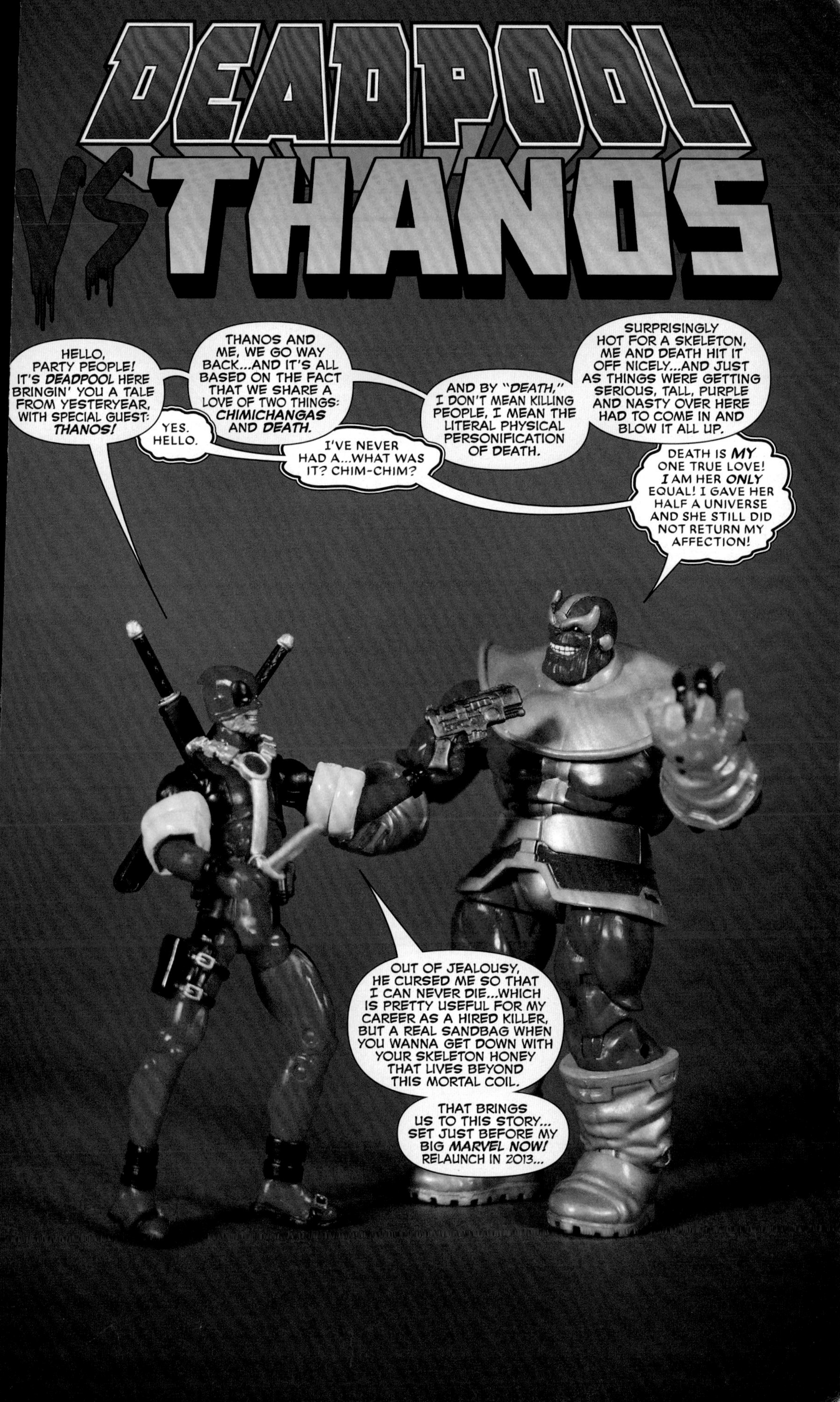
DEADPOOL VS THANOS
HELLO, PARTY PEOPLE! IT'S DEADPOOL HERE BRINGIN' YOU A TALE FROM YESTERYEAR, WITH SPECIAL GUEST: THANOS!
YES. HELLO.
THANOS AND ME, WE GO WAY BACK...AND IT'S ALL BASED ON THE FACT THAT WE SHARE A LOVE OF TWO THINGS: CHIMICHANGAS AND DEATH.
I'VE NEVER HAD A...WHAT WAS IT? CHIM-CHIM?
AND BY "DEATH," I DON'T MEAN KILLING PEOPLE, I MEAN THE LITERAL PHYSICAL PERSONIFICATION OF DEATH.
SURPRISINGLY HOT FOR A SKELETON, ME AND DEATH HIT IT OFF NICELY...AND JUST AS THINGS WERE GETTING SERIOUS, TALL, PURPLE AND NASTY OVER HERE HAD TO COME IN AND BLOW IT ALL UP.
DEATH IS MY ONE TRUE LOVE! I AM HER ONLY EQUAL! I GAVE HER HALF A UNIVERSE AND SHE STILL DID NOT RETURN MY AFFECTION!
OUT OF JEALOUSY, HE CURSED ME SO THAT I CAN NEVER DIE...WHICH IS PRETTY USEFUL FOR MY CAREER AS A HIRED KILLER, BUT A REAL SANDBAG WHEN YOU WANNA GET DOWN WITH YOUR SKELETON HONEY THAT LIVES BEYOND THIS MORTAL COIL.
THAT BRINGS US TO THIS STORY... SET JUST BEFORE MY BIG MARVEL NOW! RELAUNCH IN 2013...

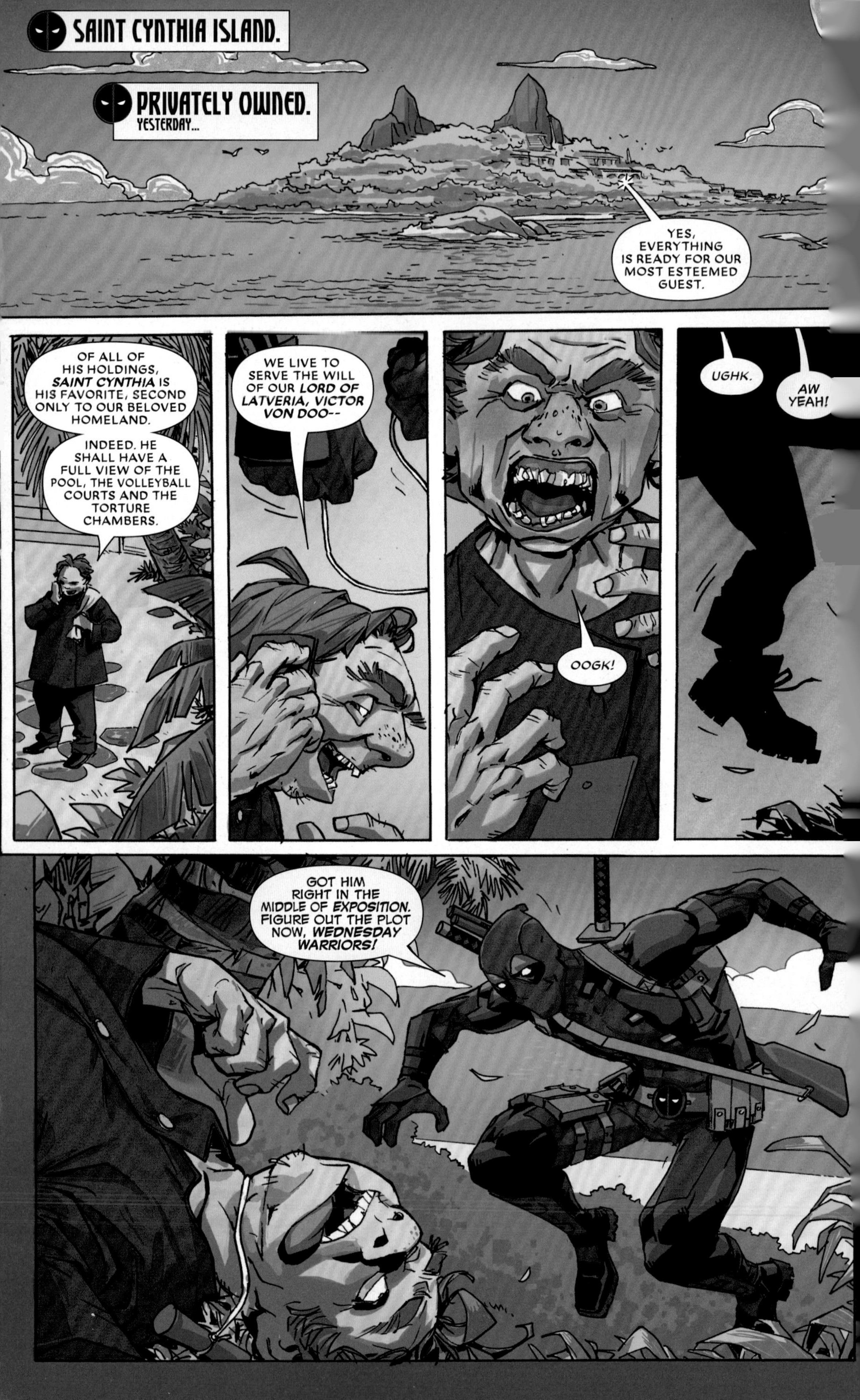
SAINT CYNTHIA ISLAND.
PRIVATELY OWNED. YESTERDAY...
YES, EVERYTHING IS READY FOR OUR MOST ESTEEMED GUEST.
OF ALL OF HIS HOLDINGS, SAINT CYNTHIA IS HIS FAVORITE, SECOND ONLY TO OUR BELOVED HOMELAND.
INDEED. HE SHALL HAVE A FULL VIEW OF THE POOL, THE VOLLEYBALL COURTS AND THE TORTURE CHAMBERS.
WE LIVE TO SERVE THE WILL OF OUR LORD OF LATVERIA, VICTOR VON DOO--
OOGK!
UGHK.
AW YEAH!
GOT HIM RIGHT IN THE MIDDLE OF EXPOSITION. FIGURE OUT THE PLOT NOW, WEDNESDAY WARRIORS!

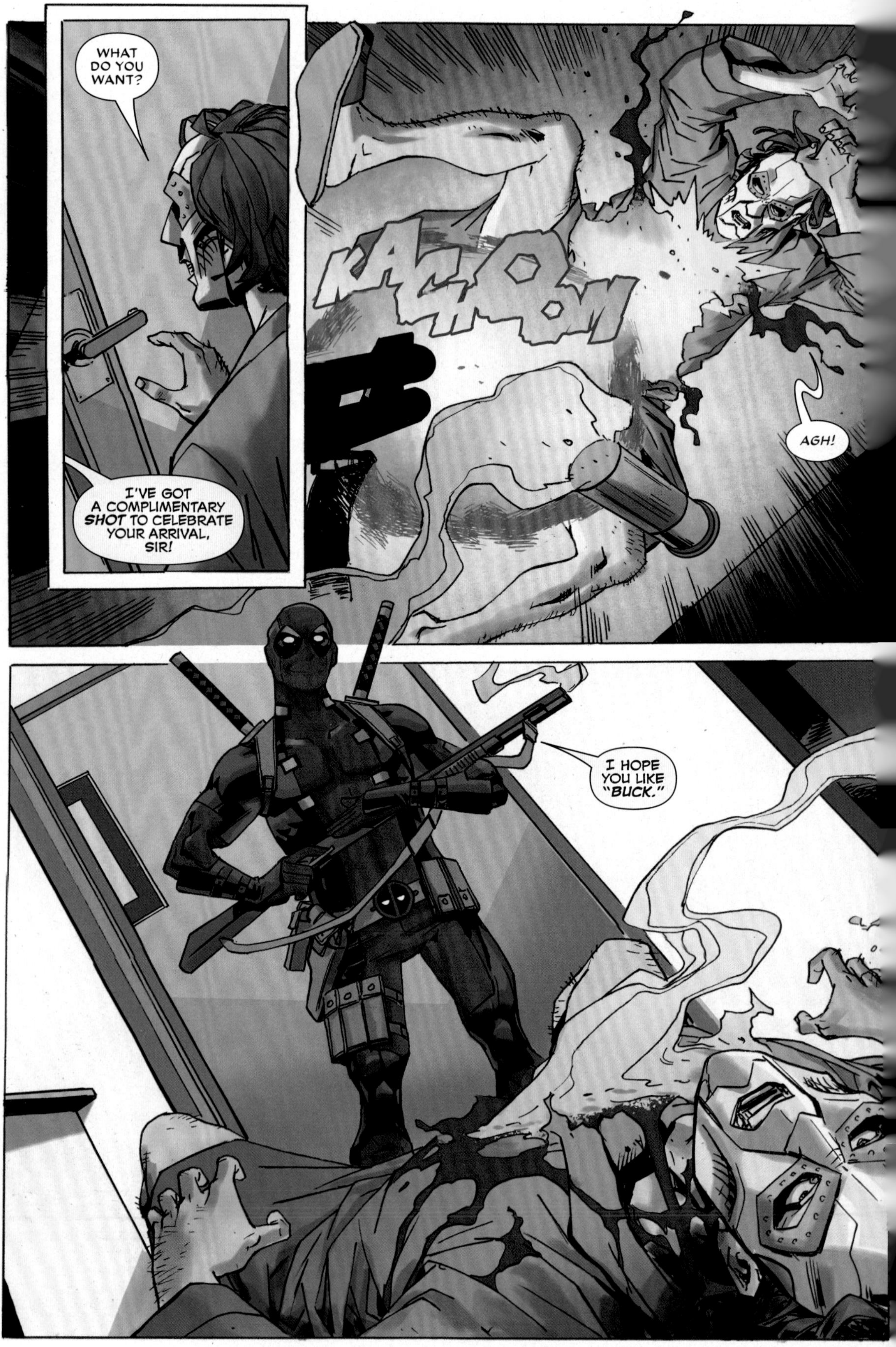
WHAT DO YOU WANT?
I'VE GOT A COMPLIMENTARY *SHOT* TO CELEBRATE YOUR ARRIVAL, SIR!
KACHOOM
AGH!
I HOPE YOU LIKE "*BUCK.*"

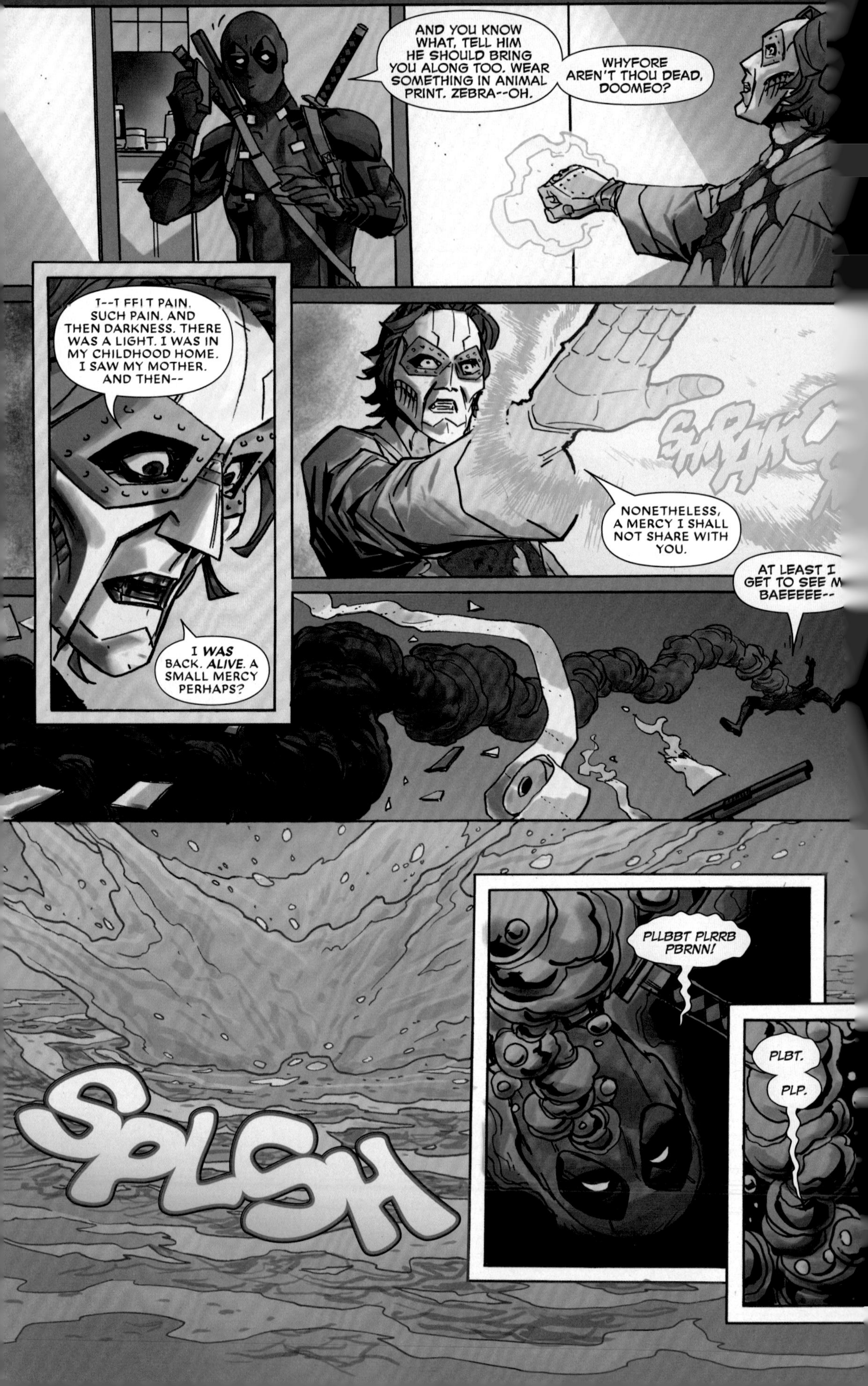
AND YOU KNOW WHAT, TELL HIM HE SHOULD BRING YOU ALONG TOO. WEAR SOMETHING IN ANIMAL PRINT. ZEBRA--OH.
WHYFORE AREN'T THOU DEAD, DOOMEO?
I--I FELT PAIN. SUCH PAIN. AND THEN DARKNESS. THERE WAS A LIGHT. I WAS IN MY CHILDHOOD HOME. I SAW MY MOTHER. AND THEN--
I *WAS* BACK. *ALIVE.* A SMALL MERCY PERHAPS?
NONETHELESS, A MERCY I SHALL NOT SHARE WITH YOU.
AT LEAST I GET TO SEE M BAEEEEE--
SPLSH
PLLBBT PLRRB PBRNN!
PLBT.
PLP.

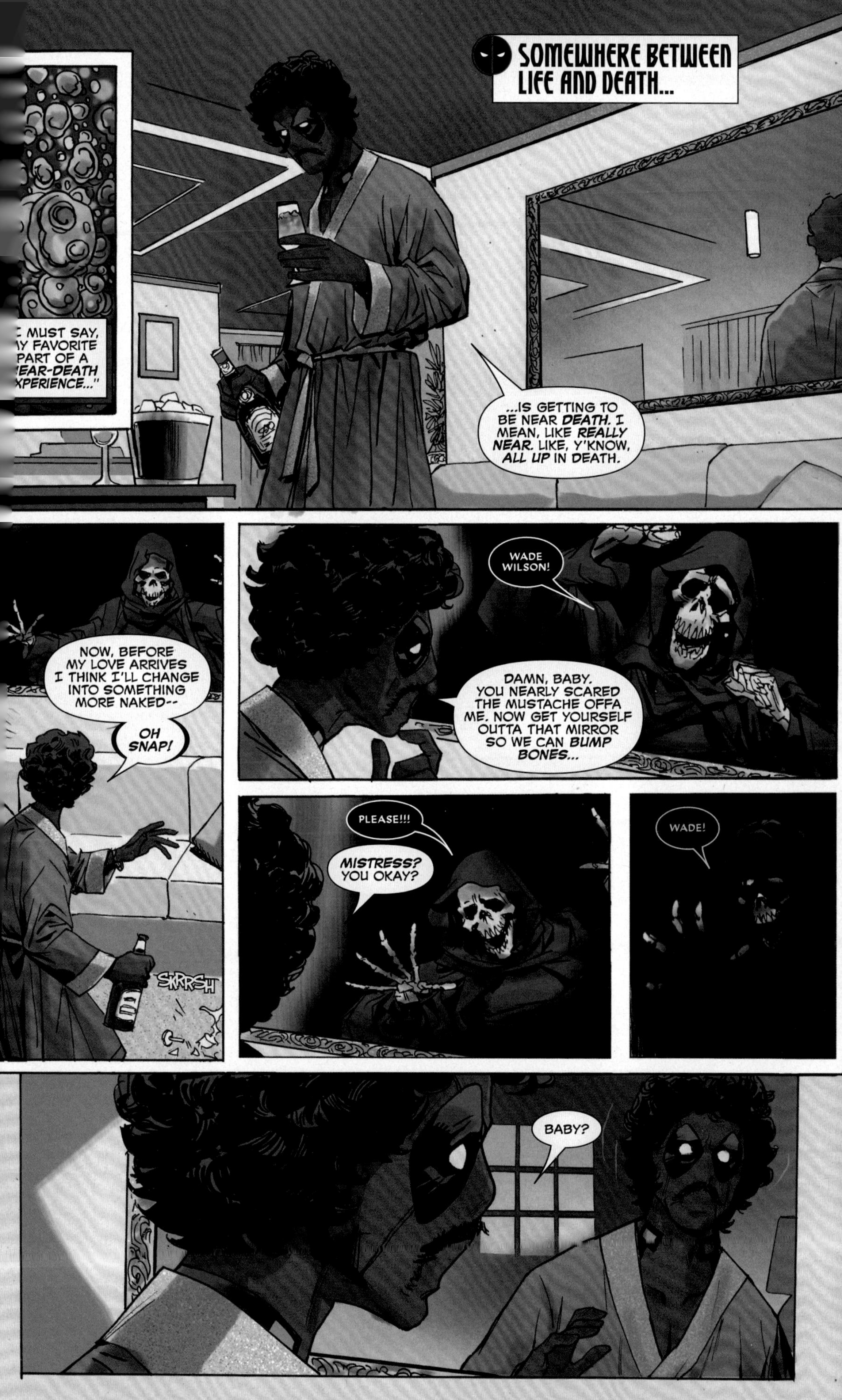
SOMEWHERE BETWEEN LIFE AND DEATH...
MUST SAY, MY FAVORITE PART OF A EAR-DEATH XPERIENCE..."
...IS GETTING TO BE NEAR DEATH. I MEAN, LIKE REALLY NEAR. LIKE, Y'KNOW, ALL UP IN DEATH.
NOW, BEFORE MY LOVE ARRIVES I THINK I'LL CHANGE INTO SOMETHING MORE NAKED--
OH SNAP!
SKRRSH
WADE WILSON!
DAMN, BABY. YOU NEARLY SCARED THE MUSTACHE OFFA ME. NOW GET YOURSELF OUTTA THAT MIRROR SO WE CAN BUMP BONES...
PLEASE!!!
MISTRESS? YOU OKAY?
WADE!
BABY?

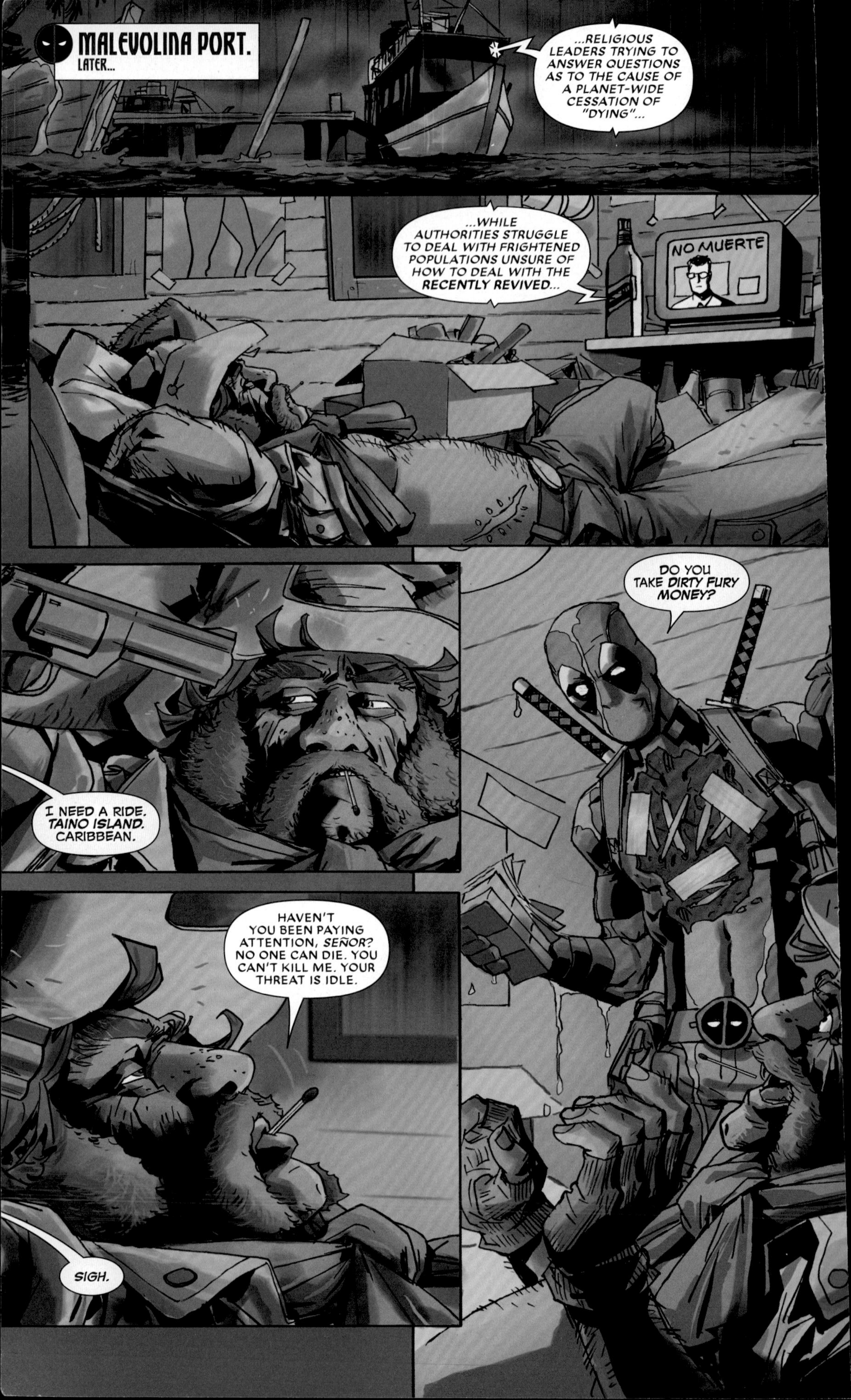
MALEVOLINA PORT.
LATER...
...RELIGIOUS LEADERS TRYING TO ANSWER QUESTIONS AS TO THE CAUSE OF A PLANET-WIDE CESSATION OF "DYING"...
...WHILE AUTHORITIES STRUGGLE TO DEAL WITH FRIGHTENED POPULATIONS UNSURE OF HOW TO DEAL WITH THE RECENTLY REVIVED...
NO MUERTE
I NEED A RIDE. TAINO ISLAND. CARIBBEAN.
DO YOU TAKE DIRTY FURY MONEY?
HAVEN'T YOU BEEN PAYING ATTENTION, SEÑOR? NO ONE CAN DIE. YOU CAN'T KILL ME. YOUR THREAT IS IDLE.
SIGH.

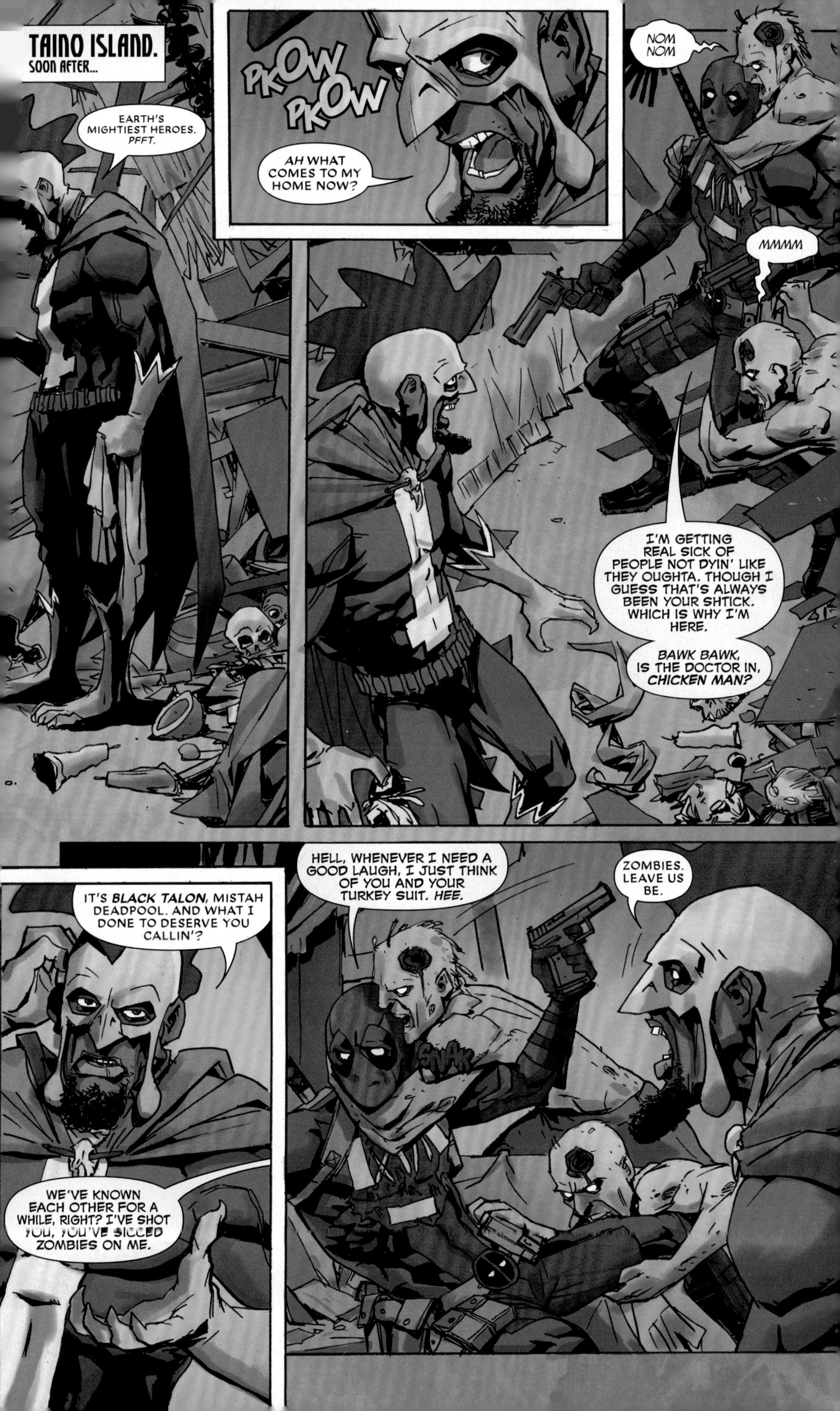
TAINO ISLAND.
SOON AFTER...
EARTH'S MIGHTIEST HEROES. PFFT.
PKOW PKOW
AH WHAT COMES TO MY HOME NOW?
NOM NOM
MMMM
I'M GETTING REAL SICK OF PEOPLE NOT DYIN' LIKE THEY OUGHTA. THOUGH I GUESS THAT'S ALWAYS BEEN YOUR SHTICK. WHICH IS WHY I'M HERE.
BAWK BAWK, IS THE DOCTOR IN, CHICKEN MAN?
IT'S BLACK TALON, MISTAH DEADPOOL. AND WHAT I DONE TO DESERVE YOU CALLIN'?
WE'VE KNOWN EACH OTHER FOR A WHILE, RIGHT? I'VE SHOT YOU, YOU'VE SICCED ZOMBIES ON ME.
HELL, WHENEVER I NEED A GOOD LAUGH, I JUST THINK OF YOU AND YOUR TURKEY SUIT. HEE.
ZOMBIES. LEAVE US BE.
SNAK

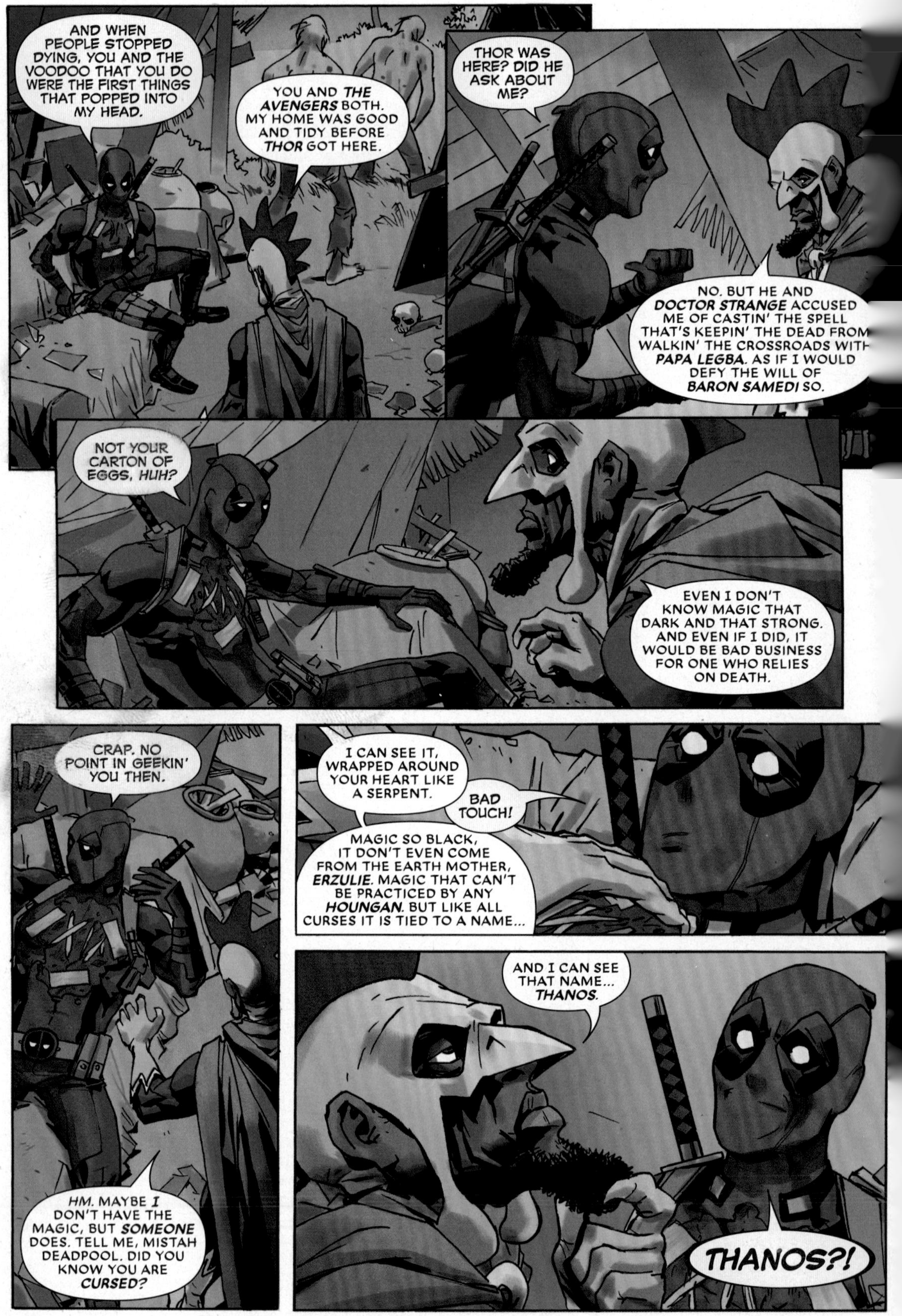
AND WHEN PEOPLE STOPPED DYING, YOU AND THE VOODOO THAT YOU DO WERE THE FIRST THINGS THAT POPPED INTO MY HEAD.
YOU AND THE AVENGERS BOTH. MY HOME WAS GOOD AND TIDY BEFORE THOR GOT HERE.
THOR WAS HERE? DID HE ASK ABOUT ME?
NO. BUT HE AND DOCTOR STRANGE ACCUSED ME OF CASTIN' THE SPELL THAT'S KEEPIN' THE DEAD FROM WALKIN' THE CROSSROADS WITH PAPA LEGBA. AS IF I WOULD DEFY THE WILL OF BARON SAMEDI SO.
NOT YOUR CARTON OF EGGS, HUH?
EVEN I DON'T KNOW MAGIC THAT DARK AND THAT STRONG. AND EVEN IF I DID, IT WOULD BE BAD BUSINESS FOR ONE WHO RELIES ON DEATH.
CRAP. NO POINT IN GEEKIN' YOU THEN.
HM. MAYBE I DON'T HAVE THE MAGIC, BUT SOMEONE DOES. TELL ME, MISTAH DEADPOOL. DID YOU KNOW YOU ARE CURSED?
I CAN SEE IT, WRAPPED AROUND YOUR HEART LIKE A SERPENT.
BAD TOUCH!
MAGIC SO BLACK, IT DON'T EVEN COME FROM THE EARTH MOTHER, ERZULIE. MAGIC THAT CAN'T BE PRACTICED BY ANY HOUNGAN. BUT LIKE ALL CURSES IT IS TIED TO A NAME...
AND I CAN SEE THAT NAME... THANOS.
THANOS?!

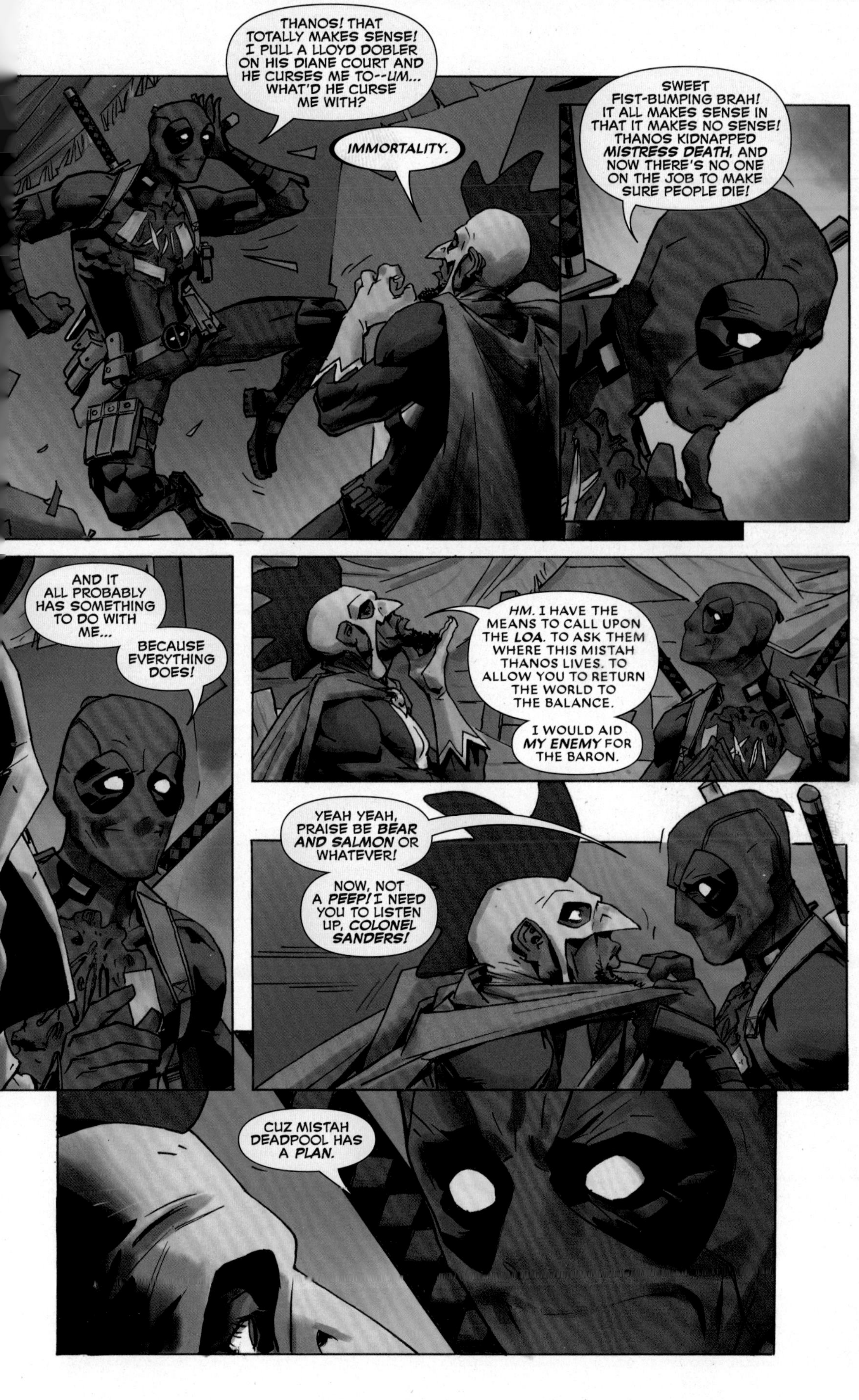
THANOS! THAT TOTALLY MAKES SENSE! I PULL A LLOYD DOBLER ON HIS DIANE COURT AND HE CURSES ME TO--UM... WHAT'D HE CURSE ME WITH?
IMMORTALITY.
SWEET FIST-BUMPING BRAH! IT ALL MAKES SENSE IN THAT IT MAKES NO SENSE! THANOS KIDNAPPED MISTRESS DEATH, AND NOW THERE'S NO ONE ON THE JOB TO MAKE SURE PEOPLE DIE!
AND IT ALL PROBABLY HAS SOMETHING TO DO WITH ME...
BECAUSE EVERYTHING DOES!
HM. I HAVE THE MEANS TO CALL UPON THE LOA. TO ASK THEM WHERE THIS MISTAH THANOS LIVES. TO ALLOW YOU TO RETURN THE WORLD TO THE BALANCE.
I WOULD AID MY ENEMY FOR THE BARON.
YEAH YEAH, PRAISE BE BEAR AND SALMON OR WHATEVER!
NOW, NOT A PEEP! I NEED YOU TO LISTEN UP, COLONEL SANDERS!
CUZ MISTAH DEADPOOL HAS A PLAN.

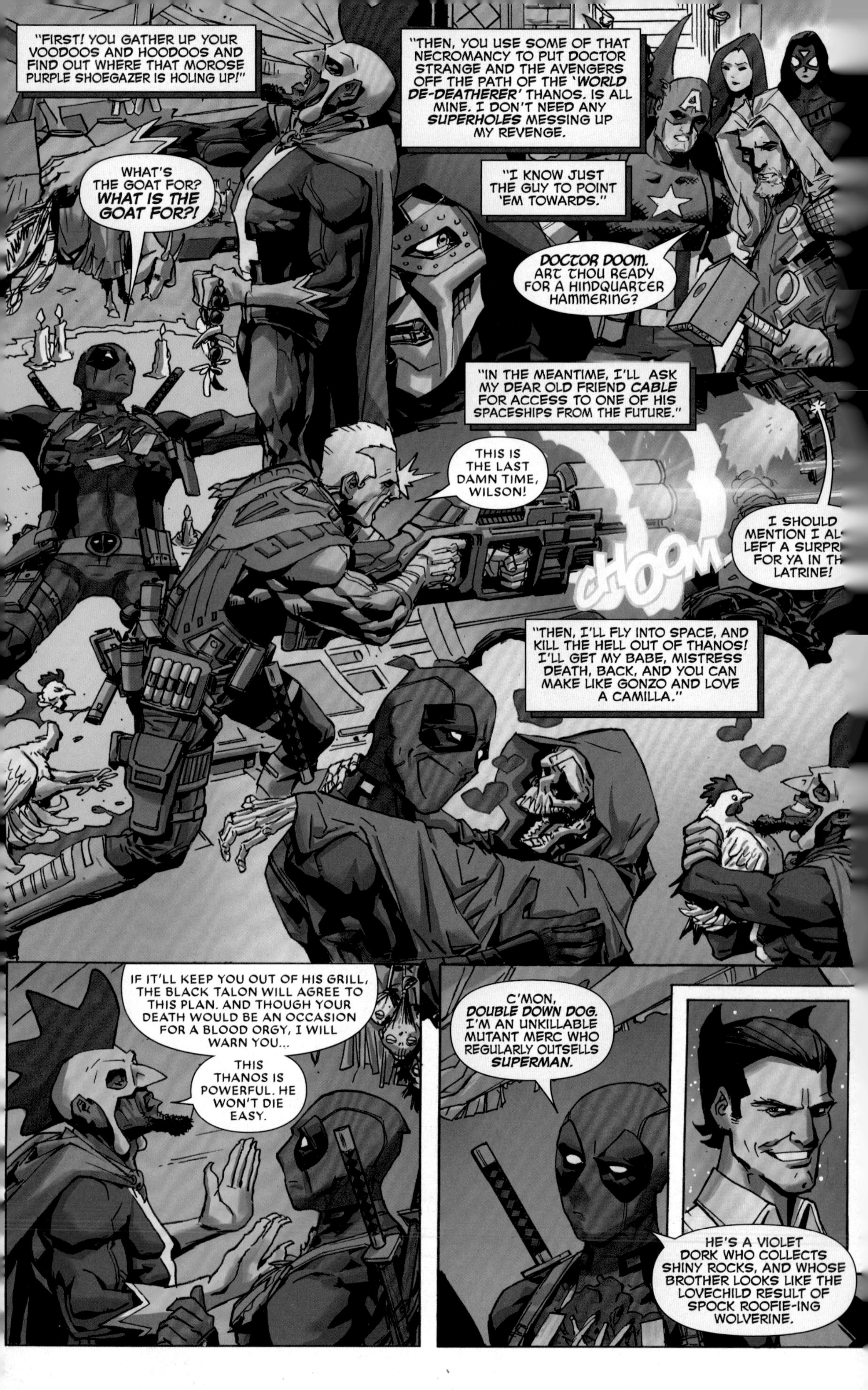
"FIRST! YOU GATHER UP YOUR VOODOOS AND HOODOOS AND FIND OUT WHERE THAT MOROSE PURPLE SHOEGAZER IS HOLING UP!"
WHAT'S THE GOAT FOR? WHAT IS THE GOAT FOR?!
"THEN, YOU USE SOME OF THAT NECROMANCY TO PUT DOCTOR STRANGE AND THE AVENGERS OFF THE PATH OF THE 'WORLD DE-DEATHERER' THANOS. IS ALL MINE. I DON'T NEED ANY SUPERHOLES MESSING UP MY REVENGE.
"I KNOW JUST THE GUY TO POINT 'EM TOWARDS."
DOCTOR DOOM. ART THOU READY FOR A HINDQUARTER HAMMERING?
"IN THE MEANTIME, I'LL ASK MY DEAR OLD FRIEND CABLE FOR ACCESS TO ONE OF HIS SPACESHIPS FROM THE FUTURE."
THIS IS THE LAST DAMN TIME, WILSON!
CHOOM
I SHOULD MENTION I AL LEFT A SURPR FOR YA IN TH LATRINE!
"THEN, I'LL FLY INTO SPACE, AND KILL THE HELL OUT OF THANOS! I'LL GET MY BABE, MISTRESS DEATH, BACK, AND YOU CAN MAKE LIKE GONZO AND LOVE A CAMILLA."
IF IT'LL KEEP YOU OUT OF HIS GRILL, THE BLACK TALON WILL AGREE TO THIS PLAN. AND THOUGH YOUR DEATH WOULD BE AN OCCASION FOR A BLOOD ORGY, I WILL WARN YOU...
THIS THANOS IS POWERFUL. HE WON'T DIE EASY.
C'MON, DOUBLE DOWN DOG. I'M AN UNKILLABLE MUTANT MERC WHO REGULARLY OUTSELLS SUPERMAN.
HE'S A VIOLET DORK WHO COLLECTS SHINY ROCKS, AND WHOSE BROTHER LOOKS LIKE THE LOVECHILD RESULT OF SPOCK ROOFIE-ING WOLVERINE.

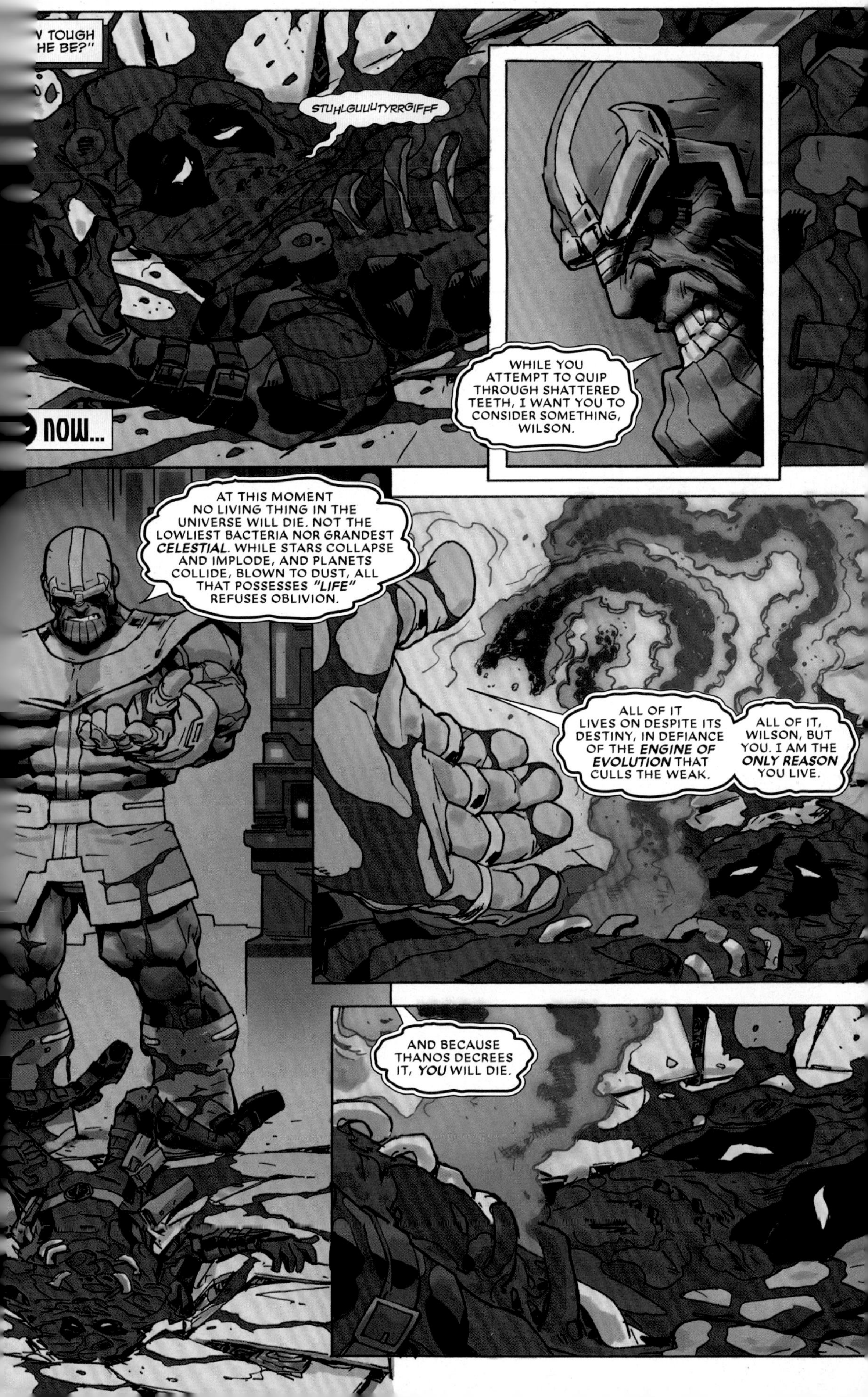
W TOUGH
HE BE?"
STUHLGUUUTYRRGIFFF
NOW...
WHILE YOU ATTEMPT TO QUIP THROUGH SHATTERED TEETH, I WANT YOU TO CONSIDER SOMETHING, WILSON.
AT THIS MOMENT NO LIVING THING IN THE UNIVERSE WILL DIE. NOT THE LOWLIEST BACTERIA NOR GRANDEST *CELESTIAL*. WHILE STARS COLLAPSE AND IMPLODE, AND PLANETS COLLIDE, BLOWN TO DUST, ALL THAT POSSESSES *"LIFE"* REFUSES OBLIVION.
ALL OF IT LIVES ON DESPITE ITS DESTINY, IN DEFIANCE OF THE *ENGINE OF EVOLUTION* THAT CULLS THE WEAK.
ALL OF IT, WILSON, BUT YOU. I AM THE *ONLY REASON* YOU LIVE.
AND BECAUSE THANOS DECREES IT, *YOU* WILL DIE.

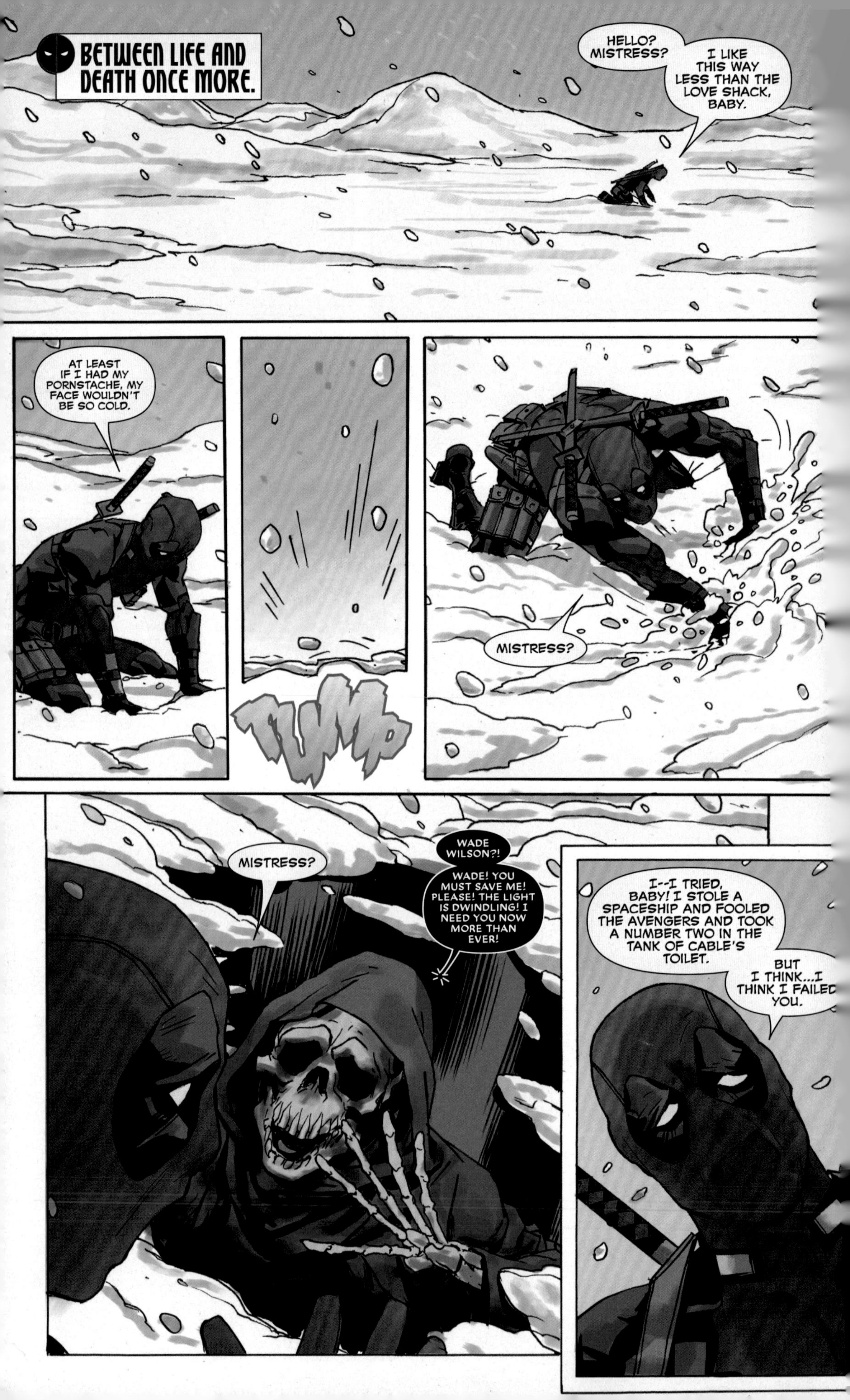

BETWEEN LIFE AND DEATH ONCE MORE.
HELLO? MISTRESS?
I LIKE THIS WAY LESS THAN THE LOVE SHACK, BABY.
AT LEAST IF I HAD MY PORNSTACHE, MY FACE WOULDN'T BE SO COLD.
TUMP
MISTRESS?
MISTRESS?
WADE WILSON?!
WADE! YOU MUST SAVE ME! PLEASE! THE LIGHT IS DWINDLING! I NEED YOU NOW MORE THAN EVER!
I--I TRIED, BABY! I STOLE A SPACESHIP AND FOOLED THE AVENGERS AND TOOK A NUMBER TWO IN THE TANK OF CABLE'S TOILET.
BUT I THINK...I THINK I FAILED YOU.

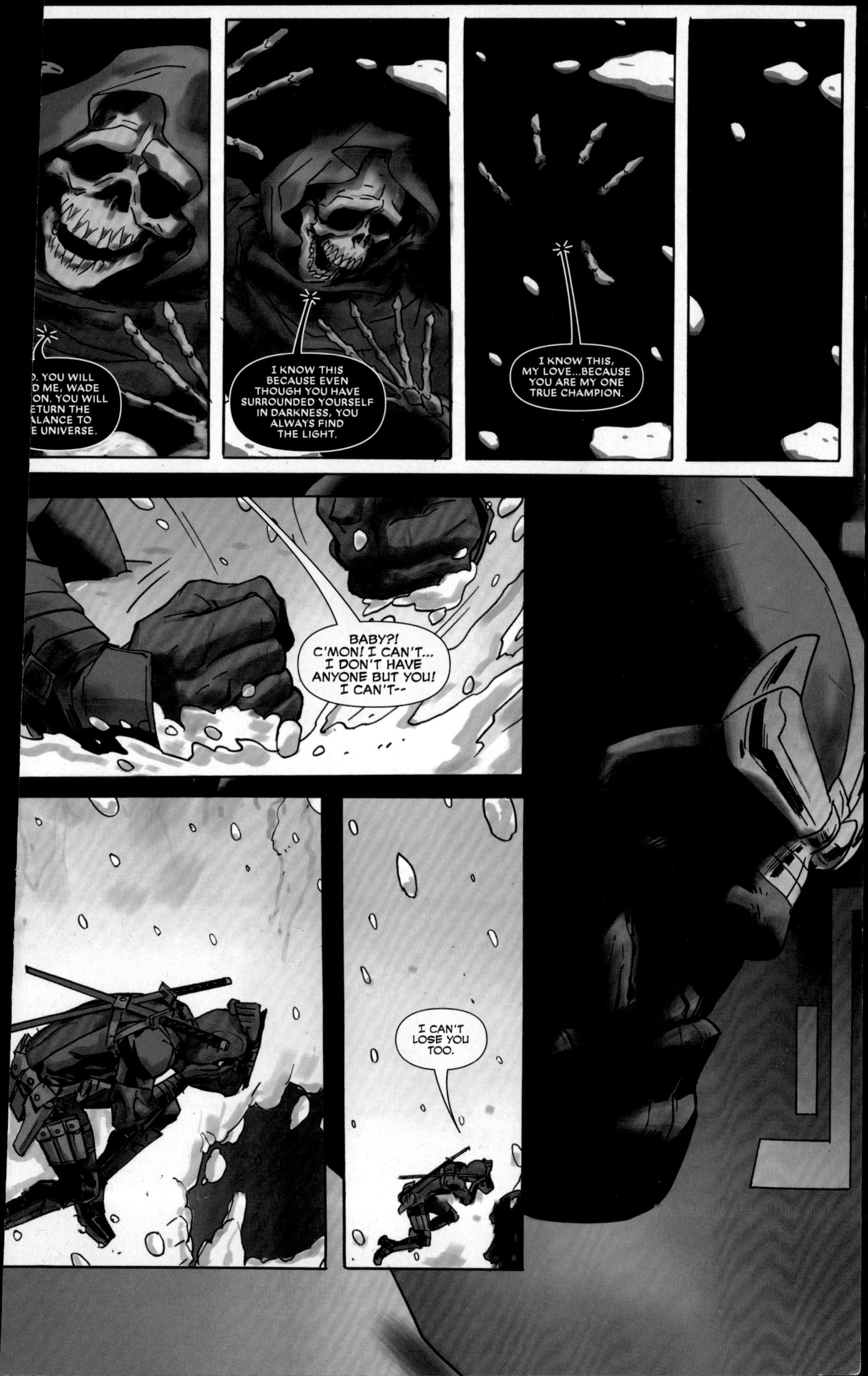

D. YOU WILL D ME, WADE ON. YOU WILL ETURN THE ALANCE TO E UNIVERSE.
I KNOW THIS BECAUSE EVEN THOUGH YOU HAVE SURROUNDED YOURSELF IN DARKNESS, YOU ALWAYS FIND THE LIGHT.
I KNOW THIS, MY LOVE...BECAUSE YOU ARE MY ONE TRUE CHAMPION.
BABY?! C'MON! I CAN'T... I DON'T HAVE ANYONE BUT YOU! I CAN'T--
I CAN'T LOSE YOU TOO.

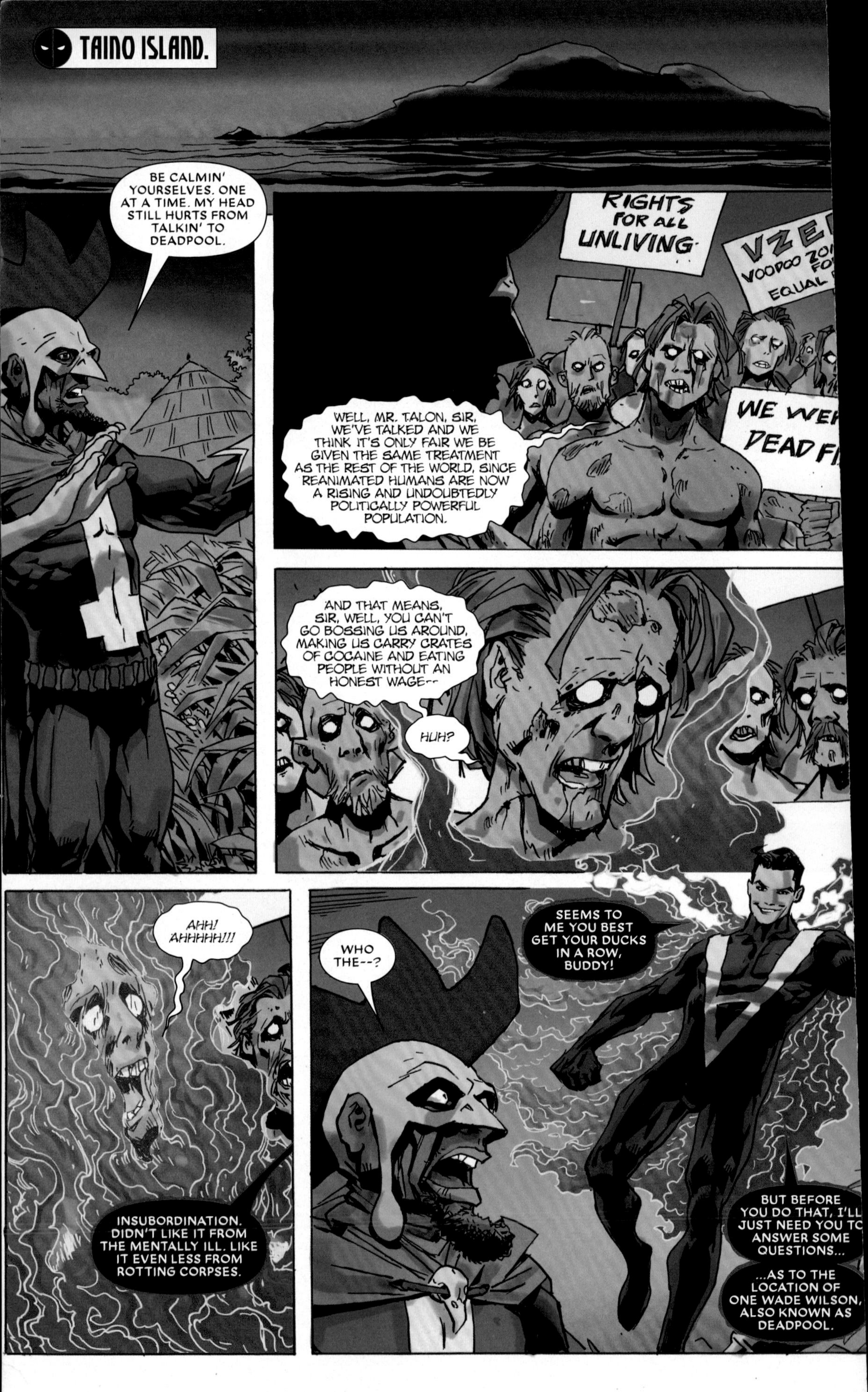
TAINO ISLAND.
BE CALMIN' YOURSELVES. ONE AT A TIME. MY HEAD STILL HURTS FROM TALKIN' TO DEADPOOL.
RIGHTS FOR ALL UNLIVING
WELL, MR. TALON, SIR, WE'VE TALKED AND WE THINK IT'S ONLY FAIR WE BE GIVEN THE SAME TREATMENT AS THE REST OF THE WORLD, SINCE REANIMATED HUMANS ARE NOW A RISING AND UNDOUBTEDLY POLITICALLY POWERFUL POPULATION.
AND THAT MEANS, SIR, WELL, YOU CAN'T GO BOSSING US AROUND, MAKING US CARRY CRATES OF COCAINE AND EATING PEOPLE WITHOUT AN HONEST WAGE--
HUH?
AHH! AHHHHH!!!
INSUBORDINATION. DIDN'T LIKE IT FROM THE MENTALLY ILL. LIKE IT EVEN LESS FROM ROTTING CORPSES.
WHO THE--?
SEEMS TO ME YOU BEST GET YOUR DUCKS IN A ROW, BUDDY!
BUT BEFORE YOU DO THAT, I'LL JUST NEED YOU TO ANSWER SOME QUESTIONS...
...AS TO THE LOCATION OF ONE WADE WILSON, ALSO KNOWN AS DEADPOOL.

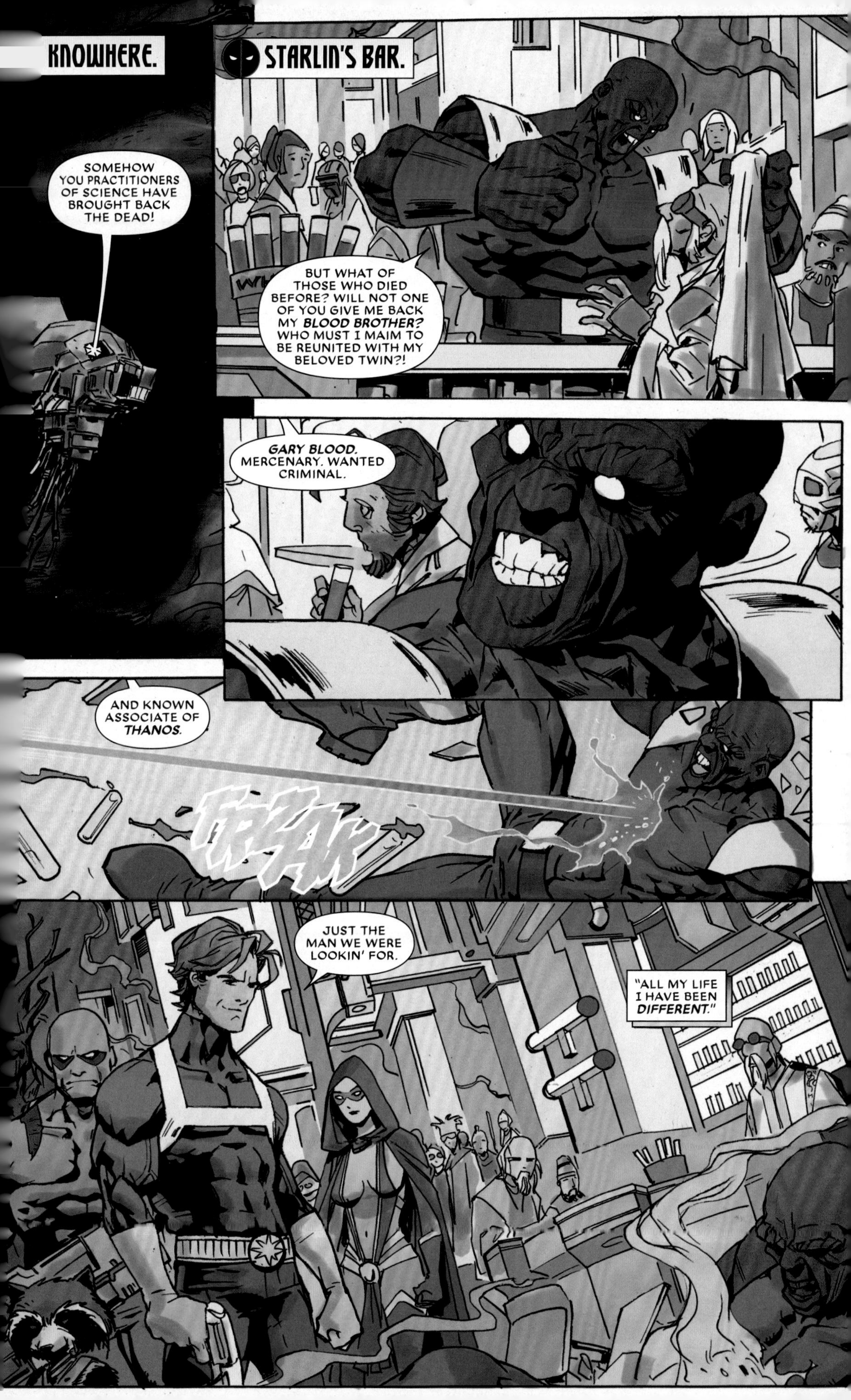
KNOWHERE.
STARLIN'S BAR.
SOMEHOW YOU PRACTITIONERS OF SCIENCE HAVE BROUGHT BACK THE DEAD!
BUT WHAT OF THOSE WHO DIED BEFORE? WILL NOT ONE OF YOU GIVE ME BACK MY *BLOOD BROTHER?* WHO MUST I MAIM TO BE REUNITED WITH MY BELOVED TWIN?!
GARY BLOOD. MERCENARY. WANTED CRIMINAL.
AND KNOWN ASSOCIATE OF *THANOS*.
FRZAK
JUST THE MAN WE WERE LOOKIN' FOR.
"ALL MY LIFE I HAVE BEEN *DIFFERENT*."

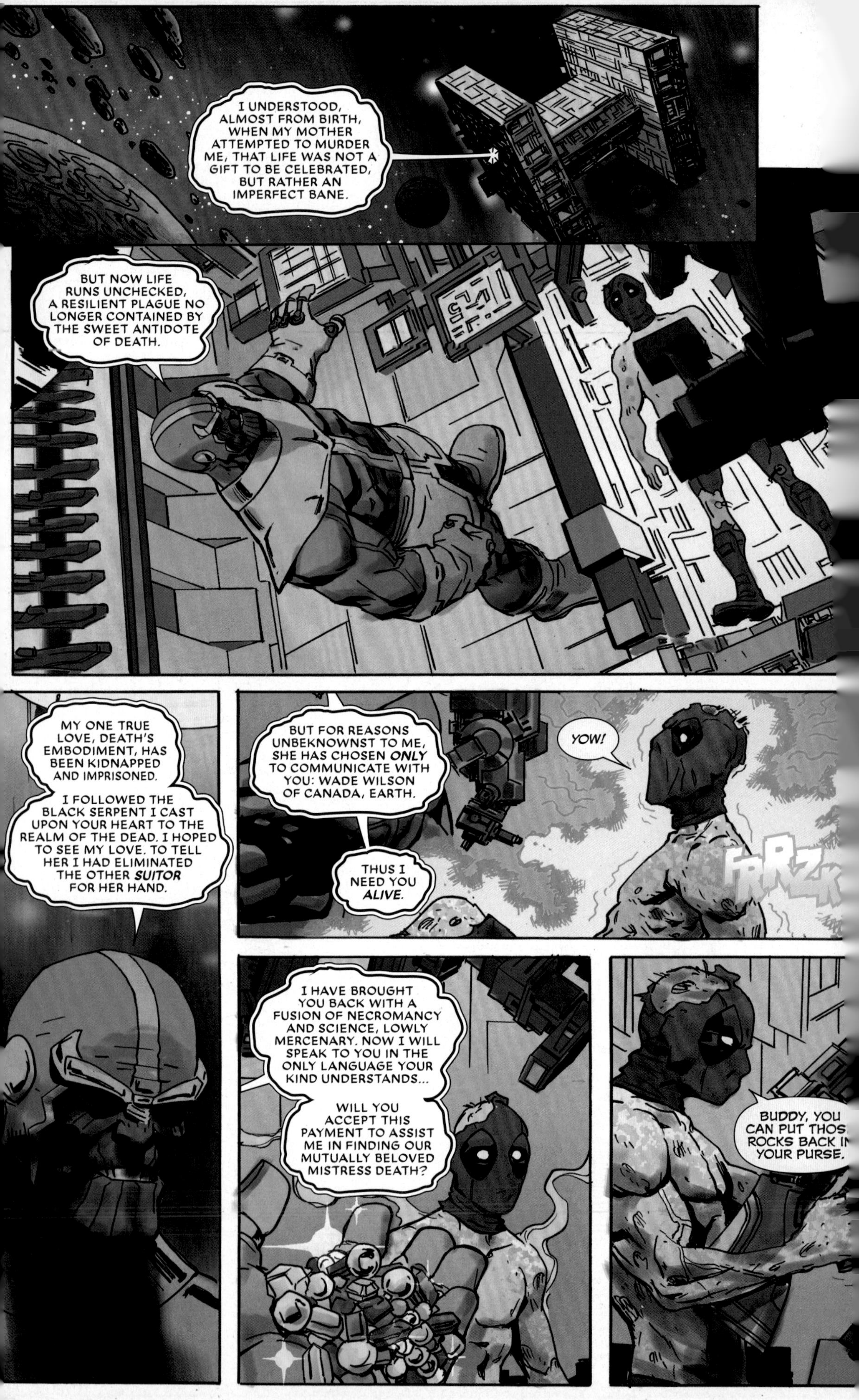

I UNDERSTOOD, ALMOST FROM BIRTH, WHEN MY MOTHER ATTEMPTED TO MURDER ME, THAT LIFE WAS NOT A GIFT TO BE CELEBRATED, BUT RATHER AN IMPERFECT BANE.
BUT NOW LIFE RUNS UNCHECKED, A RESILIENT PLAGUE NO LONGER CONTAINED BY THE SWEET ANTIDOTE OF DEATH.
MY ONE TRUE LOVE, DEATH'S EMBODIMENT, HAS BEEN KIDNAPPED AND IMPRISONED.
I FOLLOWED THE BLACK SERPENT I CAST UPON YOUR HEART TO THE REALM OF THE DEAD. I HOPED TO SEE MY LOVE. TO TELL HER I HAD ELIMINATED THE OTHER *SUITOR* FOR HER HAND.
BUT FOR REASONS UNBEKNOWNST TO ME, SHE HAS CHOSEN *ONLY* TO COMMUNICATE WITH YOU: WADE WILSON OF CANADA, EARTH.
THUS I NEED YOU *ALIVE*.
YOW!
FRRZK
I HAVE BROUGHT YOU BACK WITH A FUSION OF NECROMANCY AND SCIENCE, LOWLY MERCENARY. NOW I WILL SPEAK TO YOU IN THE ONLY LANGUAGE YOUR KIND UNDERSTANDS...
WILL YOU ACCEPT THIS PAYMENT TO ASSIST ME IN FINDING OUR MUTUALLY BELOVED MISTRESS DEATH?
BUDDY, YOU CAN PUT THOS ROCKS BACK IN YOUR PURSE.

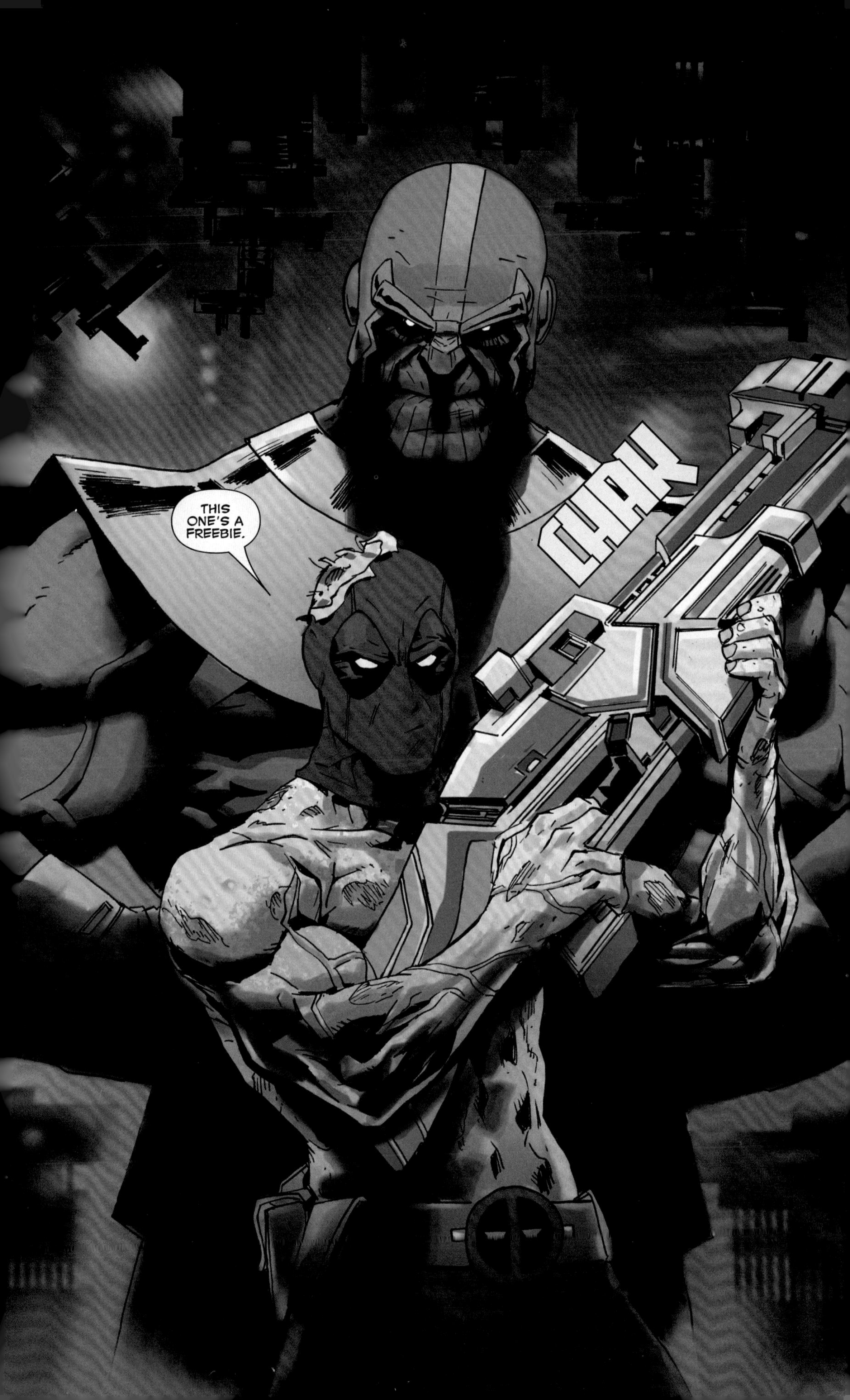
THIS ONE'S A FREEBIE.
CHAK

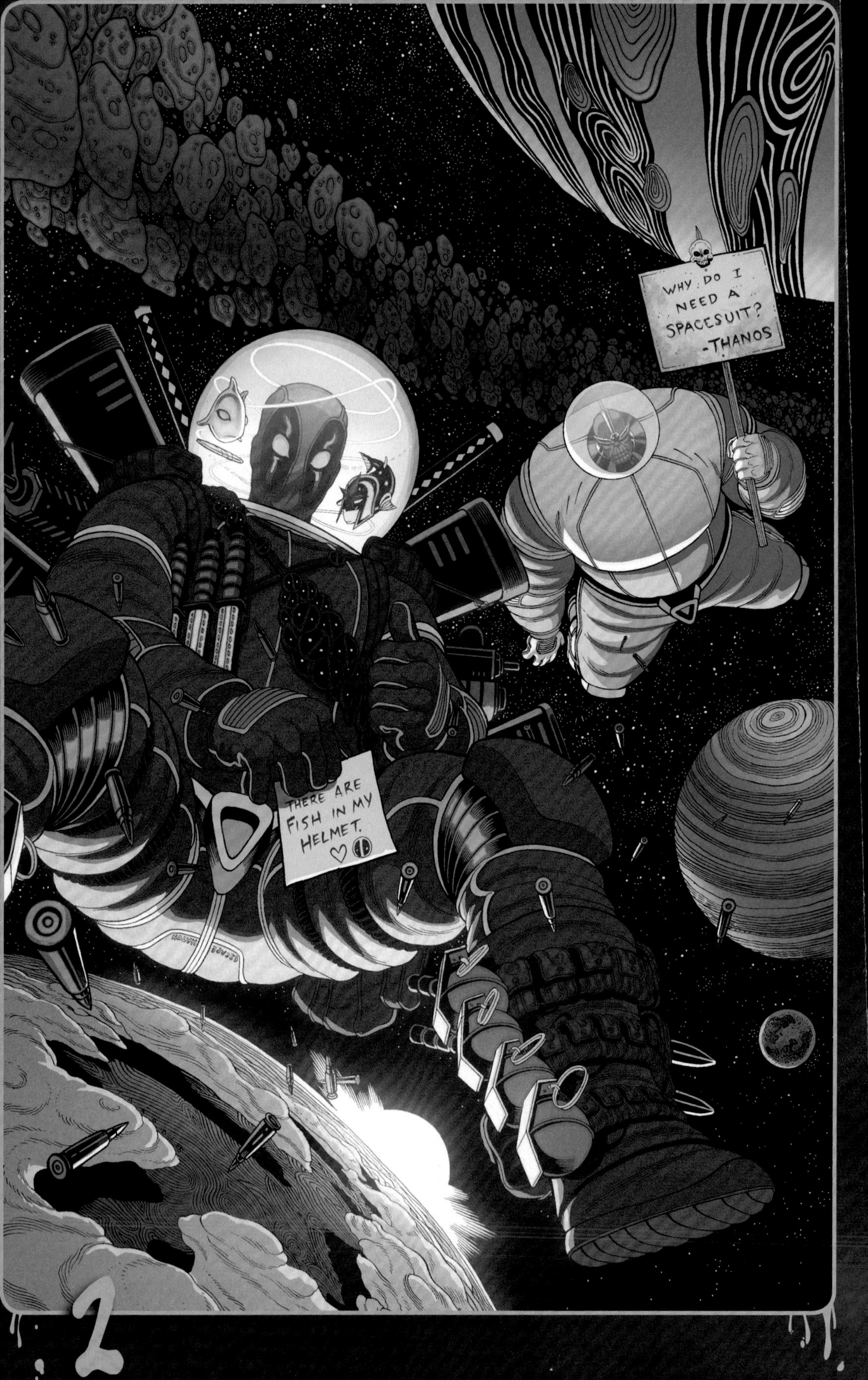
WHY DO I NEED A SPACESUIT? -THANOS
THERE ARE FISH IN MY HELMET. ♡
2

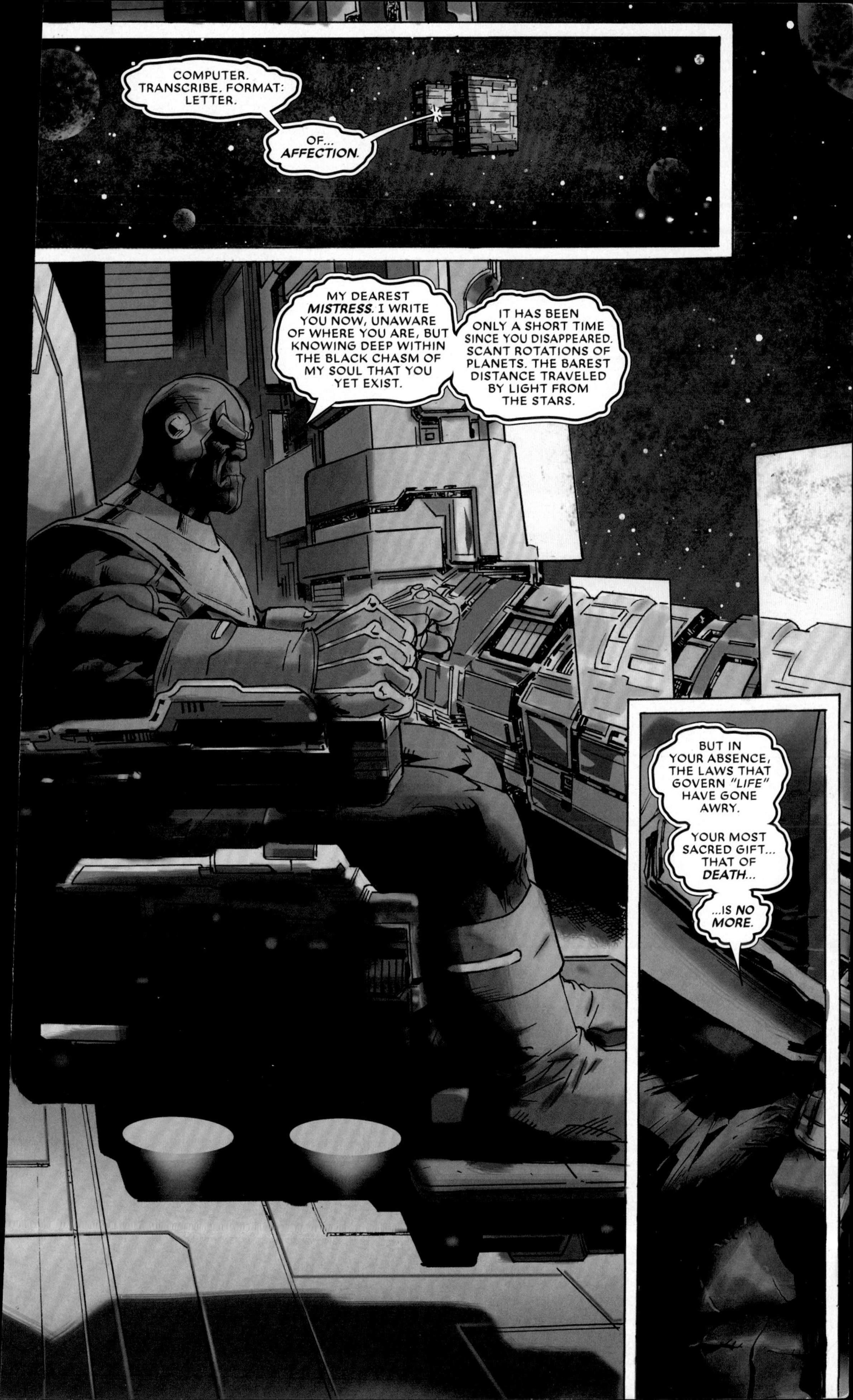
COMPUTER. TRANSCRIBE. FORMAT: LETTER.
OF... AFFECTION.
MY DEAREST MISTRESS. I WRITE YOU NOW, UNAWARE OF WHERE YOU ARE, BUT KNOWING DEEP WITHIN THE BLACK CHASM OF MY SOUL THAT YOU YET EXIST.
IT HAS BEEN ONLY A SHORT TIME SINCE YOU DISAPPEARED. SCANT ROTATIONS OF PLANETS. THE BAREST DISTANCE TRAVELED BY LIGHT FROM THE STARS.
BUT IN YOUR ABSENCE, THE LAWS THAT GOVERN "LIFE" HAVE GONE AWRY.
YOUR MOST SACRED GIFT... THAT OF DEATH...
...IS NO MORE.

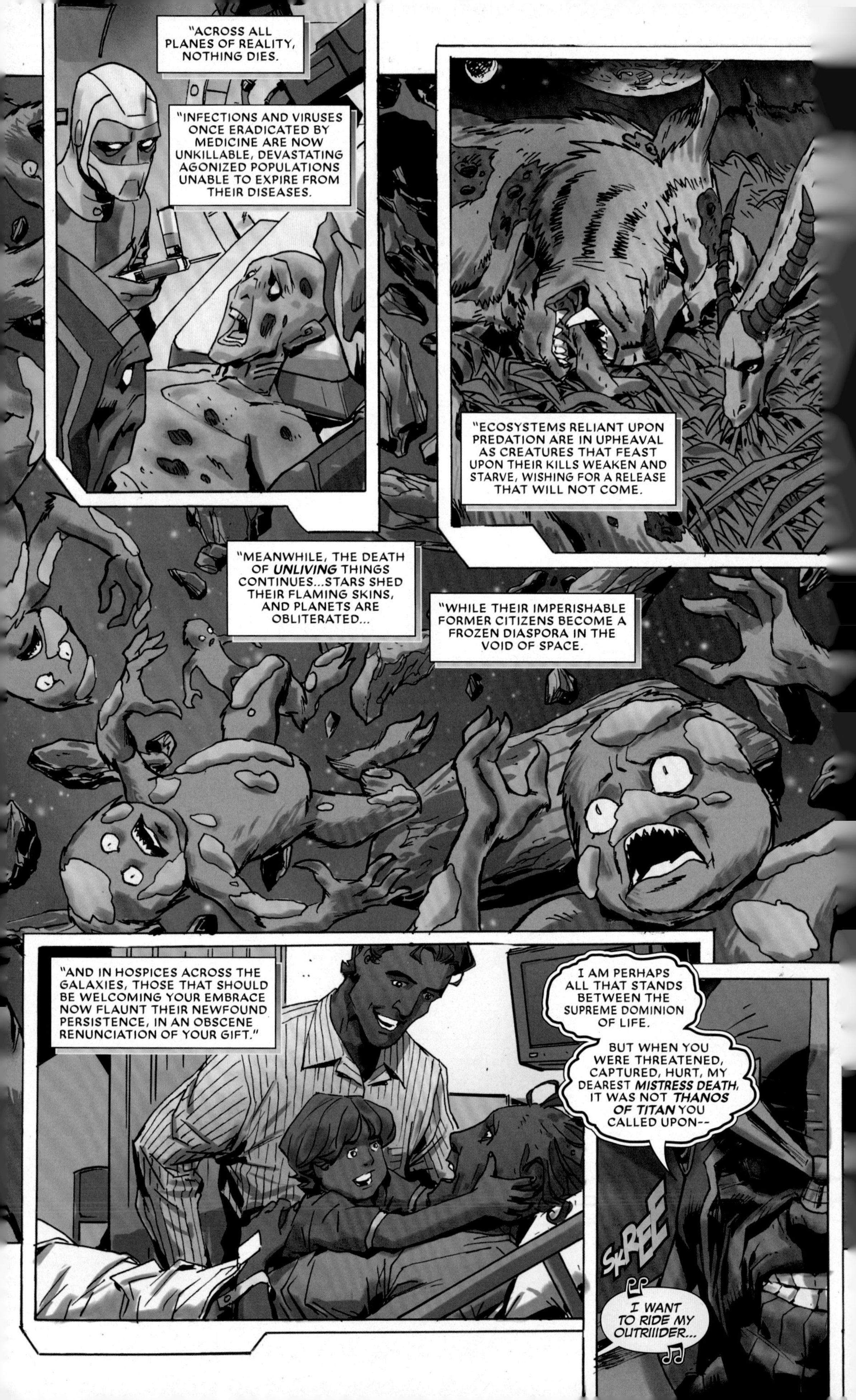
"ACROSS ALL PLANES OF REALITY, NOTHING DIES.
"INFECTIONS AND VIRUSES ONCE ERADICATED BY MEDICINE ARE NOW UNKILLABLE, DEVASTATING AGONIZED POPULATIONS UNABLE TO EXPIRE FROM THEIR DISEASES.
"ECOSYSTEMS RELIANT UPON PREDATION ARE IN UPHEAVAL AS CREATURES THAT FEAST UPON THEIR KILLS WEAKEN AND STARVE, WISHING FOR A RELEASE THAT WILL NOT COME.
"MEANWHILE, THE DEATH OF *UNLIVING* THINGS CONTINUES...STARS SHED THEIR FLAMING SKINS, AND PLANETS ARE OBLITERATED...
"WHILE THEIR IMPERISHABLE FORMER CITIZENS BECOME A FROZEN DIASPORA IN THE VOID OF SPACE.
"AND IN HOSPICES ACROSS THE GALAXIES, THOSE THAT SHOULD BE WELCOMING YOUR EMBRACE NOW FLAUNT THEIR NEWFOUND PERSISTENCE, IN AN OBSCENE RENUNCIATION OF YOUR GIFT."
I AM PERHAPS ALL THAT STANDS BETWEEN THE SUPREME DOMINION OF LIFE.
BUT WHEN YOU WERE THREATENED, CAPTURED, HURT, MY DEAREST *MISTRESS DEATH*, IT WAS NOT *THANOS OF TITAN* YOU CALLED UPON--
SKREEE
I WANT TO RIDE MY OUTRIIIDER...

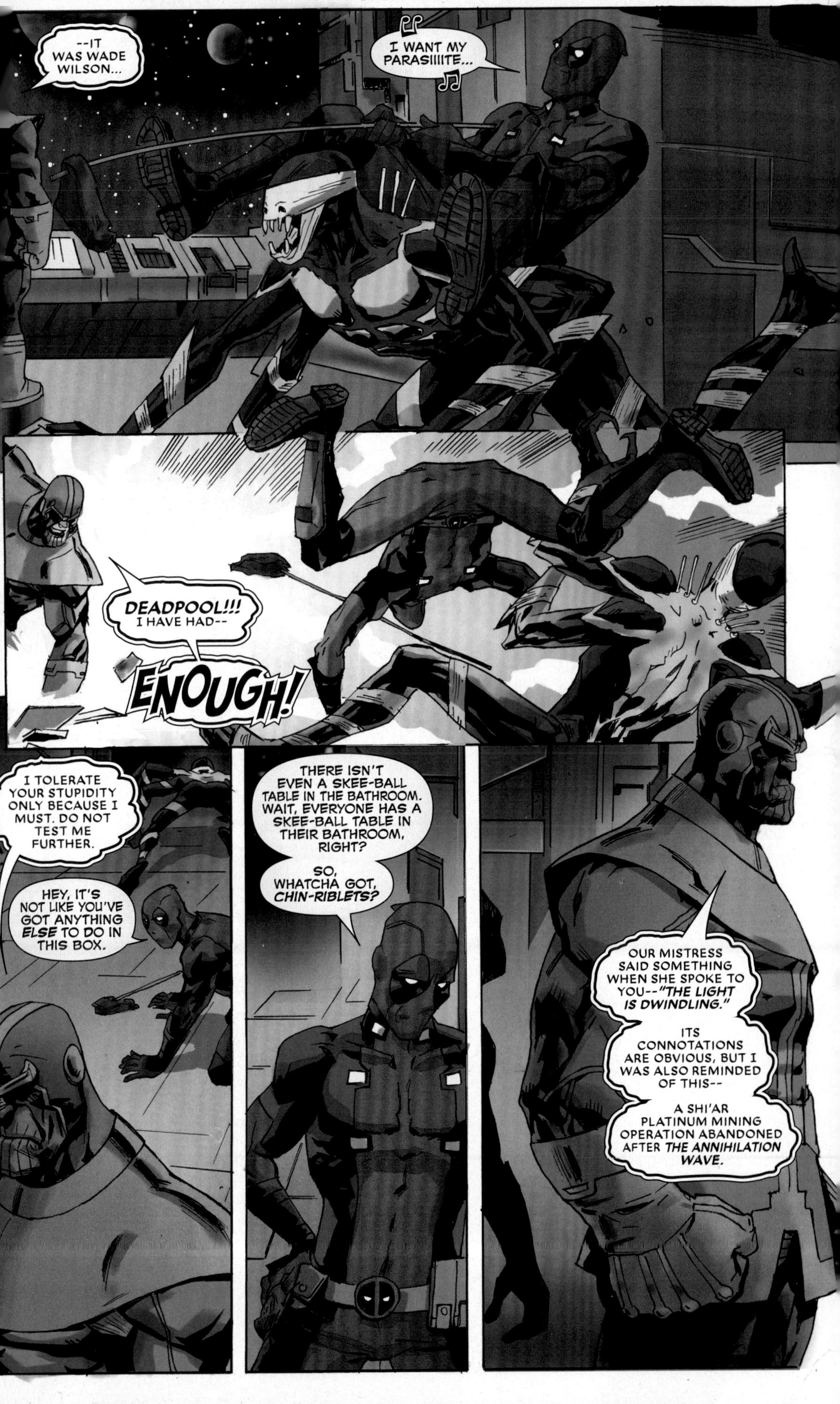
--IT WAS WADE WILSON...
I WANT MY PARASIIIIITE...
DEADPOOL!!! I HAVE HAD--
ENOUGH!
I TOLERATE YOUR STUPIDITY ONLY BECAUSE I MUST. DO NOT TEST ME FURTHER.
HEY, IT'S NOT LIKE YOU'VE GOT ANYTHING ELSE TO DO IN THIS BOX.
THERE ISN'T EVEN A SKEE-BALL TABLE IN THE BATHROOM. WAIT, EVERYONE HAS A SKEE-BALL TABLE IN THEIR BATHROOM, RIGHT?
SO, WHATCHA GOT, CHIN-RIBLETS?
OUR MISTRESS SAID SOMETHING WHEN SHE SPOKE TO YOU--"THE LIGHT IS DWINDLING."
ITS CONNOTATIONS ARE OBVIOUS, BUT I WAS ALSO REMINDED OF THIS--
A SHI'AR PLATINUM MINING OPERATION ABANDONED AFTER THE ANNIHILATION WAVE.

"ITS POSITION IN ORBIT BEHIND A GAS GIANT GAVE IT A *NICKNAME*...

"THE DWINDLING LIGHT."

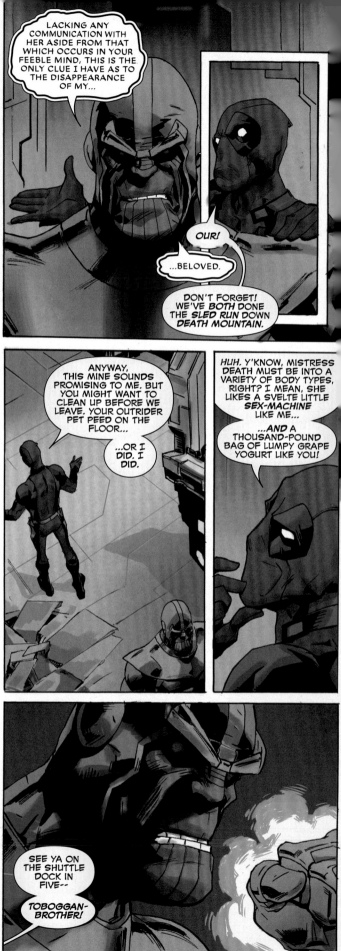

LACKING ANY COMMUNICATION WITH HER ASIDE FROM THAT WHICH OCCURS IN YOUR *FEEBLE* MIND, THIS IS THE ONLY CLUE I HAVE AS TO THE DISAPPEARANCE OF MY...

OUR!

...BELOVED.

DON'T FORGET! WE'VE *BOTH* DONE THE *SLED RUN* DOWN *DEATH MOUNTAIN.*

ANYWAY, THIS MINE SOUNDS PROMISING TO ME. BUT YOU MIGHT WANT TO CLEAN UP BEFORE WE LEAVE. YOUR OUTRIDER PET PEED ON THE FLOOR...

...OR I DID. I DID.

HUH. Y'KNOW, MISTRESS DEATH MUST BE INTO A VARIETY OF BODY TYPES, RIGHT? I MEAN, SHE LIKES A SVELTE LITTLE *SEX-MACHINE* LIKE ME...

...AND A THOUSAND-POUND BAG OF LUMPY GRAPE YOGURT LIKE YOU!

SEE YA ON THE SHUTTLE DOCK IN FIVE--

TOBOGGAN-BROTHER!

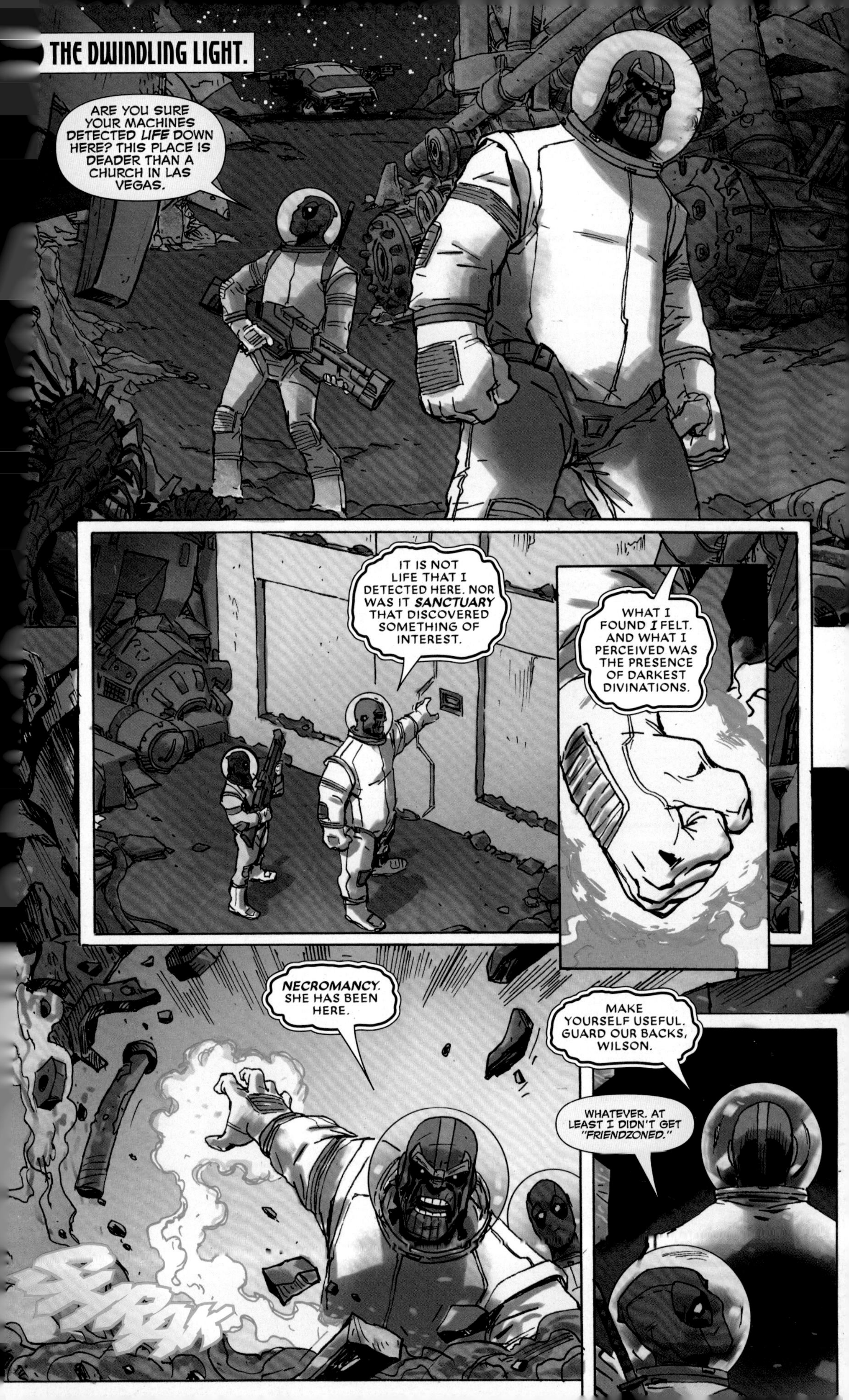
THE DWINDLING LIGHT.
ARE YOU SURE YOUR MACHINES DETECTED LIFE DOWN HERE? THIS PLACE IS DEADER THAN A CHURCH IN LAS VEGAS.
IT IS NOT LIFE THAT I DETECTED HERE. NOR WAS IT SANCTUARY THAT DISCOVERED SOMETHING OF INTEREST.
WHAT I FOUND I FELT. AND WHAT I PERCEIVED WAS THE PRESENCE OF DARKEST DIVINATIONS.
NECROMANCY. SHE HAS BEEN HERE.
MAKE YOURSELF USEFUL. GUARD OUR BACKS, WILSON.
WHATEVER. AT LEAST I DIDN'T GET "FRIENDZONED."
SPRAK

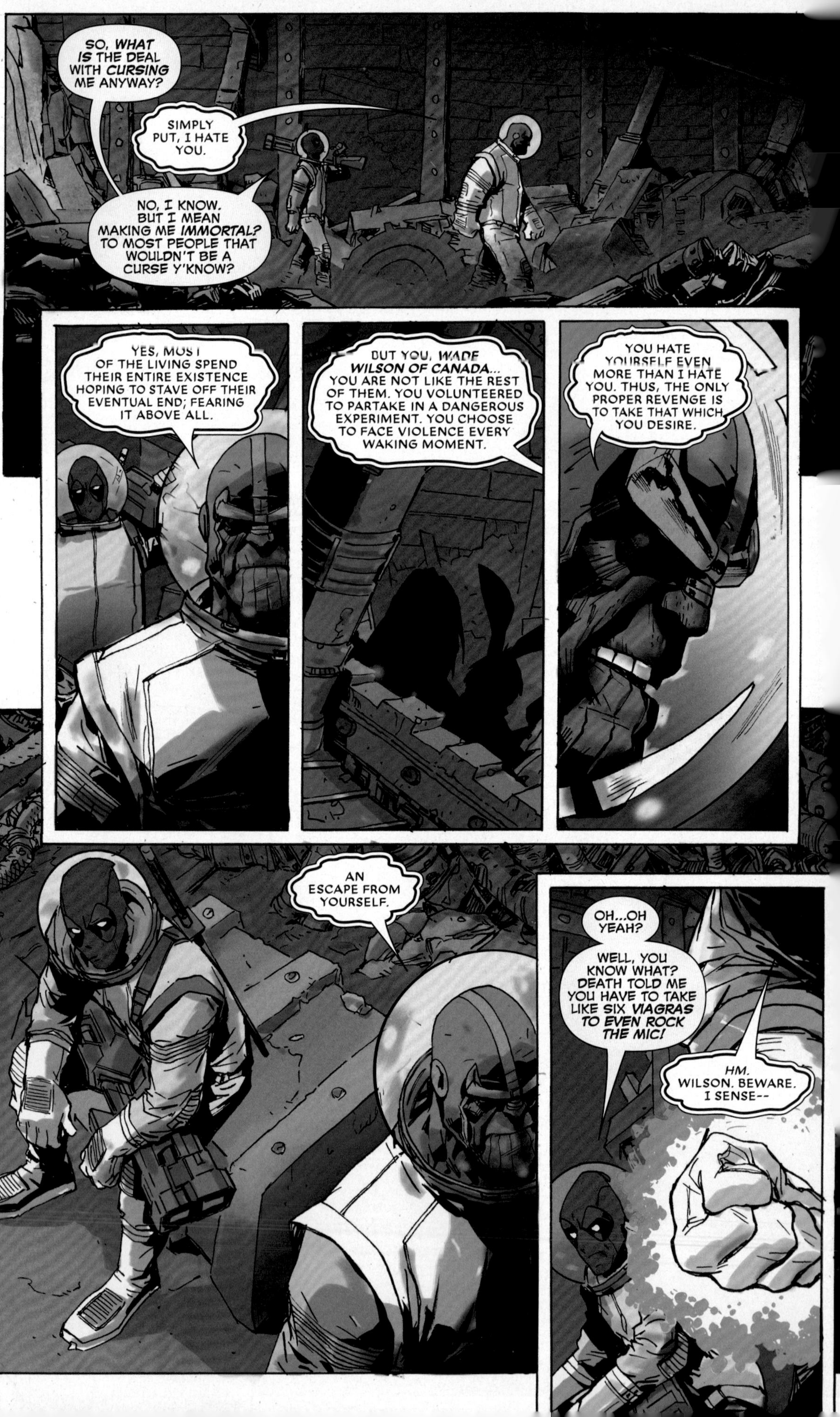
SO, WHAT IS THE DEAL WITH CURSING ME ANYWAY?
SIMPLY PUT, I HATE YOU.
NO, I KNOW. BUT I MEAN MAKING ME IMMORTAL? TO MOST PEOPLE THAT WOULDN'T BE A CURSE Y'KNOW?
YES, MOST OF THE LIVING SPEND THEIR ENTIRE EXISTENCE HOPING TO STAVE OFF THEIR EVENTUAL END; FEARING IT ABOVE ALL.
BUT YOU, WADE WILSON OF CANADA... YOU ARE NOT LIKE THE REST OF THEM. YOU VOLUNTEERED TO PARTAKE IN A DANGEROUS EXPERIMENT. YOU CHOOSE TO FACE VIOLENCE EVERY WAKING MOMENT.
YOU HATE YOURSELF EVEN MORE THAN I HATE YOU. THUS, THE ONLY PROPER REVENGE IS TO TAKE THAT WHICH YOU DESIRE.
AN ESCAPE FROM YOURSELF.
OH...OH YEAH?
WELL, YOU KNOW WHAT? DEATH TOLD ME YOU HAVE TO TAKE LIKE SIX VIAGRAS TO EVEN ROCK THE MIC!
HM. WILSON. BEWARE. I SENSE--

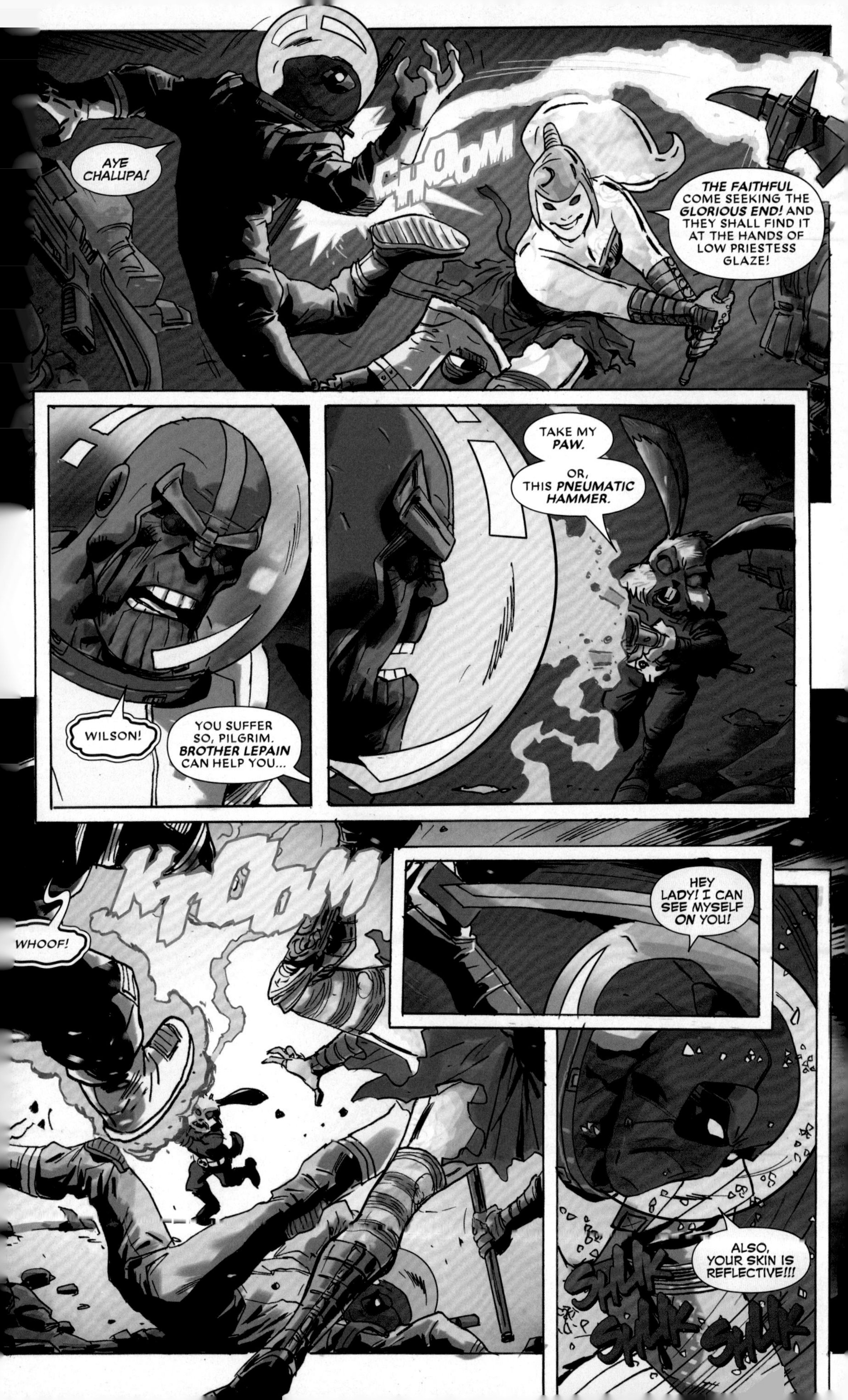

AYE CHALUPA!
CHOOM
THE FAITHFUL COME SEEKING THE GLORIOUS END! AND THEY SHALL FIND IT AT THE HANDS OF LOW PRIESTESS GLAZE!
WILSON!
YOU SUFFER SO, PILGRIM. BROTHER LEPAIN CAN HELP YOU...
TAKE MY PAW.
OR, THIS PNEUMATIC HAMMER.
KTOOM
WHOOF!
HEY LADY! I CAN SEE MYSELF ON YOU!
ALSO, YOUR SKIN IS REFLECTIVE!!!
SHLK SHLK SHLK

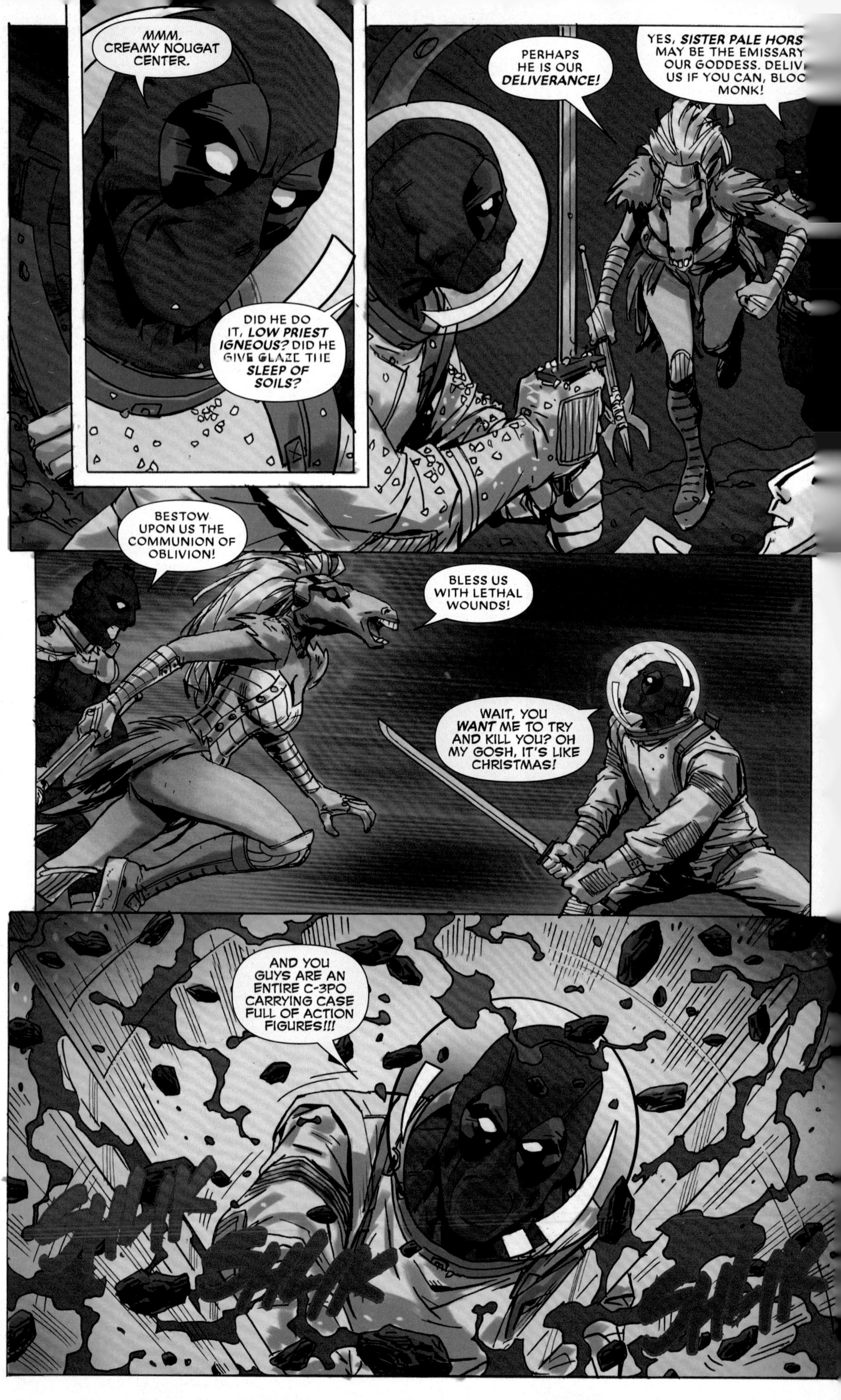

MMM. CREAMY NOUGAT CENTER.
DID HE DO IT, LOW PRIEST IGNEOUS? DID HE GIVE GLAZE THE SLEEP OF SOILS?
PERHAPS HE IS OUR DELIVERANCE!
YES, SISTER PALE HORS MAY BE THE EMISSARY OUR GODDESS. DELIV US IF YOU CAN, BLOO MONK!
BESTOW UPON US THE COMMUNION OF OBLIVION!
BLESS US WITH LETHAL WOUNDS!
WAIT, YOU WANT ME TO TRY AND KILL YOU? OH MY GOSH, IT'S LIKE CHRISTMAS!
AND YOU GUYS ARE AN ENTIRE C-3PO CARRYING CASE FULL OF ACTION FIGURES!!!

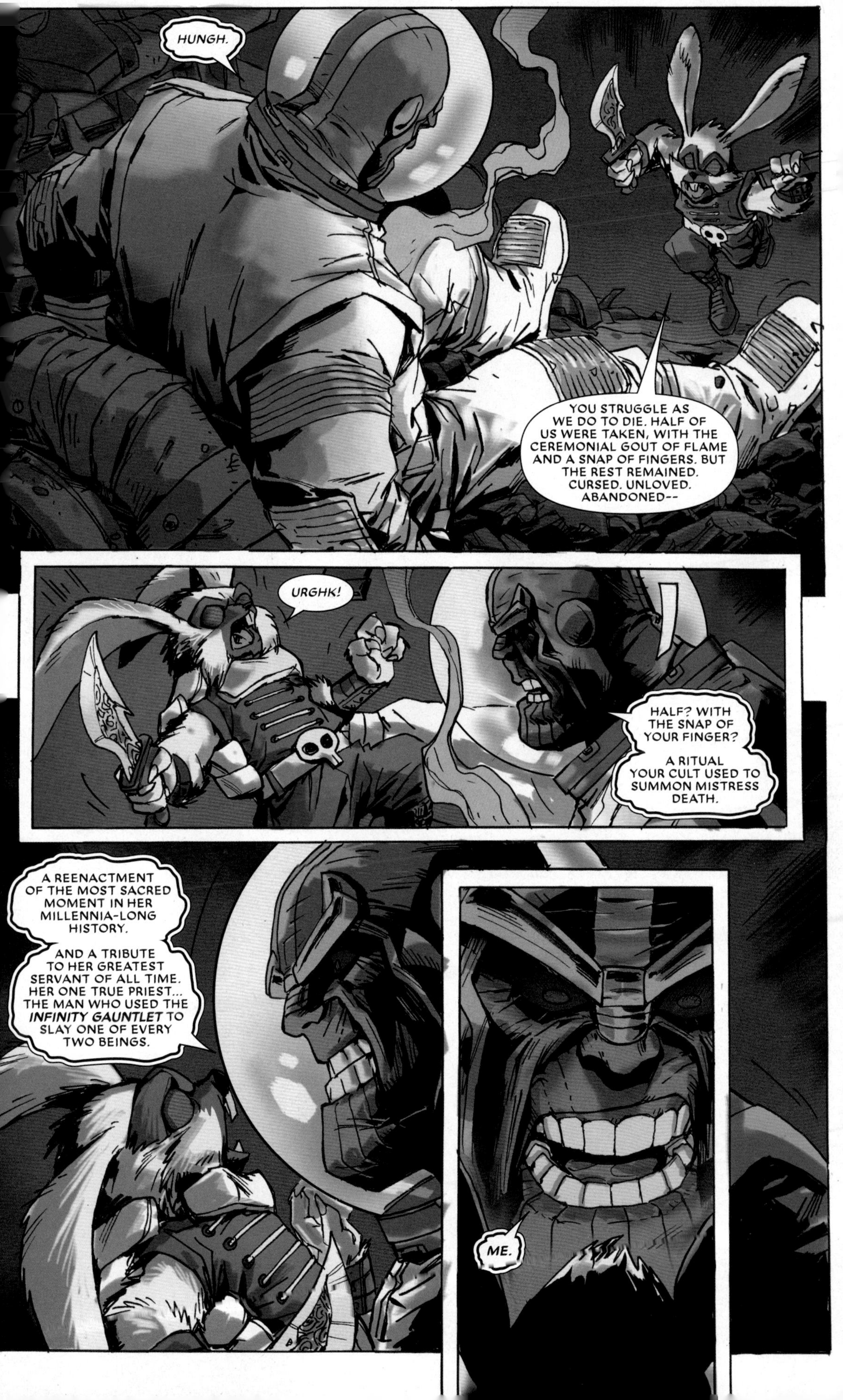
HUNGH.
YOU STRUGGLE AS WE DO TO DIE. HALF OF US WERE TAKEN, WITH THE CEREMONIAL GOUT OF FLAME AND A SNAP OF FINGERS. BUT THE REST REMAINED. CURSED. UNLOVED. ABANDONED--
URGHK!
HALF? WITH THE SNAP OF YOUR FINGER?
A RITUAL YOUR CULT USED TO SUMMON MISTRESS DEATH.
A REENACTMENT OF THE MOST SACRED MOMENT IN HER MILLENNIA-LONG HISTORY.
AND A TRIBUTE TO HER GREATEST SERVANT OF ALL TIME. HER ONE TRUE PRIEST... THE MAN WHO USED THE *INFINITY GAUNTLET* TO SLAY ONE OF EVERY TWO BEINGS.
ME.

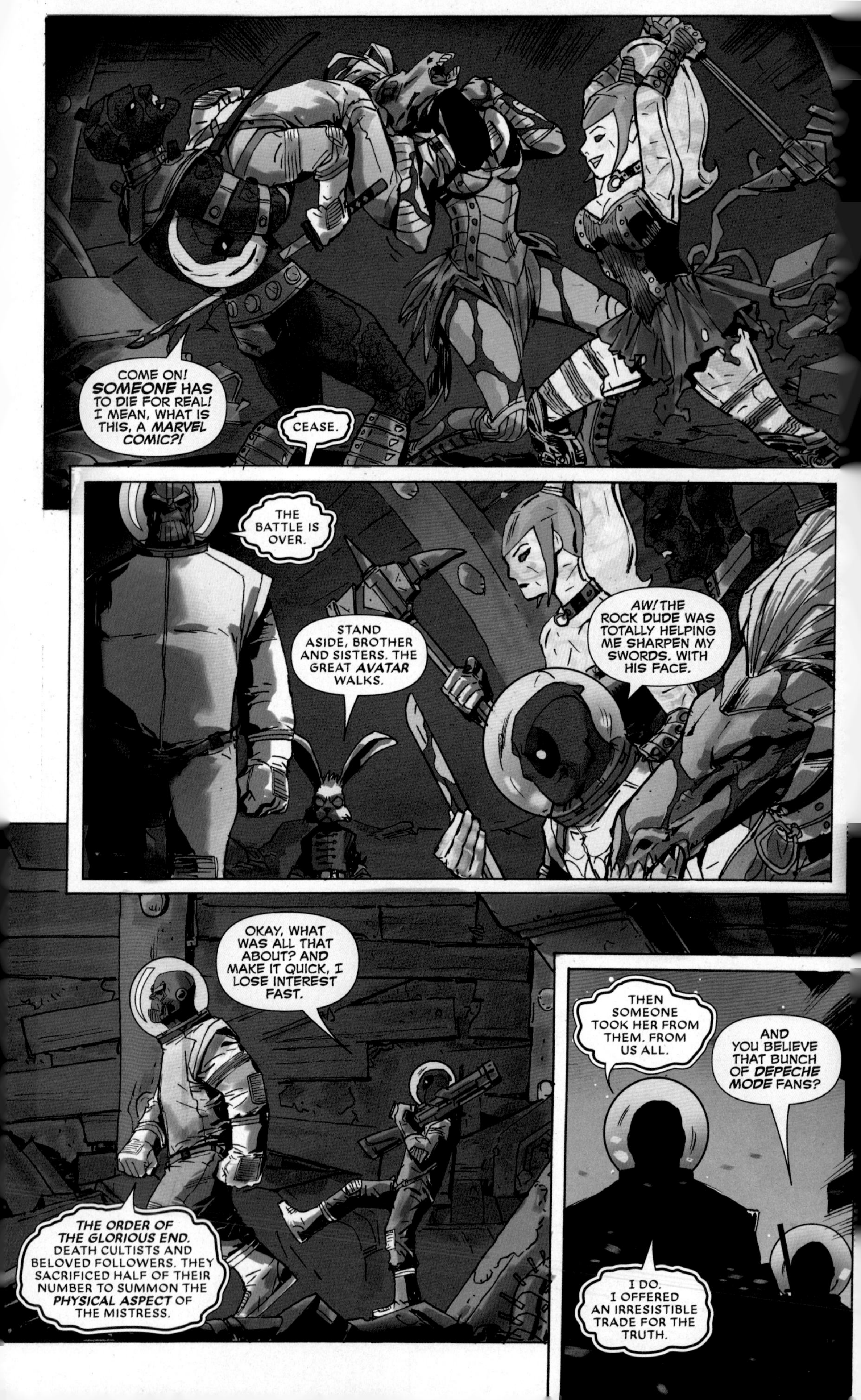
COME ON! SOMEONE HAS TO DIE FOR REAL! I MEAN, WHAT IS THIS, A MARVEL COMIC?!
CEASE.
THE BATTLE IS OVER.
STAND ASIDE, BROTHER AND SISTERS. THE GREAT AVATAR WALKS.
AW! THE ROCK DUDE WAS TOTALLY HELPING ME SHARPEN MY SWORDS. WITH HIS FACE.
OKAY, WHAT WAS ALL THAT ABOUT? AND MAKE IT QUICK, I LOSE INTEREST FAST.
THE ORDER OF THE GLORIOUS END. DEATH CULTISTS AND BELOVED FOLLOWERS. THEY SACRIFICED HALF OF THEIR NUMBER TO SUMMON THE PHYSICAL ASPECT OF THE MISTRESS.
THEN SOMEONE TOOK HER FROM THEM. FROM US ALL.
AND YOU BELIEVE THAT BUNCH OF DEPECHE MODE FANS?
I DO. I OFFERED AN IRRESISTIBLE TRADE FOR THE TRUTH.

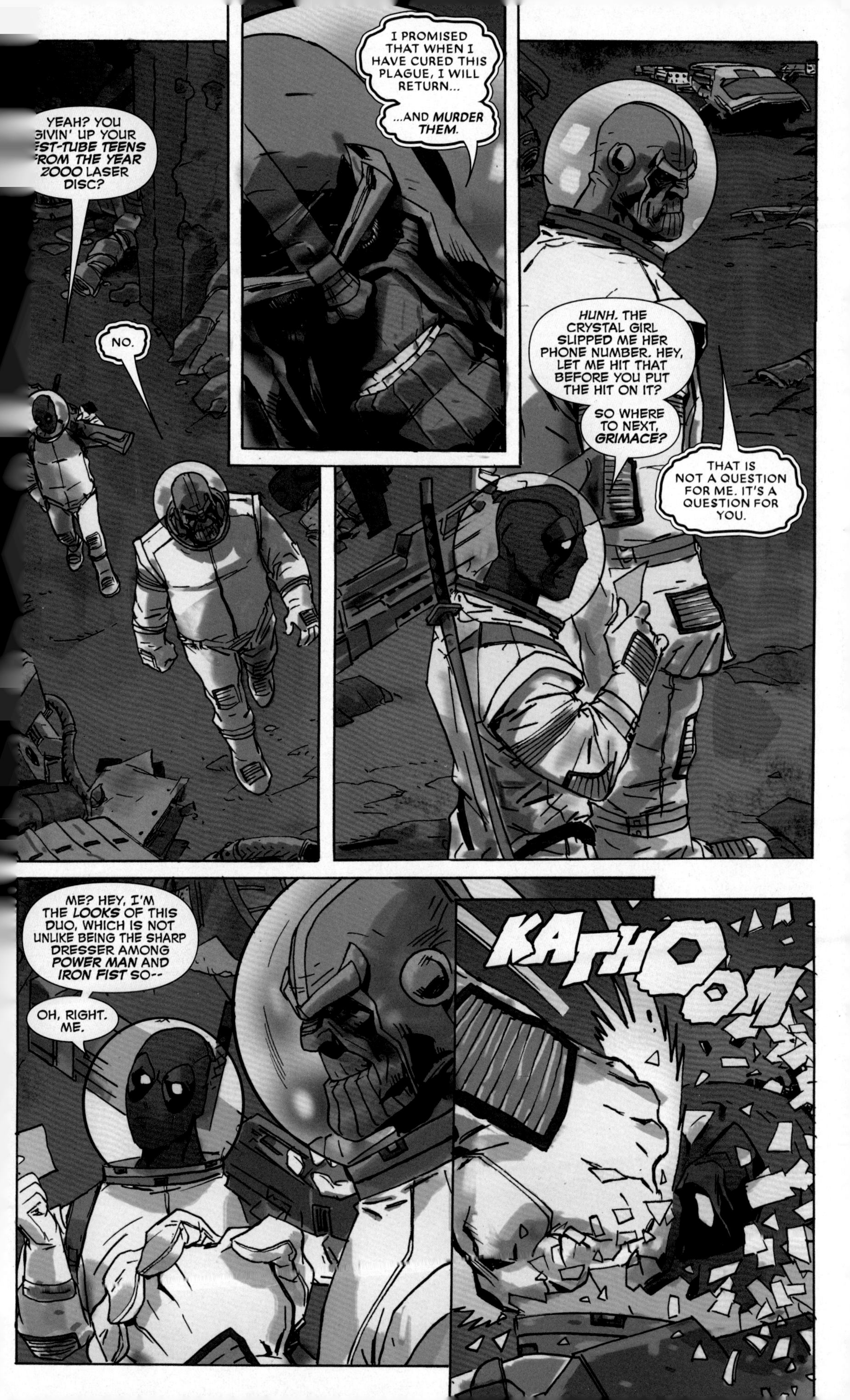
YEAH? YOU GIVIN' UP YOUR TEST-TUBE TEENS FROM THE YEAR 2000 LASER DISC?
I PROMISED THAT WHEN I HAVE CURED THIS PLAGUE, I WILL RETURN...
...AND MURDER THEM.
NO.
HUNH. THE CRYSTAL GIRL SLIPPED ME HER PHONE NUMBER. HEY, LET ME HIT THAT BEFORE YOU PUT THE HIT ON IT?
SO WHERE TO NEXT, GRIMACE?
THAT IS NOT A QUESTION FOR ME. IT'S A QUESTION FOR YOU.
ME? HEY, I'M THE LOOKS OF THIS DUO, WHICH IS NOT UNLIKE BEING THE SHARP DRESSER AMONG POWER MAN AND IRON FIST SO--
OH, RIGHT. ME.
KATHOOM

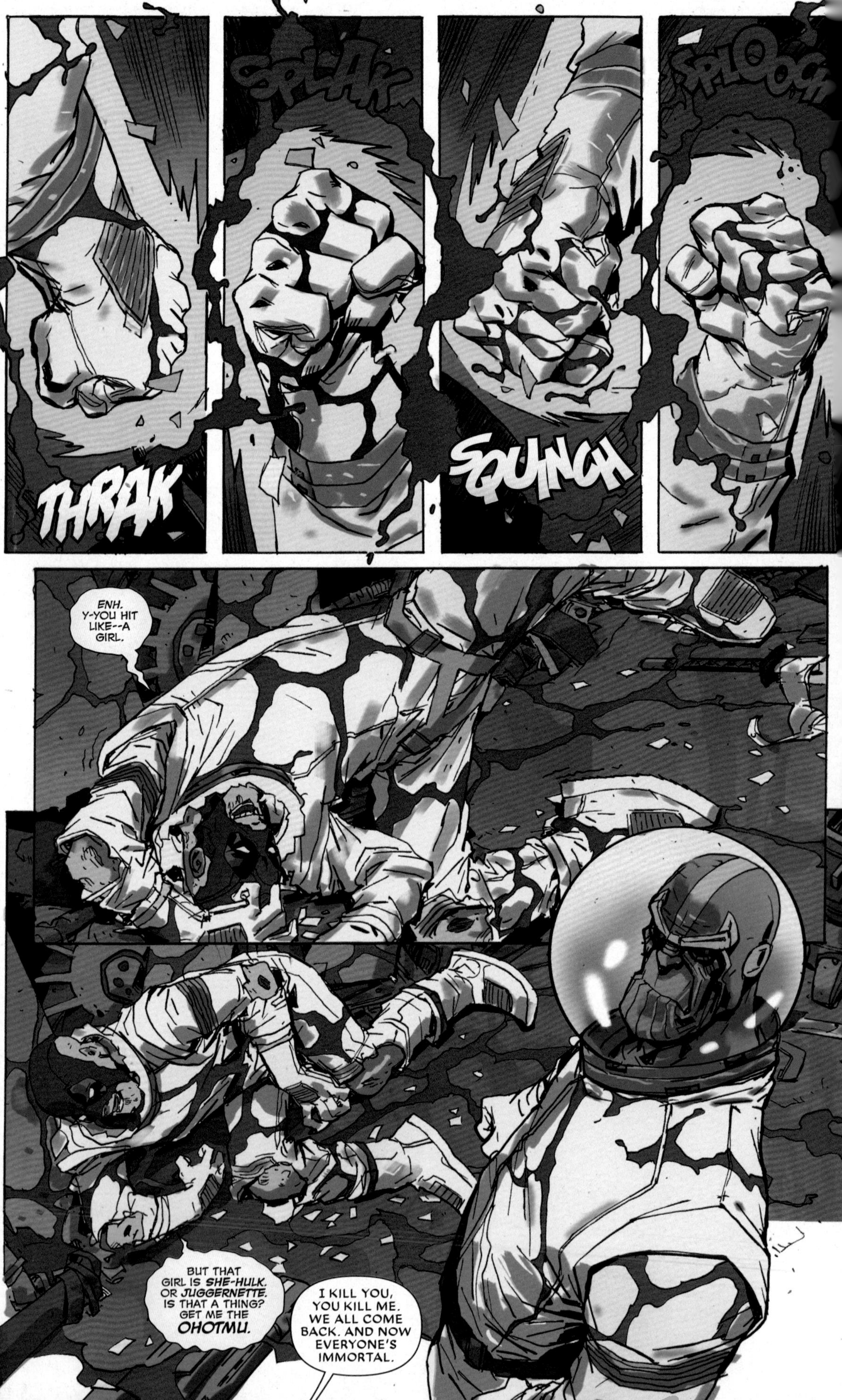
THRAK
SPLAK
SQUINCH
SPLOOCH
ENH. Y-YOU HIT LIKE--A GIRL.
BUT THAT GIRL IS SHE-HULK. OR JUGGERNETTE. IS THAT A THING? GET ME THE OHOTMU.
I KILL YOU, YOU KILL ME. WE ALL COME BACK. AND NOW EVERYONE'S IMMORTAL.

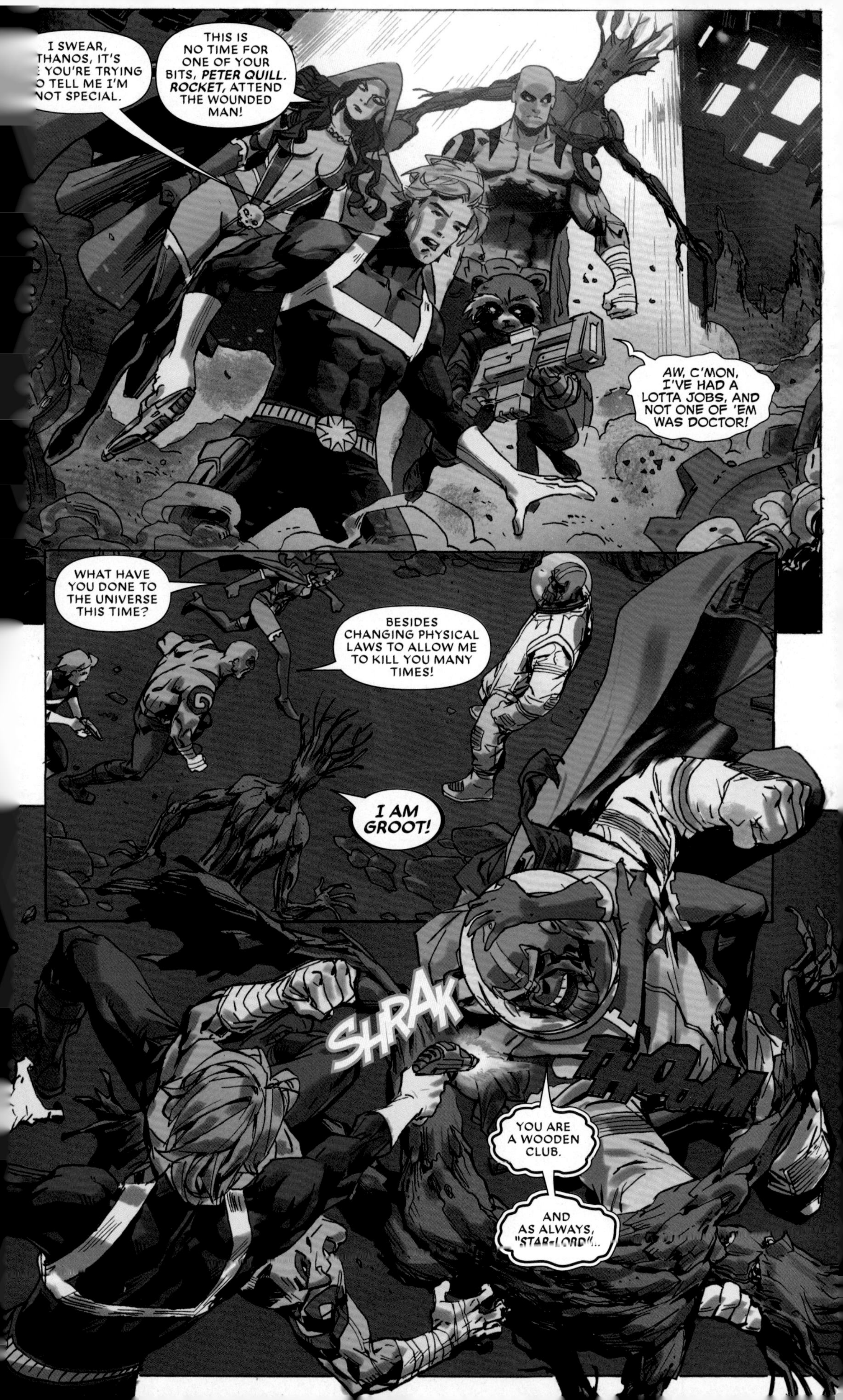
I SWEAR, THANOS, IT'S E YOU'RE TRYING O TELL ME I'M NOT SPECIAL.
THIS IS NO TIME FOR ONE OF YOUR BITS, PETER QUILL. ROCKET, ATTEND THE WOUNDED MAN!
AW, C'MON, I'VE HAD A LOTTA JOBS, AND NOT ONE OF 'EM WAS DOCTOR!
WHAT HAVE YOU DONE TO THE UNIVERSE THIS TIME?
BESIDES CHANGING PHYSICAL LAWS TO ALLOW ME TO KILL YOU MANY TIMES!
I AM GROOT!
SHRAK
YOU ARE A WOODEN CLUB.
AND AS ALWAYS, "STAR-LORD"...

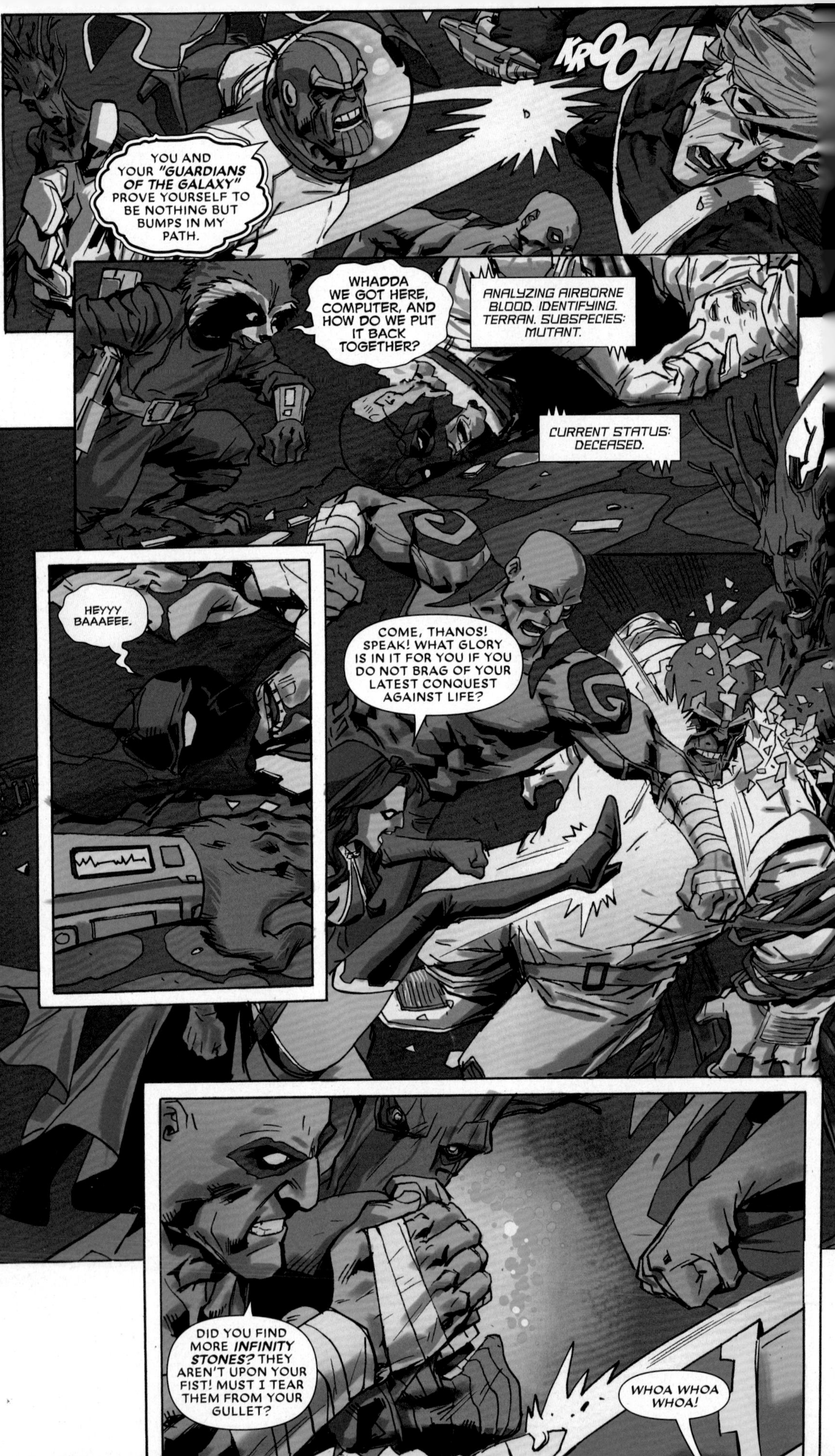
KROOOM
YOU AND YOUR "GUARDIANS OF THE GALAXY" PROVE YOURSELF TO BE NOTHING BUT BUMPS IN MY PATH.
WHADDA WE GOT HERE, COMPUTER, AND HOW DO WE PUT IT BACK TOGETHER?
ANALYZING AIRBORNE BLOOD. IDENTIFYING. TERRAN. SUBSPECIES: MUTANT.
CURRENT STATUS: DECEASED.
HEYYY BAAAEEE.
COME, THANOS! SPEAK! WHAT GLORY IS IN IT FOR YOU IF YOU DO NOT BRAG OF YOUR LATEST CONQUEST AGAINST LIFE?
DID YOU FIND MORE INFINITY STONES? THEY AREN'T UPON YOUR FIST! MUST I TEAR THEM FROM YOUR GULLET?
WHOA WHOA WHOA!

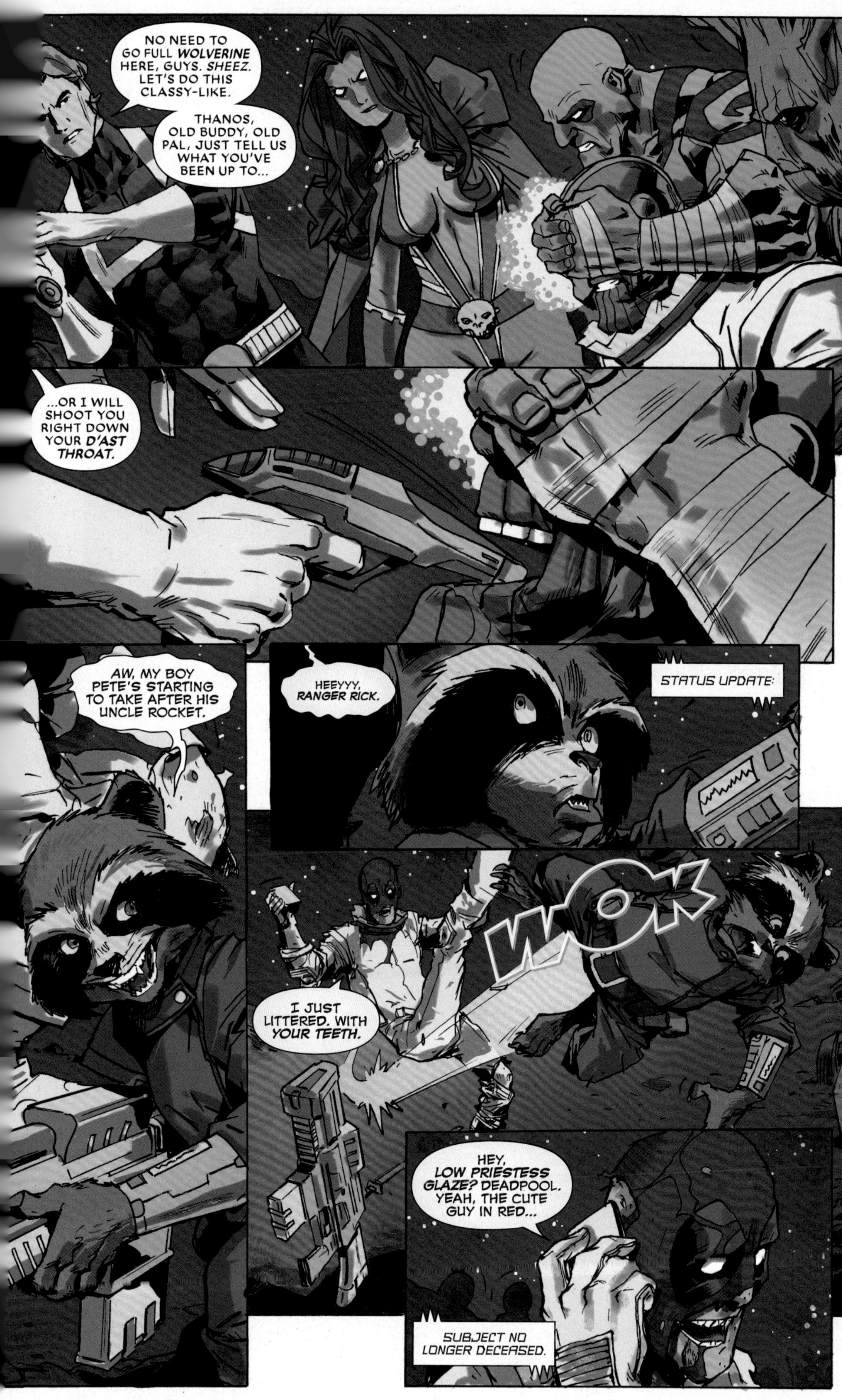
NO NEED TO GO FULL WOLVERINE HERE, GUYS. SHEEZ. LET'S DO THIS CLASSY-LIKE.
THANOS, OLD BUDDY, OLD PAL, JUST TELL US WHAT YOU'VE BEEN UP TO...
...OR I WILL SHOOT YOU RIGHT DOWN YOUR D'AST THROAT.
AW, MY BOY PETE'S STARTING TO TAKE AFTER HIS UNCLE ROCKET.
HEEYYY, RANGER RICK.
STATUS UPDATE:
WOK
I JUST LITTERED. WITH YOUR TEETH.
HEY, LOW PRIESTESS GLAZE? DEADPOOL. YEAH, THE CUTE GUY IN RED...
SUBJECT NO LONGER DECEASED.

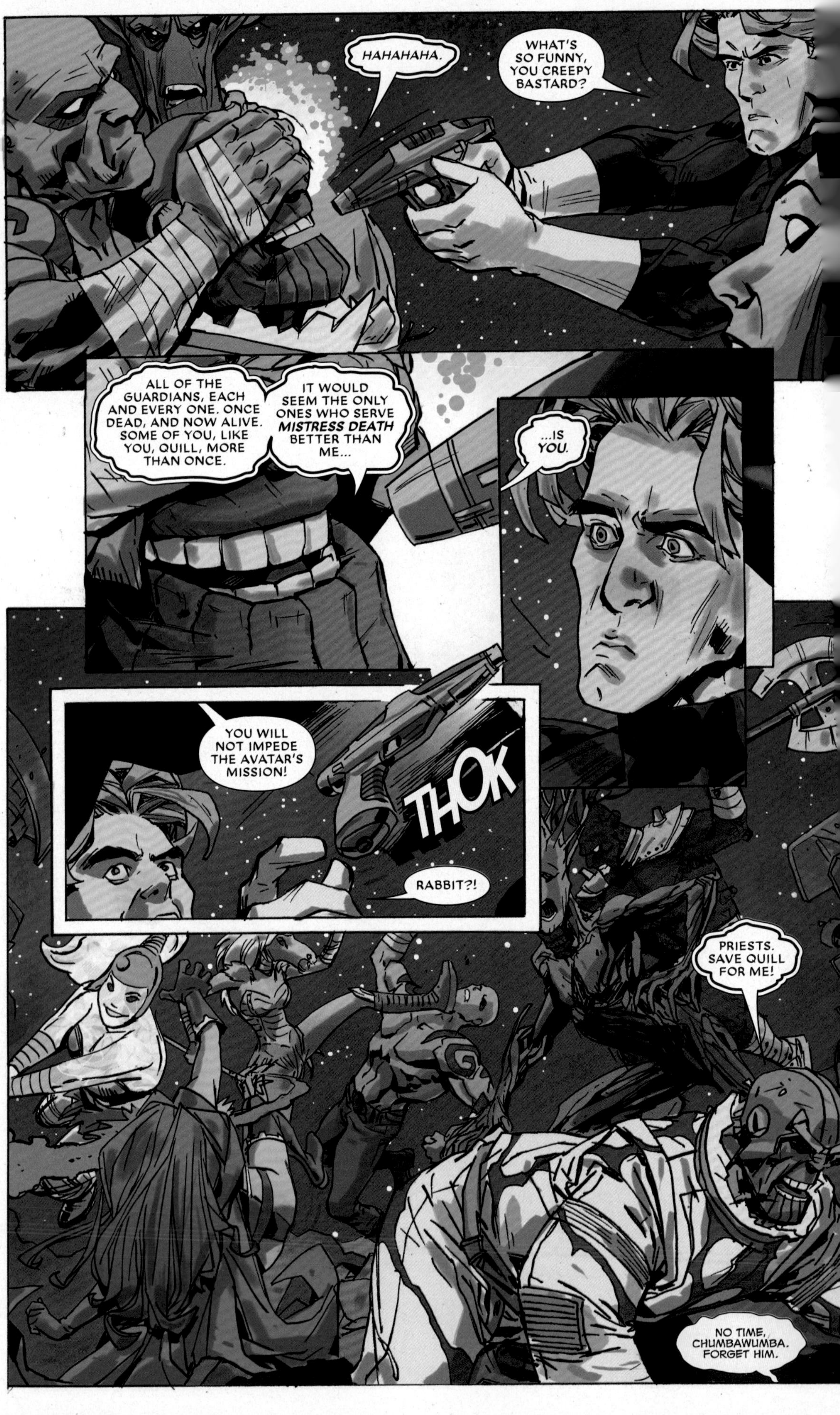
HAHAHAHA.
WHAT'S SO FUNNY, YOU CREEPY BASTARD?
ALL OF THE GUARDIANS, EACH AND EVERY ONE. ONCE DEAD, AND NOW ALIVE. SOME OF YOU, LIKE YOU, QUILL, MORE THAN ONCE.
IT WOULD SEEM THE ONLY ONES WHO SERVE MISTRESS DEATH BETTER THAN ME...
...IS YOU.
YOU WILL NOT IMPEDE THE AVATAR'S MISSION!
THOK
RABBIT?!
PRIESTS. SAVE QUILL FOR ME!
NO TIME, CHUMBAWUMBA. FORGET HIM.

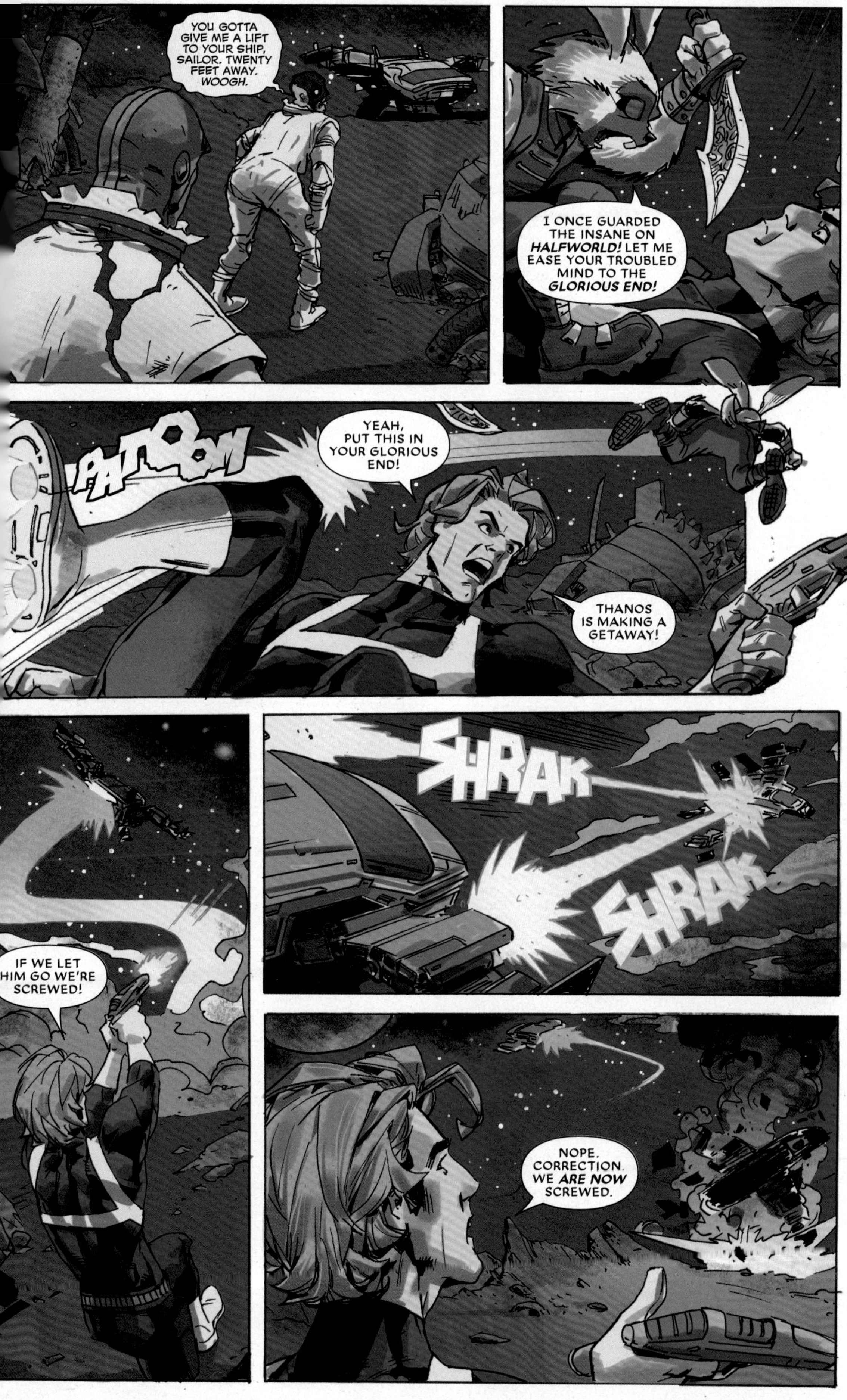
YOU GOTTA GIVE ME A LIFT TO YOUR SHIP, SAILOR. TWENTY FEET AWAY. WOOGH.
I ONCE GUARDED THE INSANE ON HALFWORLD! LET ME EASE YOUR TROUBLED MIND TO THE GLORIOUS END!
PATOOM
YEAH, PUT THIS IN YOUR GLORIOUS END!
THANOS IS MAKING A GETAWAY!
IF WE LET HIM GO WE'RE SCREWED!
SHRAK
SHRAK
NOPE. CORRECTION. WE ARE NOW SCREWED.

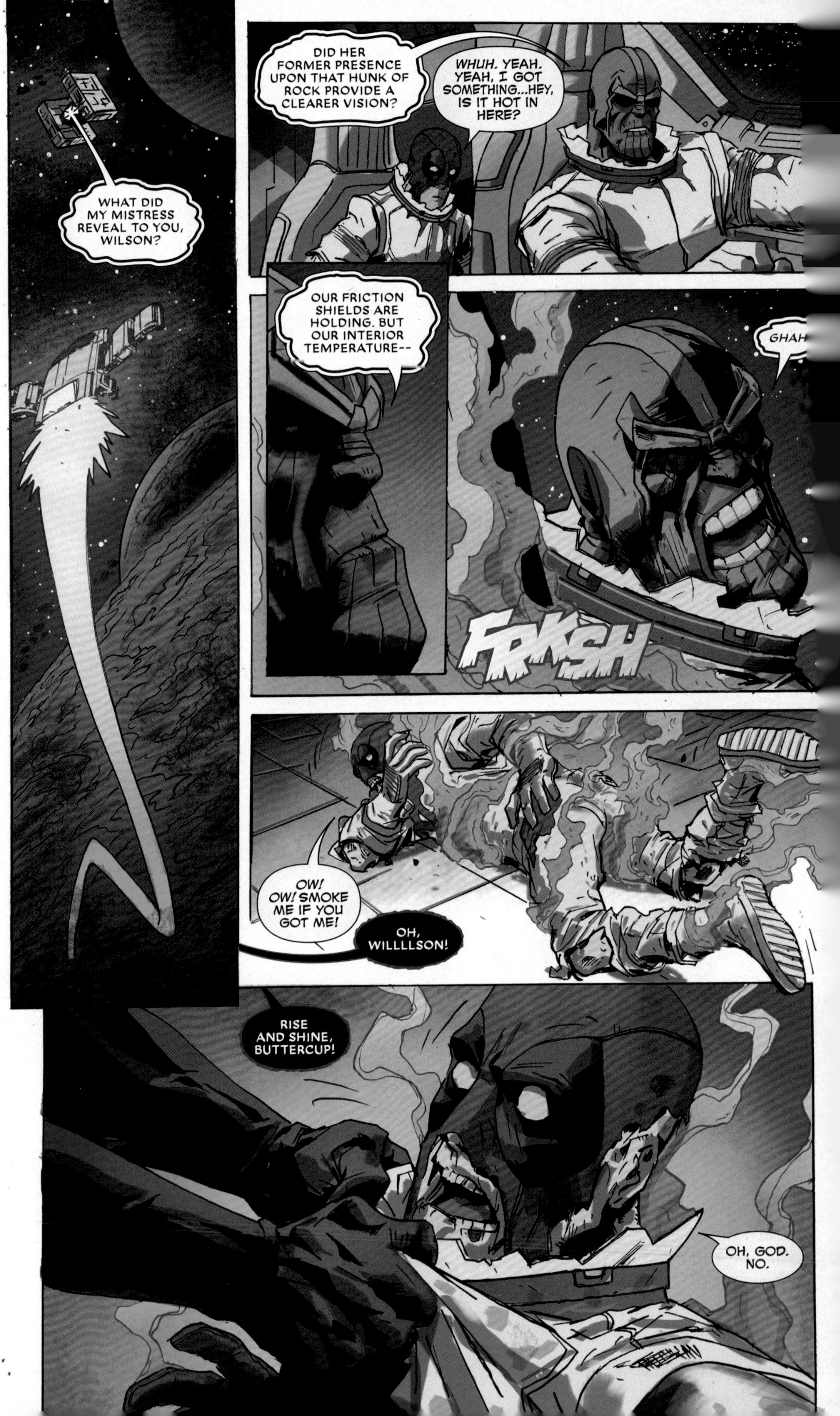
WHAT DID MY MISTRESS REVEAL TO YOU, WILSON?
DID HER FORMER PRESENCE UPON THAT HUNK OF ROCK PROVIDE A CLEARER VISION?
WHUH. YEAH. YEAH, I GOT SOMETHING...HEY, IS IT HOT IN HERE?
OUR FRICTION SHIELDS ARE HOLDING. BUT OUR INTERIOR TEMPERATURE--
GHAH
FRKSH
OW! OW! SMOKE ME IF YOU GOT ME!
OH, WILLLLSON!
RISE AND SHINE, BUTTERCUP!
OH, GOD. NO.

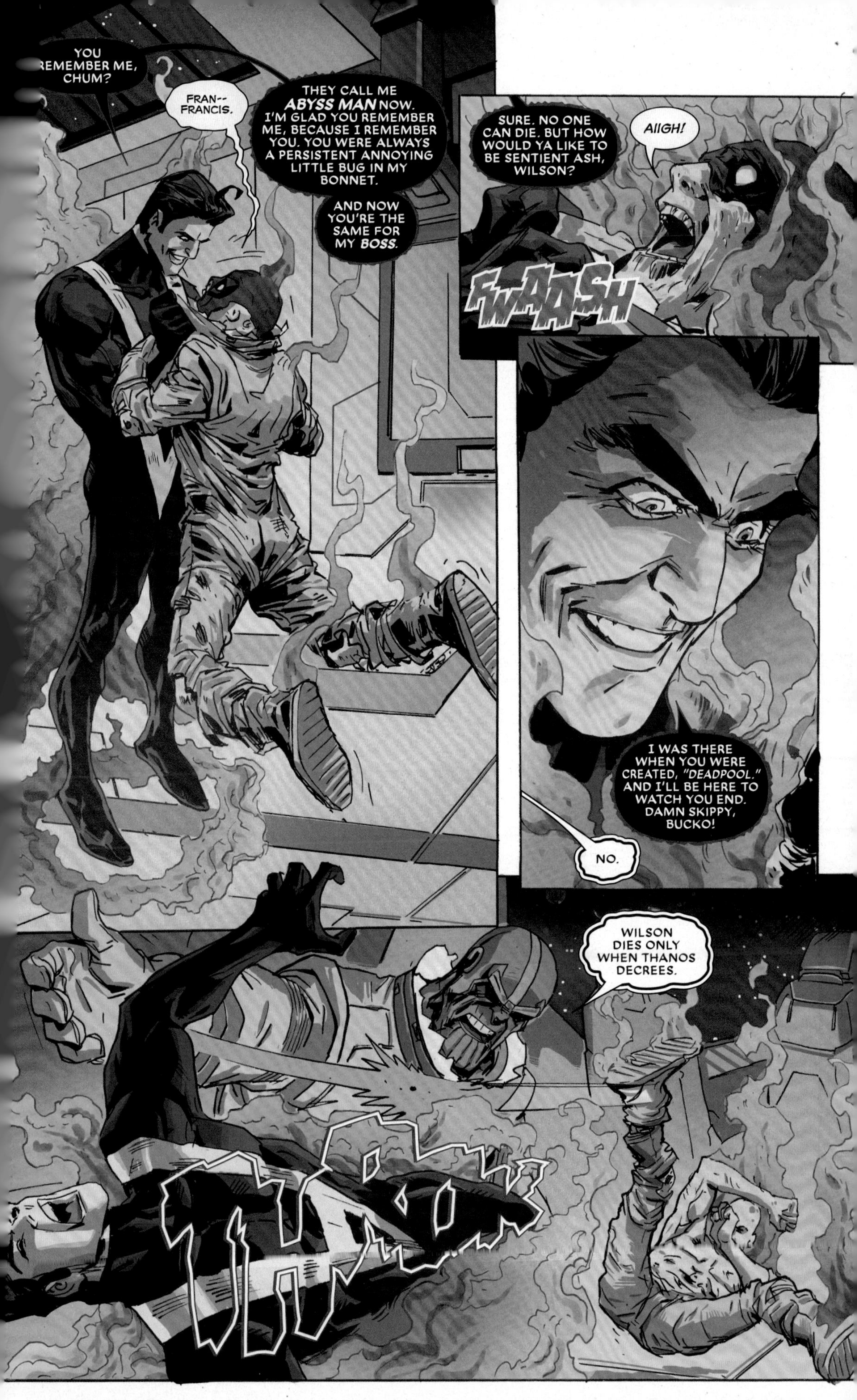
YOU REMEMBER ME, CHUM?
FRAN-- FRANCIS.
THEY CALL ME ABYSS MAN NOW. I'M GLAD YOU REMEMBER ME, BECAUSE I REMEMBER YOU. YOU WERE ALWAYS A PERSISTENT ANNOYING LITTLE BUG IN MY BONNET.
AND NOW YOU'RE THE SAME FOR MY BOSS.
SURE. NO ONE CAN DIE. BUT HOW WOULD YA LIKE TO BE SENTIENT ASH, WILSON?
AIIGH!
FWAASH
I WAS THERE WHEN YOU WERE CREATED, "DEADPOOL." AND I'LL BE HERE TO WATCH YOU END. DAMN SKIPPY, BUCKO!
NO.
WILSON DIES ONLY WHEN THANOS DECREES.
THWOK

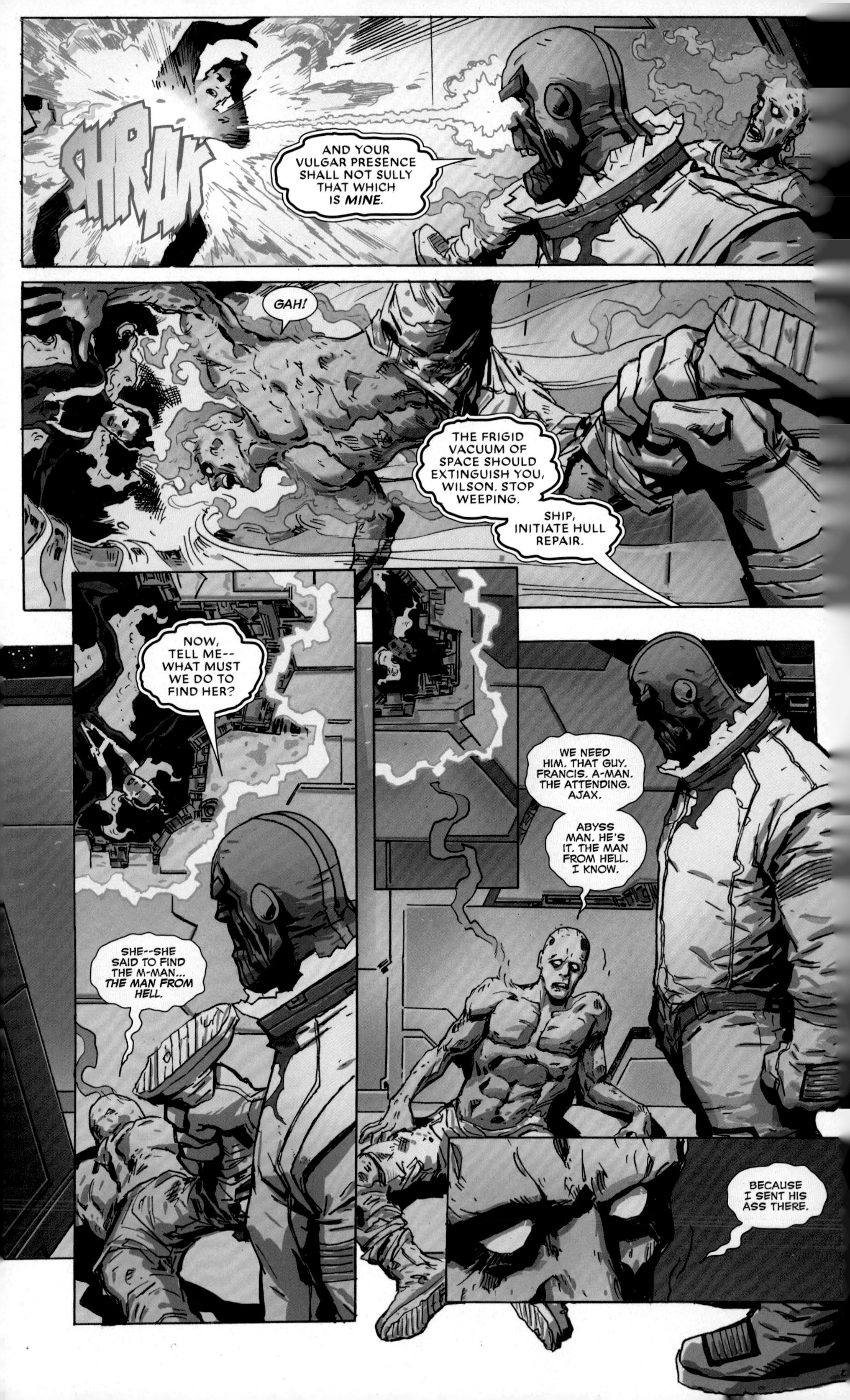
SHRAK
AND YOUR VULGAR PRESENCE SHALL NOT SULLY THAT WHICH IS *MINE*.
GAH!
THE FRIGID VACUUM OF SPACE SHOULD EXTINGUISH YOU, WILSON. STOP WEEPING.
SHIP, INITIATE HULL REPAIR.
NOW, TELL ME-- WHAT MUST WE DO TO FIND HER?
SHE--SHE SAID TO FIND THE M-MAN... *THE MAN FROM HELL.*
WE NEED HIM. THAT GUY. FRANCIS. A-MAN. THE ATTENDING. AJAX.
ABYSS MAN. HE'S IT. THE MAN FROM HELL. I KNOW.
BECAUSE I SENT HIS ASS THERE.

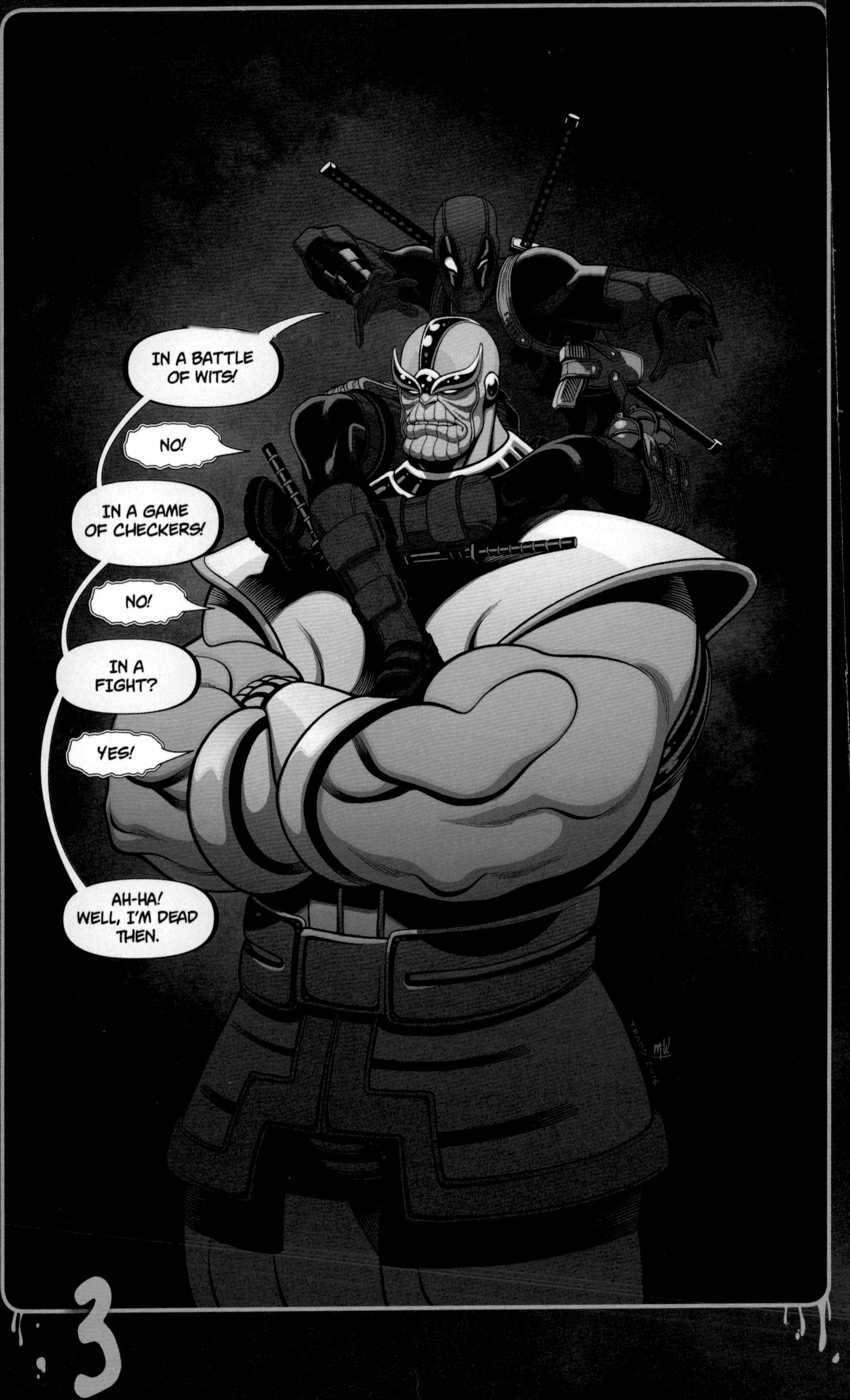
IN A BATTLE OF WITS!
NO!
IN A GAME OF CHECKERS!
NO!
IN A FIGHT?
YES!
AH-HA! WELL, I'M DEAD THEN.
3

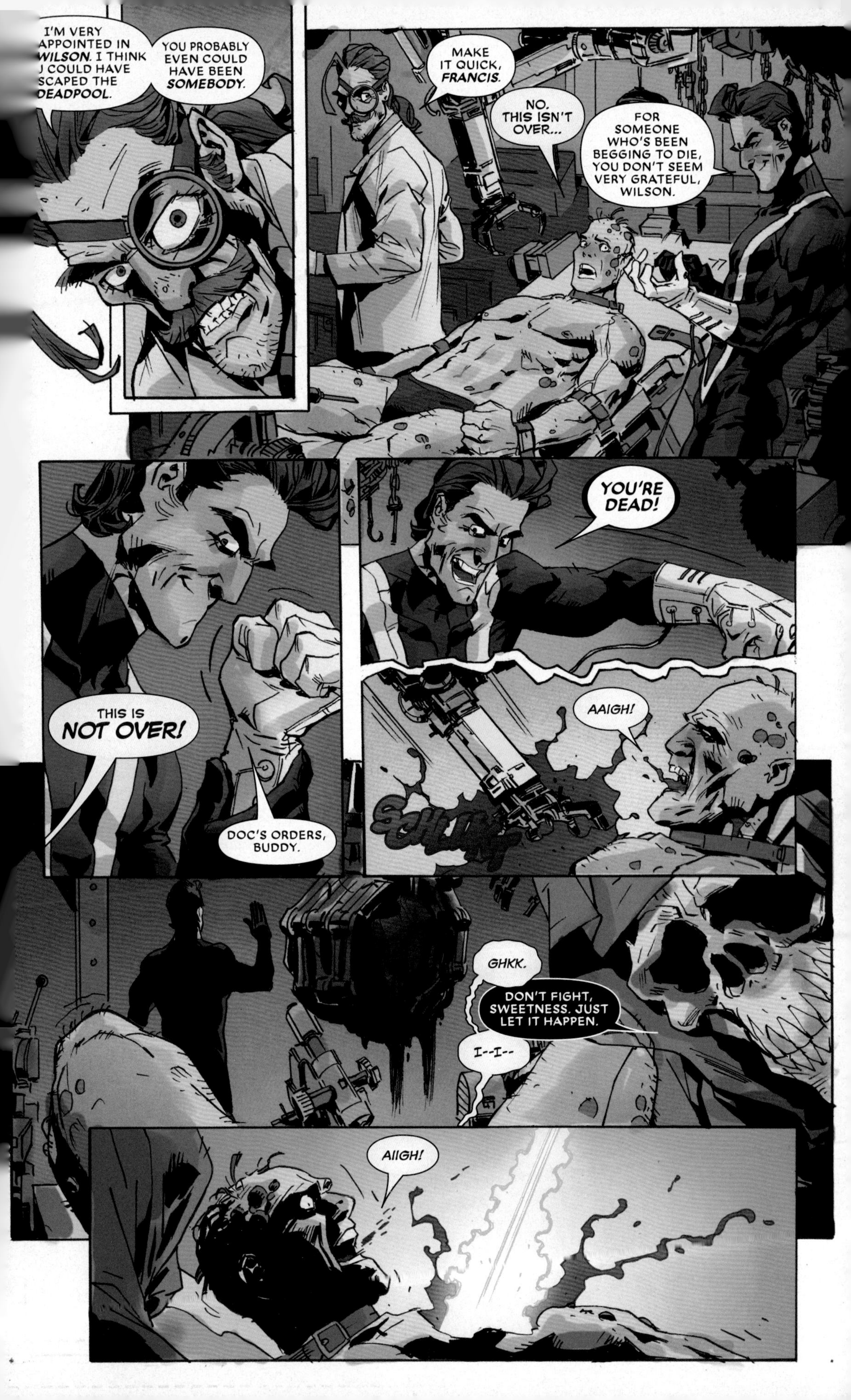
I'M VERY
APPOINTED IN
WILSON. I THINK
U COULD HAVE
SCAPED THE
DEADPOOL.
YOU PROBABLY EVEN COULD HAVE BEEN SOMEBODY.
MAKE IT QUICK, FRANCIS.
NO. THIS ISN'T OVER...
FOR SOMEONE WHO'S BEEN BEGGING TO DIE, YOU DON'T SEEM VERY GRATEFUL, WILSON.
THIS IS NOT OVER!
DOC'S ORDERS, BUDDY.
YOU'RE DEAD!
AAIGH!
GHKK.
DON'T FIGHT, SWEETNESS. JUST LET IT HAPPEN.
I--I--
AIIGH!

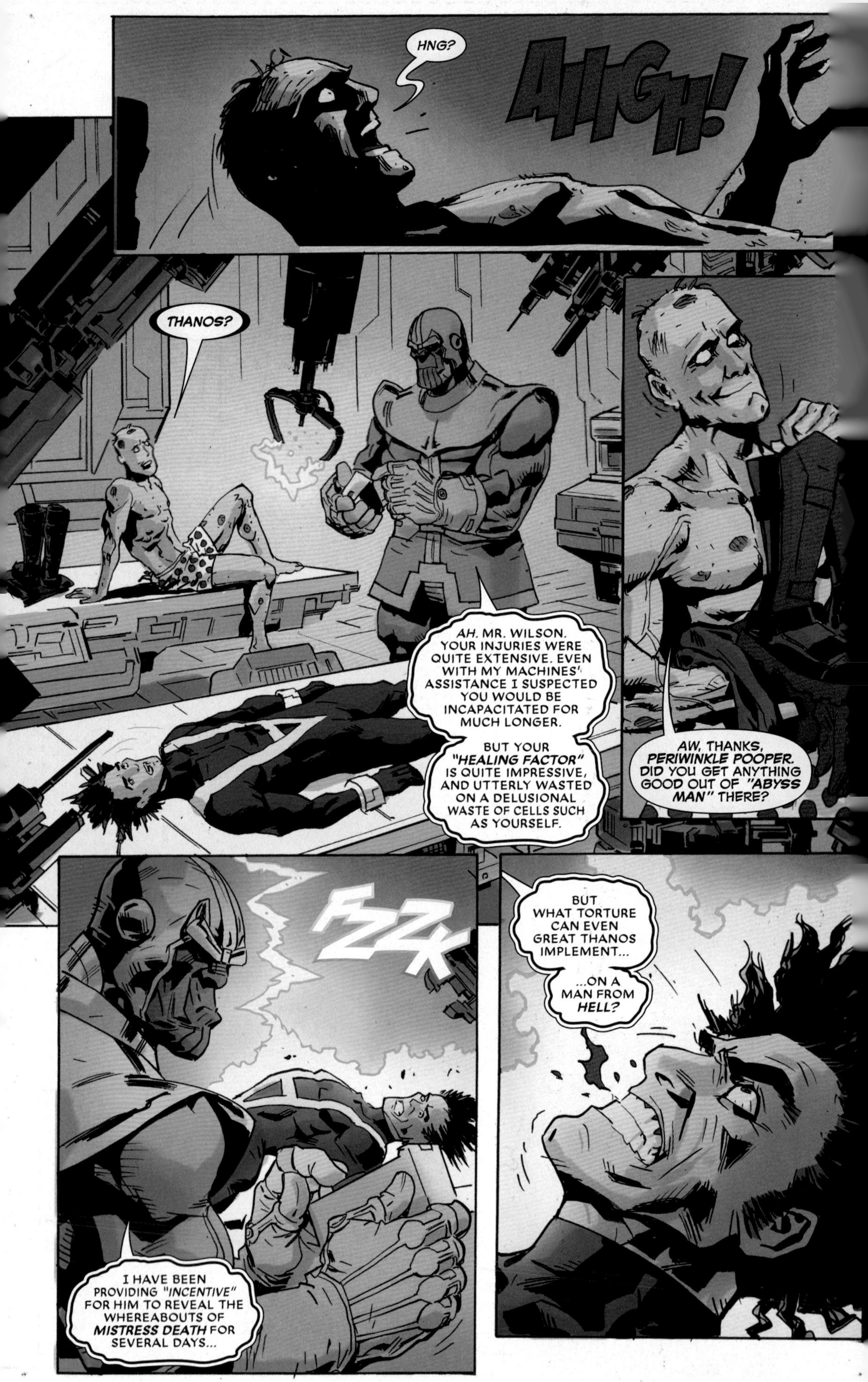
HNG?
AIIIGH!
THANOS?
AH. MR. WILSON. YOUR INJURIES WERE QUITE EXTENSIVE. EVEN WITH MY MACHINES' ASSISTANCE I SUSPECTED YOU WOULD BE INCAPACITATED FOR MUCH LONGER.
BUT YOUR "HEALING FACTOR" IS QUITE IMPRESSIVE, AND UTTERLY WASTED ON A DELUSIONAL WASTE OF CELLS SUCH AS YOURSELF.
AW, THANKS, PERIWINKLE POOPER. DID YOU GET ANYTHING GOOD OUT OF "ABYSS MAN" THERE?
FZZK
I HAVE BEEN PROVIDING "INCENTIVE" FOR HIM TO REVEAL THE WHEREABOUTS OF MISTRESS DEATH FOR SEVERAL DAYS...
BUT WHAT TORTURE CAN EVEN GREAT THANOS IMPLEMENT...
...ON A MAN FROM HELL?

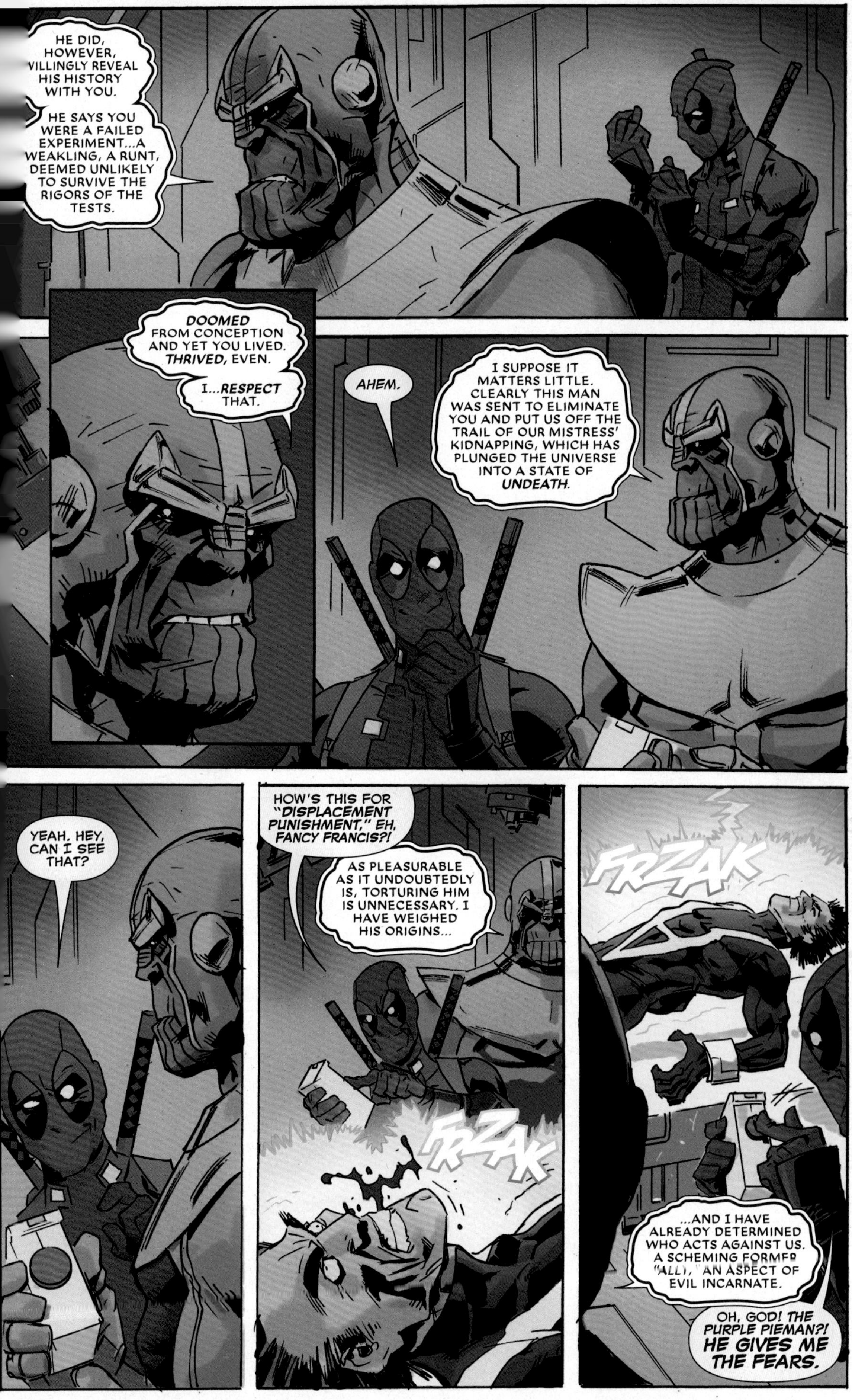
HE DID, HOWEVER, WILLINGLY REVEAL HIS HISTORY WITH YOU.
HE SAYS YOU WERE A FAILED EXPERIMENT...A WEAKLING, A RUNT, DEEMED UNLIKELY TO SURVIVE THE RIGORS OF THE TESTS.
DOOMED FROM CONCEPTION AND YET YOU LIVED. THRIVED, EVEN.
I...RESPECT THAT.
AHEM.
I SUPPOSE IT MATTERS LITTLE. CLEARLY THIS MAN WAS SENT TO ELIMINATE YOU AND PUT US OFF THE TRAIL OF OUR MISTRESS' KIDNAPPING, WHICH HAS PLUNGED THE UNIVERSE INTO A STATE OF UNDEATH.
YEAH. HEY, CAN I SEE THAT?
HOW'S THIS FOR "DISPLACEMENT PUNISHMENT," EH, FANCY FRANCIS?!
AS PLEASURABLE AS IT UNDOUBTEDLY IS, TORTURING HIM IS UNNECESSARY. I HAVE WEIGHED HIS ORIGINS...
FRZAK
FRZAK
...AND I HAVE ALREADY DETERMINED WHO ACTS AGAINST US. A SCHEMING FORMER "ALLY," AN ASPECT OF EVIL INCARNATE.
OH, GOD! THE PURPLE PIEMAN?! HE GIVES ME THE FEARS.

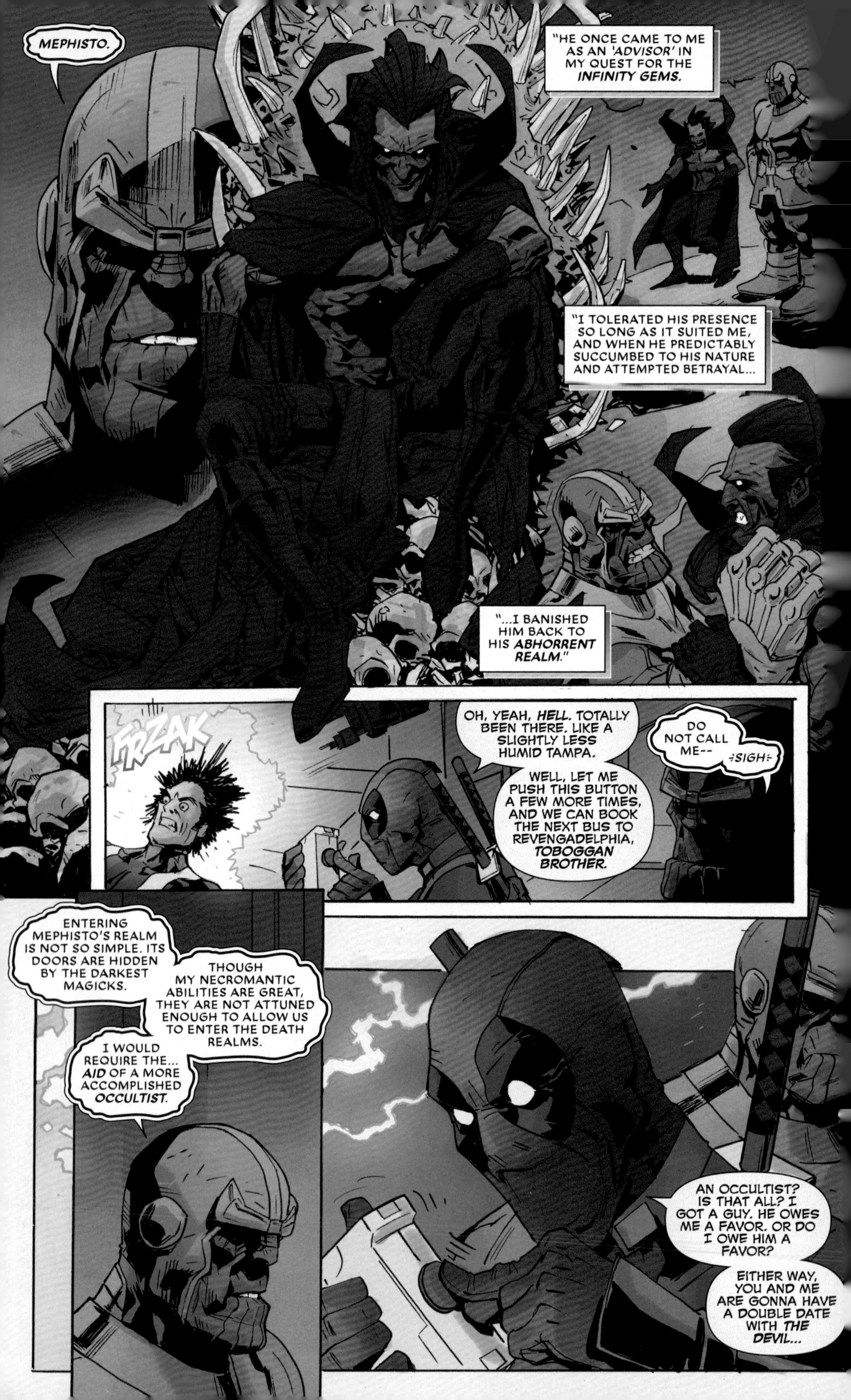
MEPHISTO.
"HE ONCE CAME TO ME AS AN 'ADVISOR' IN MY QUEST FOR THE INFINITY GEMS.
"I TOLERATED HIS PRESENCE SO LONG AS IT SUITED ME, AND WHEN HE PREDICTABLY SUCCUMBED TO HIS NATURE AND ATTEMPTED BETRAYAL...
"...I BANISHED HIM BACK TO HIS ABHORRENT REALM."
FRZAK
OH, YEAH, HELL. TOTALLY BEEN THERE. LIKE A SLIGHTLY LESS HUMID TAMPA.
WELL, LET ME PUSH THIS BUTTON A FEW MORE TIMES, AND WE CAN BOOK THE NEXT BUS TO REVENGADELPHIA, TOBOGGAN BROTHER.
DO NOT CALL ME--
SIGH
ENTERING MEPHISTO'S REALM IS NOT SO SIMPLE. ITS DOORS ARE HIDDEN BY THE DARKEST MAGICKS.
THOUGH MY NECROMANTIC ABILITIES ARE GREAT, THEY ARE NOT ATTUNED ENOUGH TO ALLOW US TO ENTER THE DEATH REALMS.
I WOULD REQUIRE THE... AID OF A MORE ACCOMPLISHED OCCULTIST.
AN OCCULTIST? IS THAT ALL? I GOT A GUY. HE OWES ME A FAVOR. OR DO I OWE HIM A FAVOR?
EITHER WAY, YOU AND ME ARE GONNA HAVE A DOUBLE DATE WITH THE DEVIL...

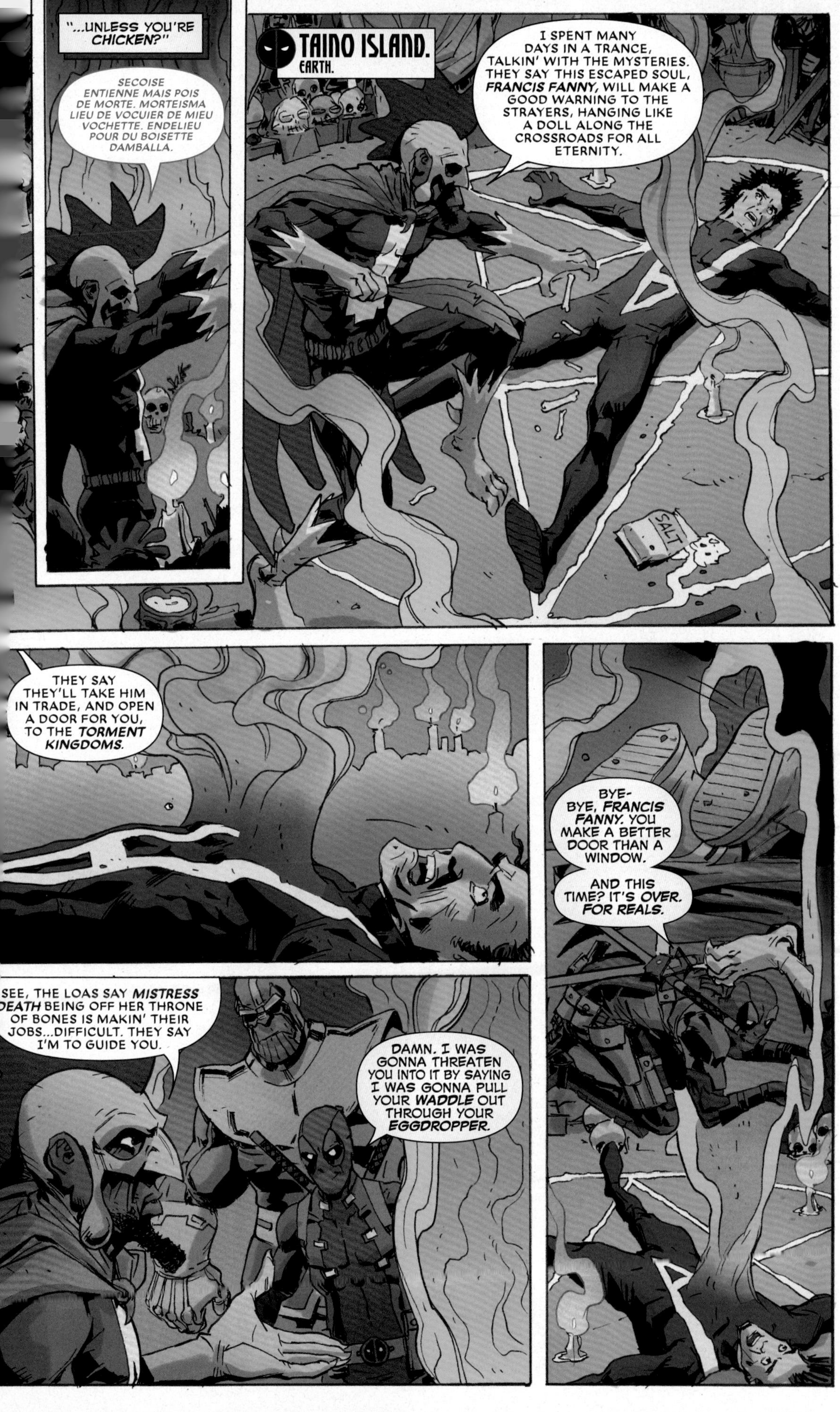
"...UNLESS YOU'RE CHICKEN?"
SECOISE ENTIENNE MAIS POIS DE MORTE. MORTEISMA LIEU DE VOCUIER DE MIEU VOCHETTE. ENDELIEU POUR DU BOISETTE DAMBALLA.
TAINO ISLAND. EARTH.
I SPENT MANY DAYS IN A TRANCE, TALKIN' WITH THE MYSTERIES. THEY SAY THIS ESCAPED SOUL, FRANCIS FANNY, WILL MAKE A GOOD WARNING TO THE STRAYERS, HANGING LIKE A DOLL ALONG THE CROSSROADS FOR ALL ETERNITY.
SALT
THEY SAY THEY'LL TAKE HIM IN TRADE, AND OPEN A DOOR FOR YOU, TO THE TORMENT KINGDOMS.
BYE-BYE, FRANCIS FANNY. YOU MAKE A BETTER DOOR THAN A WINDOW.
AND THIS TIME? IT'S OVER. FOR REALS.
SEE, THE LOAS SAY MISTRESS DEATH BEING OFF HER THRONE OF BONES IS MAKIN' THEIR JOBS...DIFFICULT. THEY SAY I'M TO GUIDE YOU.
DAMN. I WAS GONNA THREATEN YOU INTO IT BY SAYING I WAS GONNA PULL YOUR WADDLE OUT THROUGH YOUR EGGDROPPER.

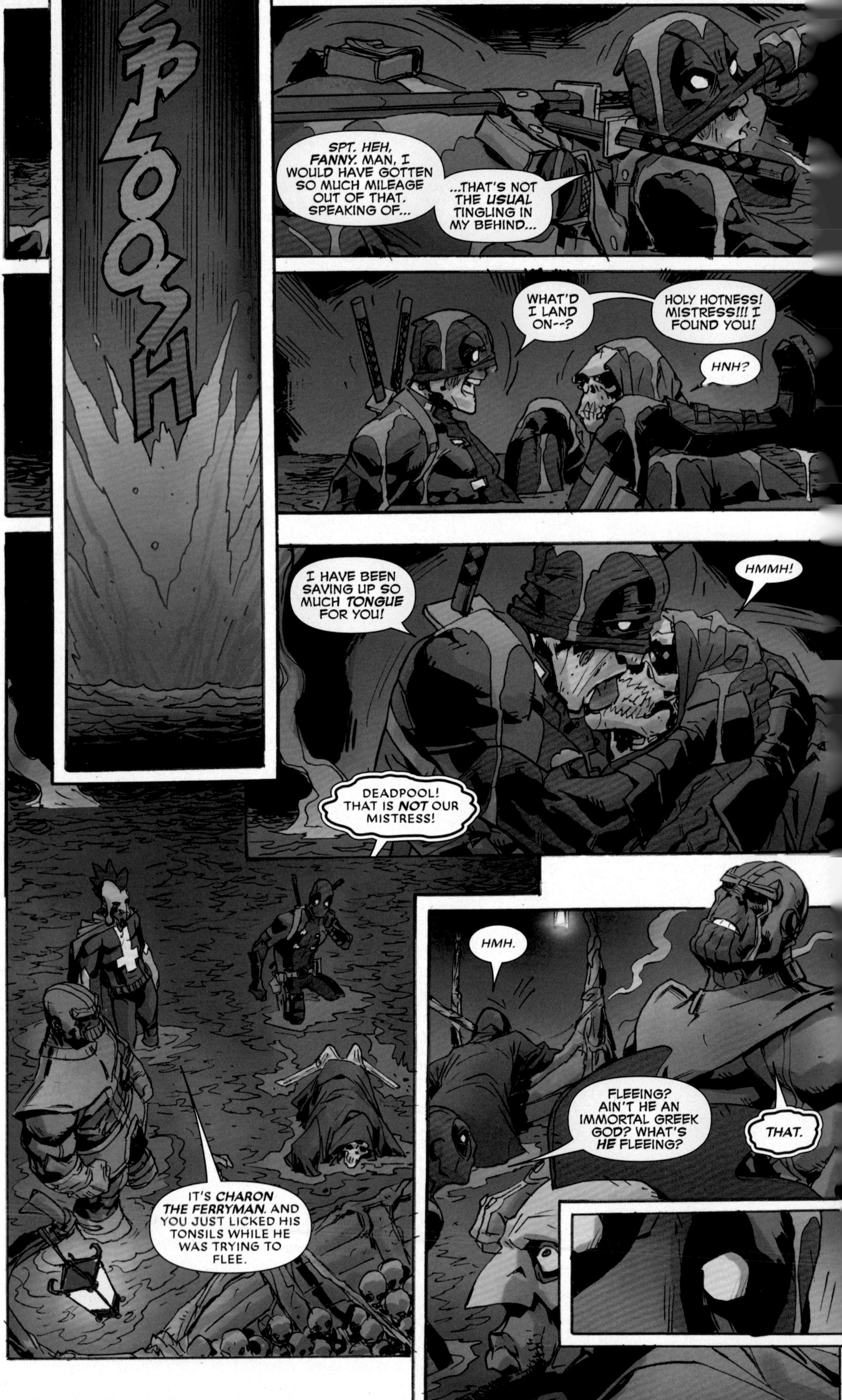
SPLOOSH
SPT. HEH, FANNY. MAN, I WOULD HAVE GOTTEN SO MUCH MILEAGE OUT OF THAT. SPEAKING OF...
...THAT'S NOT THE USUAL TINGLING IN MY BEHIND...
WHAT'D I LAND ON--?
HOLY HOTNESS! MISTRESS!!! I FOUND YOU!
HNH?
I HAVE BEEN SAVING UP SO MUCH TONGUE FOR YOU!
HMMH!
DEADPOOL! THAT IS NOT OUR MISTRESS!
IT'S CHARON THE FERRYMAN. AND YOU JUST LICKED HIS TONSILS WHILE HE WAS TRYING TO FLEE.
HMH.
FLEEING? AIN'T HE AN IMMORTAL GREEK GOD? WHAT'S HE FLEEING?
THAT.

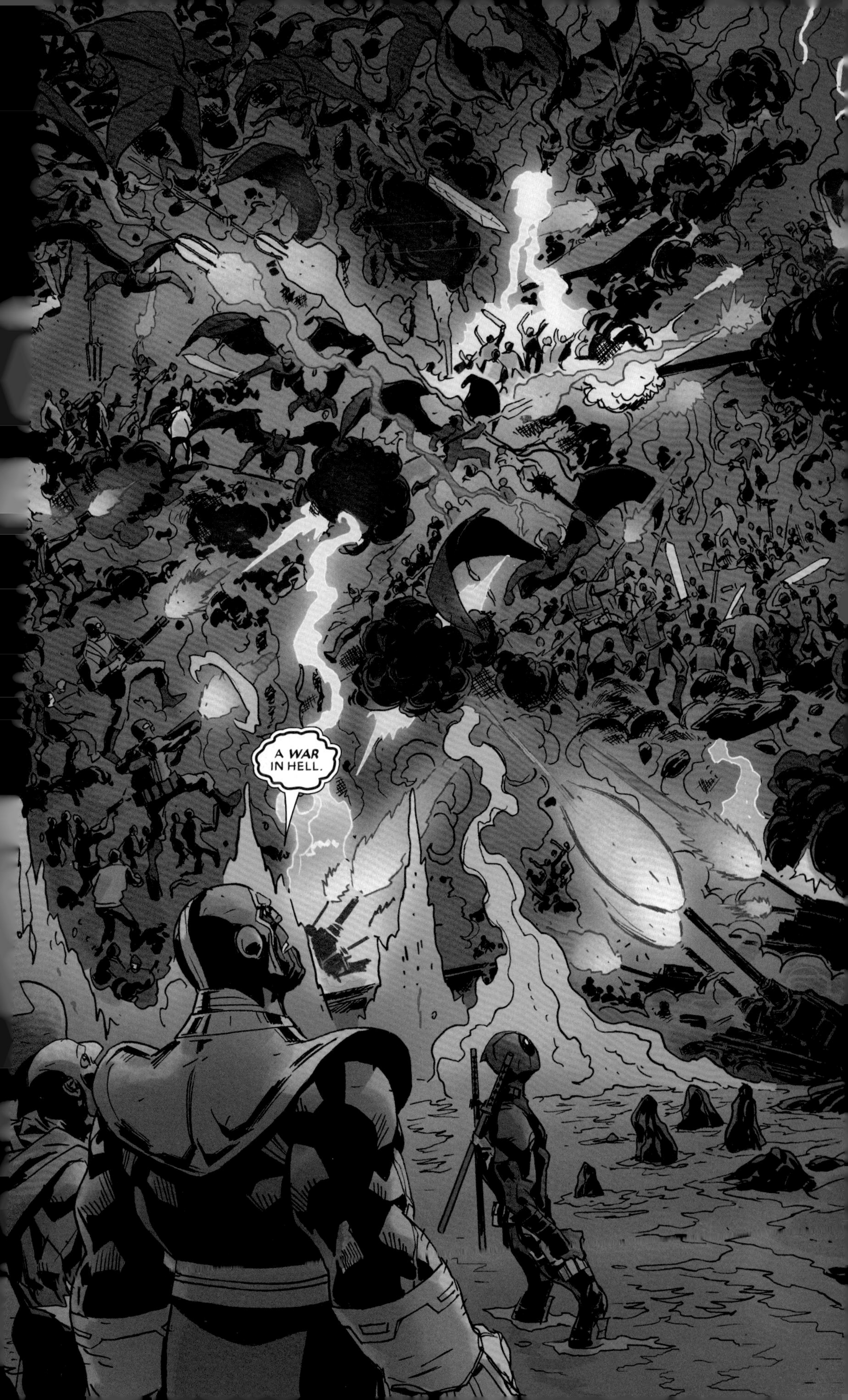
A WAR IN HELL.

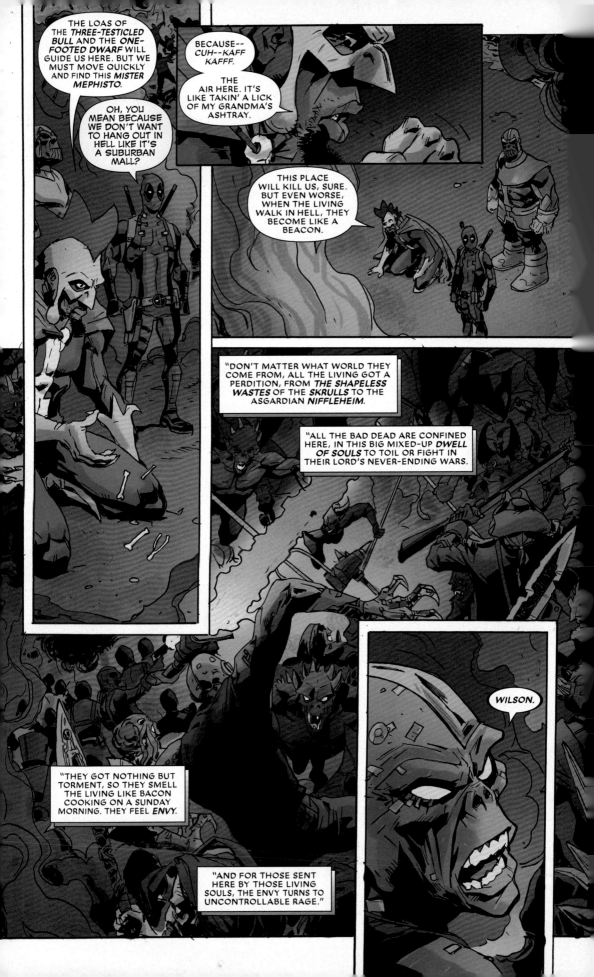

THE LOAS OF THE *THREE-TESTICLED BULL* AND THE *ONE-FOOTED DWARF* WILL GUIDE US HERE. BUT WE MUST MOVE QUICKLY AND FIND THIS *MISTER MEPHISTO.*

OH, YOU MEAN BECAUSE WE DON'T WANT TO HANG OUT IN HELL LIKE IT'S A SUBURBAN MALL?

BECAUSE-- CUH--KAFF KAFFF.

THE AIR HERE. IT'S LIKE TAKIN' A LICK OF MY GRANDMA'S ASHTRAY.

THIS PLACE WILL KILL US, SURE. BUT EVEN WORSE, WHEN THE LIVING WALK IN HELL, THEY BECOME LIKE A BEACON.

"DON'T MATTER WHAT WORLD THEY COME FROM, ALL THE LIVING GOT A PERDITION, FROM *THE SHAPELESS WASTES* OF THE *SKRULLS* TO THE ASGARDIAN *NIFFLEHEIM.*"

"ALL THE BAD DEAD ARE CONFINED HERE, IN THIS BIG MIXED-UP *DWELL OF SOULS* TO TOIL OR FIGHT IN THEIR LORD'S NEVER-ENDING WARS."

"THEY GOT NOTHING BUT TORMENT, SO THEY SMELL THE LIVING LIKE BACON COOKING ON A SUNDAY MORNING. THEY FEEL *ENVY.*"

WILSON.

"AND FOR THOSE SENT HERE BY THOSE LIVING SOULS, THE ENVY TURNS TO UNCONTROLLABLE RAGE."

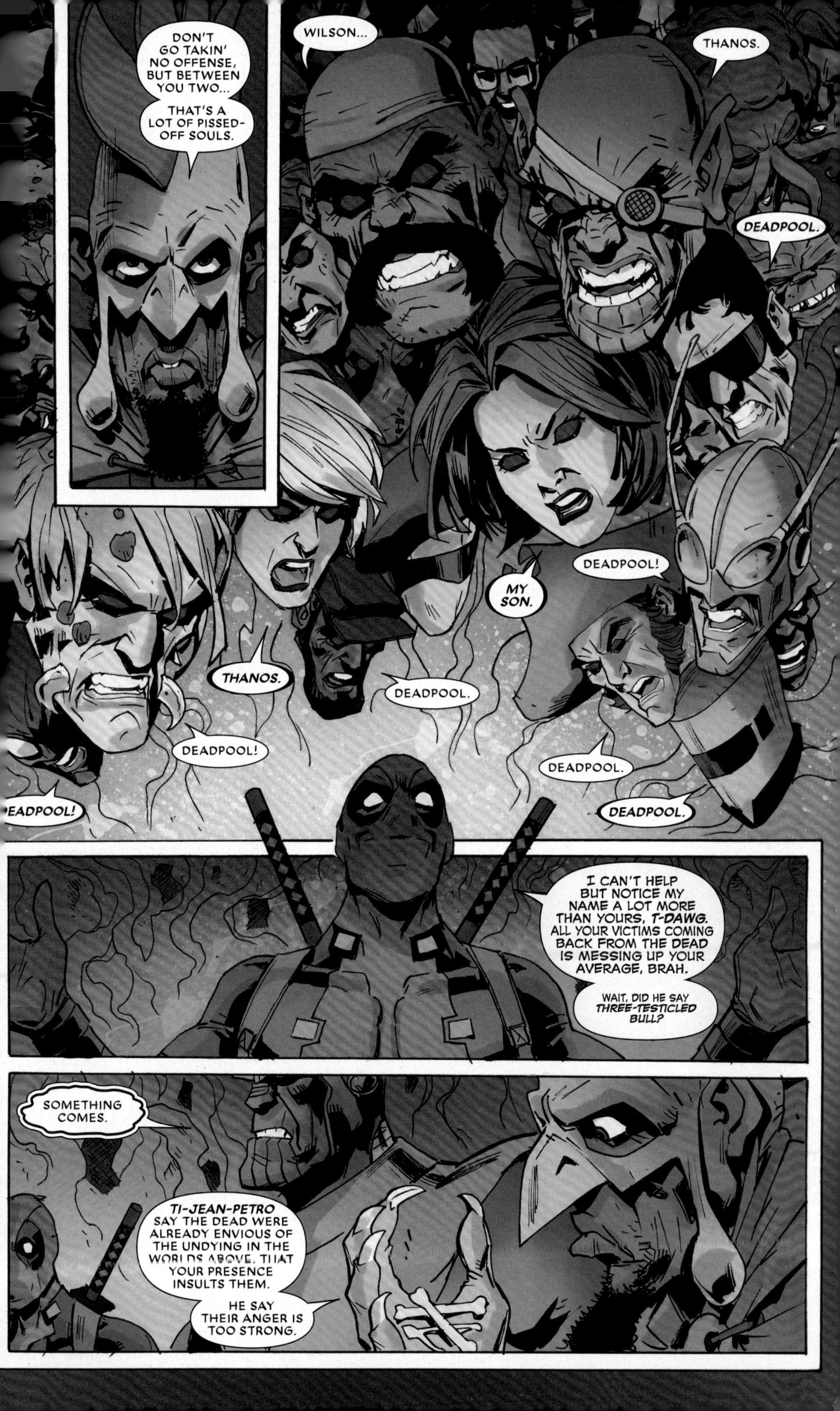
DON'T GO TAKIN' NO OFFENSE, BUT BETWEEN YOU TWO...
THAT'S A LOT OF PISSED-OFF SOULS.
WILSON...
THANOS.
DEADPOOL.
MY SON.
DEADPOOL!
THANOS.
DEADPOOL.
DEADPOOL!
DEADPOOL.
EADPOOL!
DEADPOOL.
I CAN'T HELP BUT NOTICE MY NAME A LOT MORE THAN YOURS, T-DAWG. ALL YOUR VICTIMS COMING BACK FROM THE DEAD IS MESSING UP YOUR AVERAGE, BRAH.
WAIT, DID HE SAY THREE-TESTICLED BULL?
SOMETHING COMES.
TI-JEAN-PETRO SAY THE DEAD WERE ALREADY ENVIOUS OF THE UNDYING IN THE WORLDS ABOVE. THAT YOUR PRESENCE INSULTS THEM.
HE SAY THEIR ANGER IS TOO STRONG.

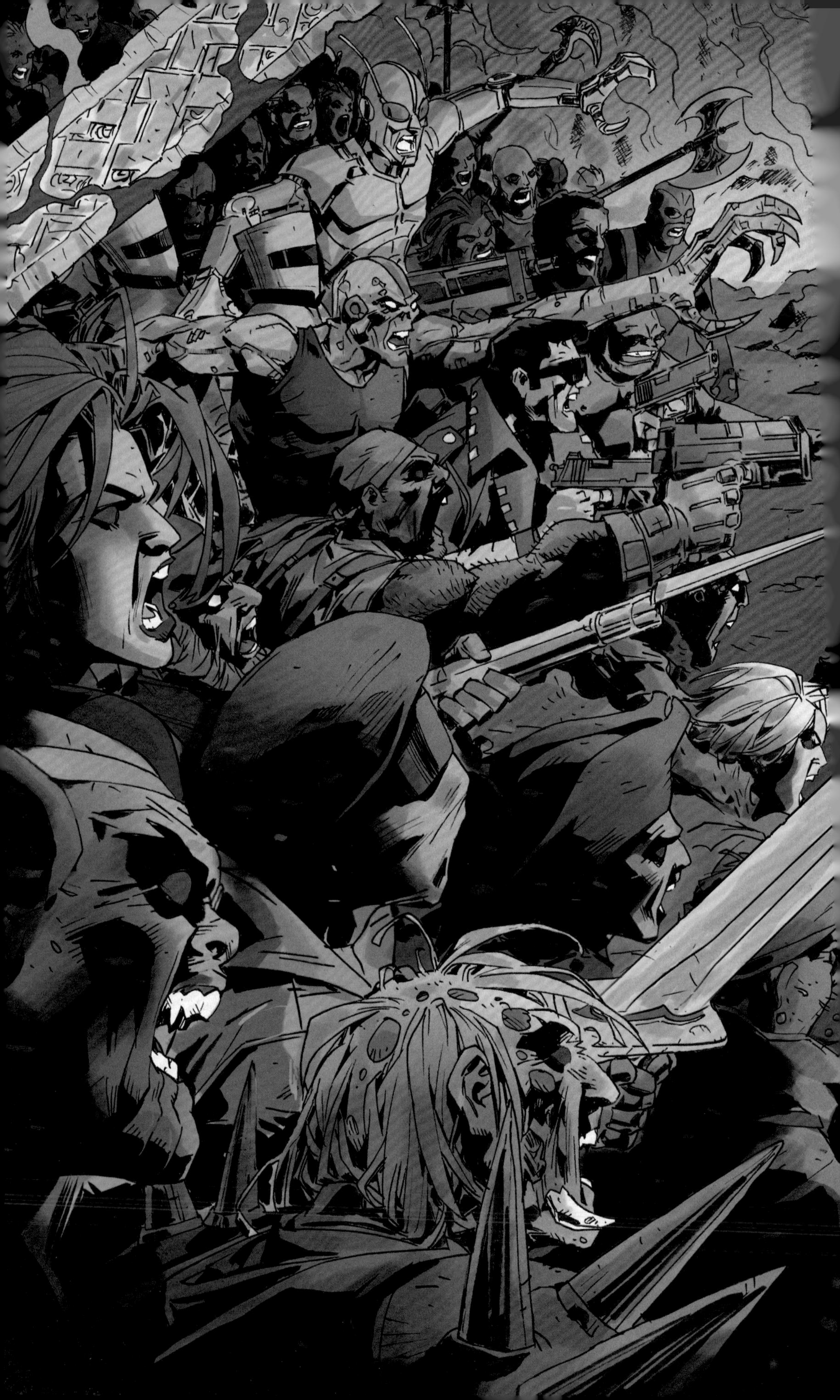

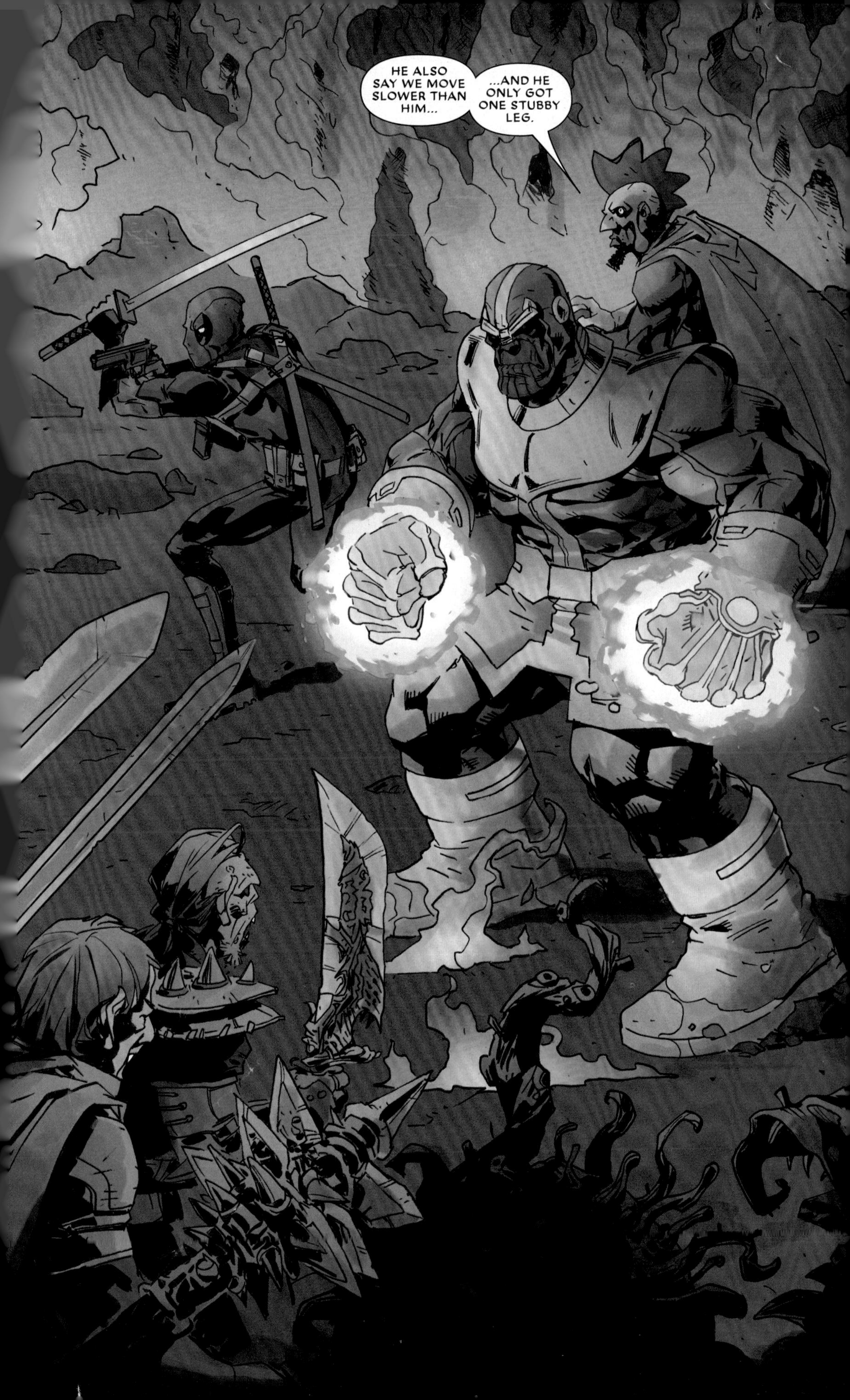
HE ALSO SAY WE MOVE SLOWER THAN HIM...
...AND HE ONLY GOT ONE STUBBY LEG.

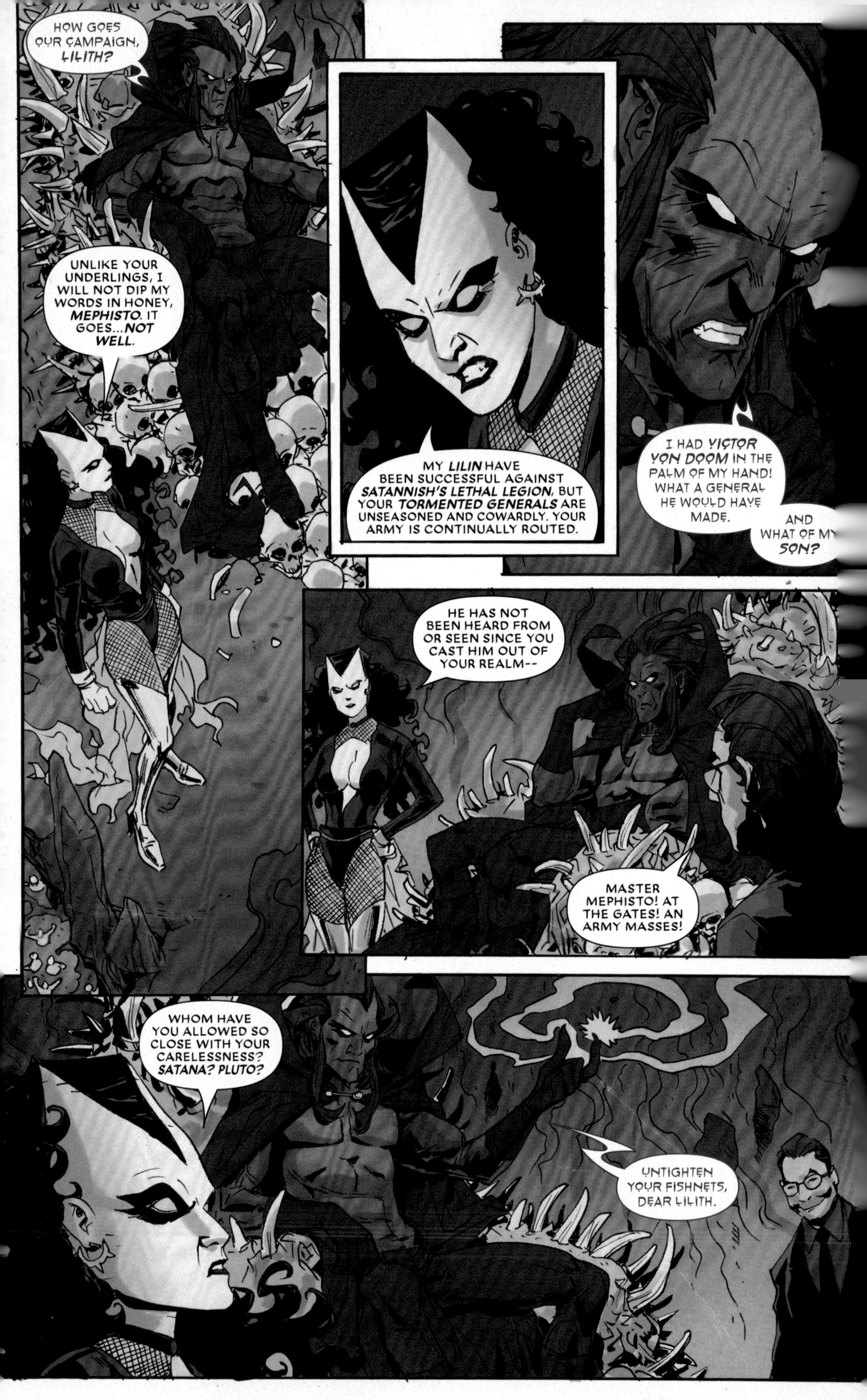
HOW GOES OUR CAMPAIGN, LILITH?
UNLIKE YOUR UNDERLINGS, I WILL NOT DIP MY WORDS IN HONEY, MEPHISTO. IT GOES...NOT WELL.
MY LILIN HAVE BEEN SUCCESSFUL AGAINST SATANNISH'S LETHAL LEGION, BUT YOUR TORMENTED GENERALS ARE UNSEASONED AND COWARDLY. YOUR ARMY IS CONTINUALLY ROUTED.
I HAD VICTOR VON DOOM IN THE PALM OF MY HAND! WHAT A GENERAL HE WOULD HAVE MADE.
AND WHAT OF MY SON?
HE HAS NOT BEEN HEARD FROM OR SEEN SINCE YOU CAST HIM OUT OF YOUR REALM--
MASTER MEPHISTO! AT THE GATES! AN ARMY MASSES!
WHOM HAVE YOU ALLOWED SO CLOSE WITH YOUR CARELESSNESS? SATANA? PLUTO?
UNTIGHTEN YOUR FISHNETS, DEAR LILITH.

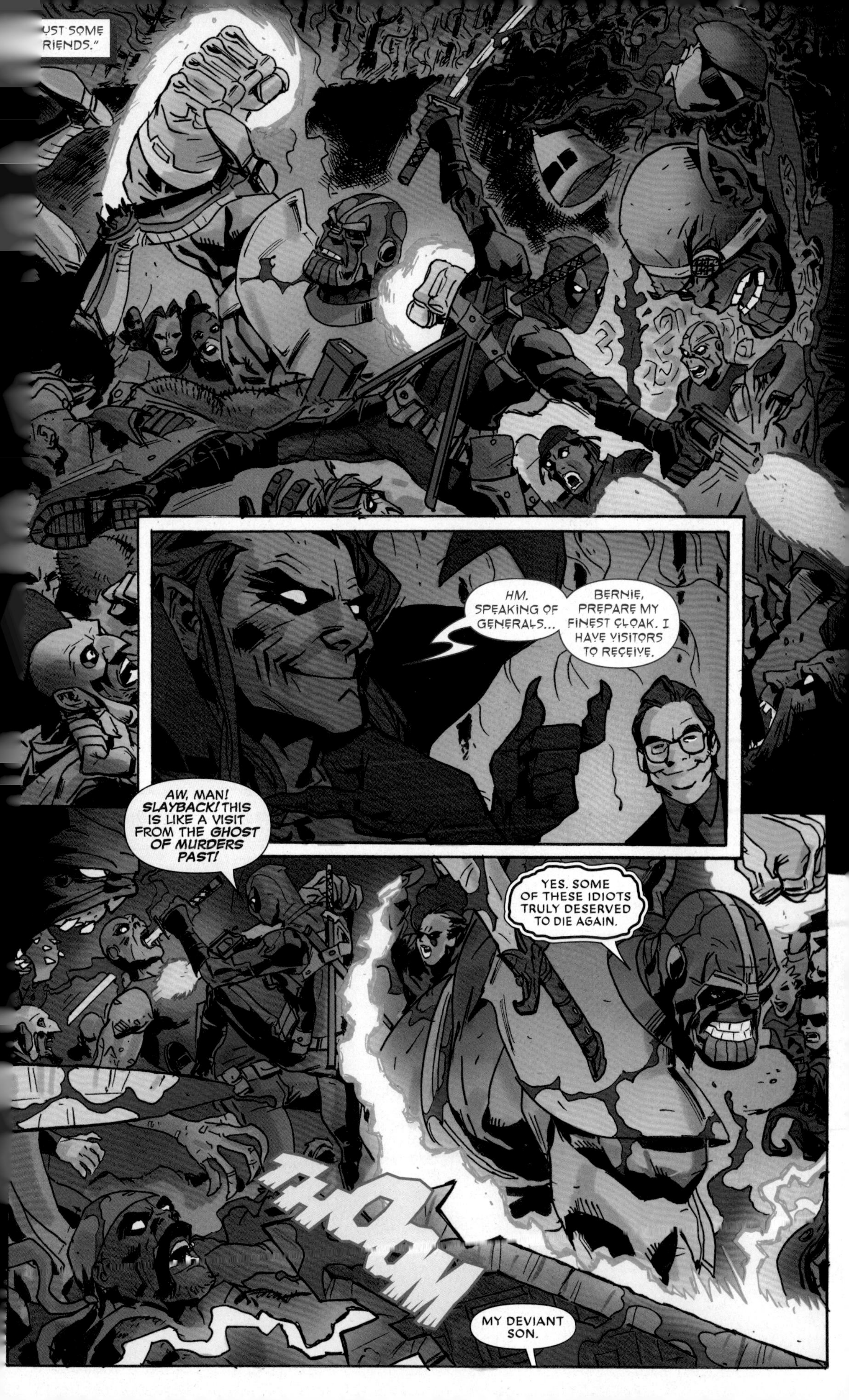
UST SOME
RIENDS."
HM. SPEAKING OF GENERALS...
BERNIE, PREPARE MY FINEST CLOAK. I HAVE VISITORS TO RECEIVE.
AW, MAN! SLAYBACK! THIS IS LIKE A VISIT FROM THE GHOST OF MURDERS PAST!
YES. SOME OF THESE IDIOTS TRULY DESERVED TO DIE AGAIN.
THOOM
MY DEVIANT SON.

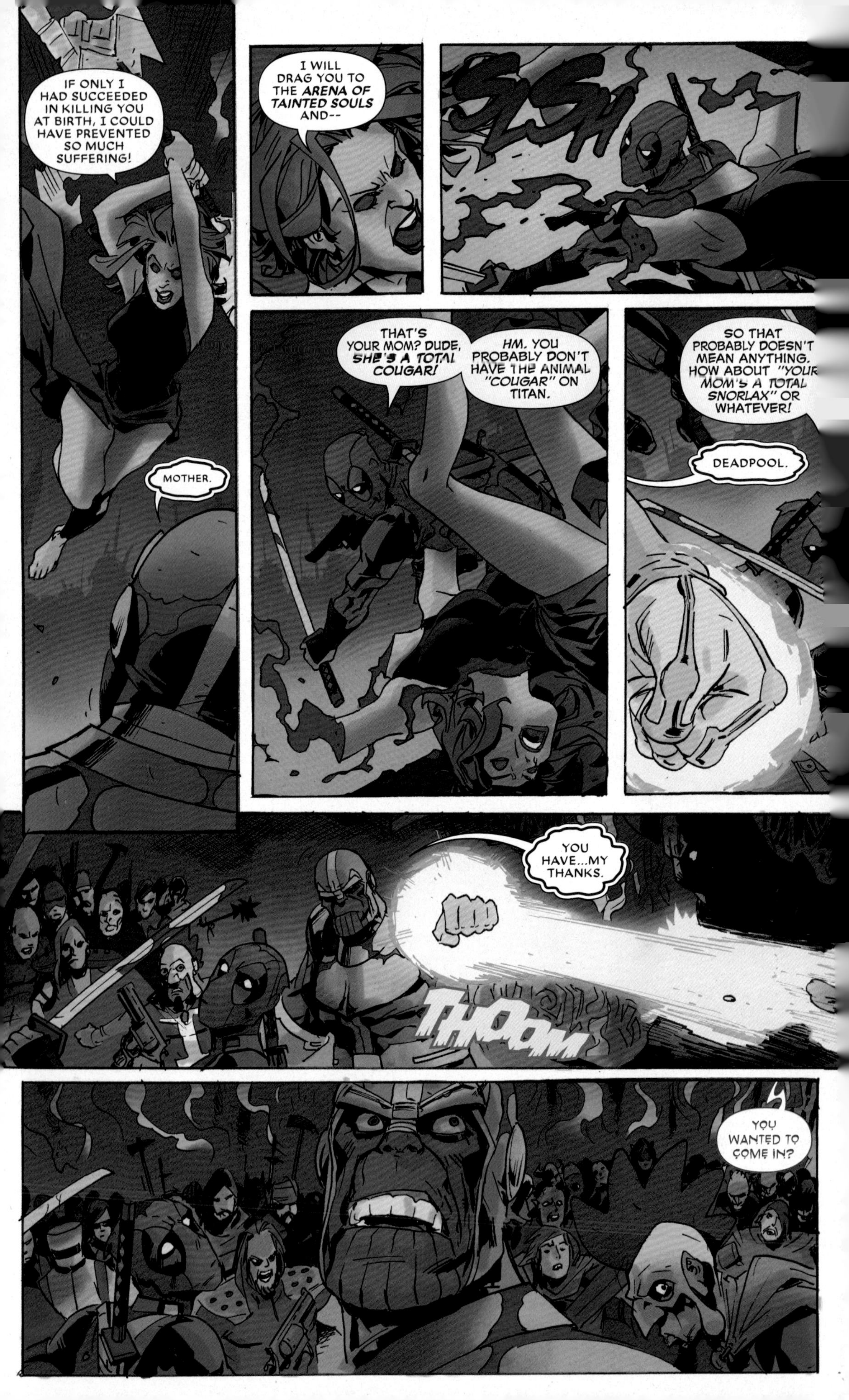

IF ONLY I HAD SUCCEEDED IN KILLING YOU AT BIRTH, I COULD HAVE PREVENTED SO MUCH SUFFERING!
MOTHER.
I WILL DRAG YOU TO THE ARENA OF TAINTED SOULS AND--
SLSH
THAT'S YOUR MOM? DUDE, SHE'S A TOTAL COUGAR!
HM. YOU PROBABLY DON'T HAVE THE ANIMAL "COUGAR" ON TITAN.
SO THAT PROBABLY DOESN'T MEAN ANYTHING. HOW ABOUT "YOUR MOM'S A TOTAL SNORLAX" OR WHATEVER!
DEADPOOL.
YOU HAVE...MY THANKS.
THOOM
YOU WANTED TO COME IN?

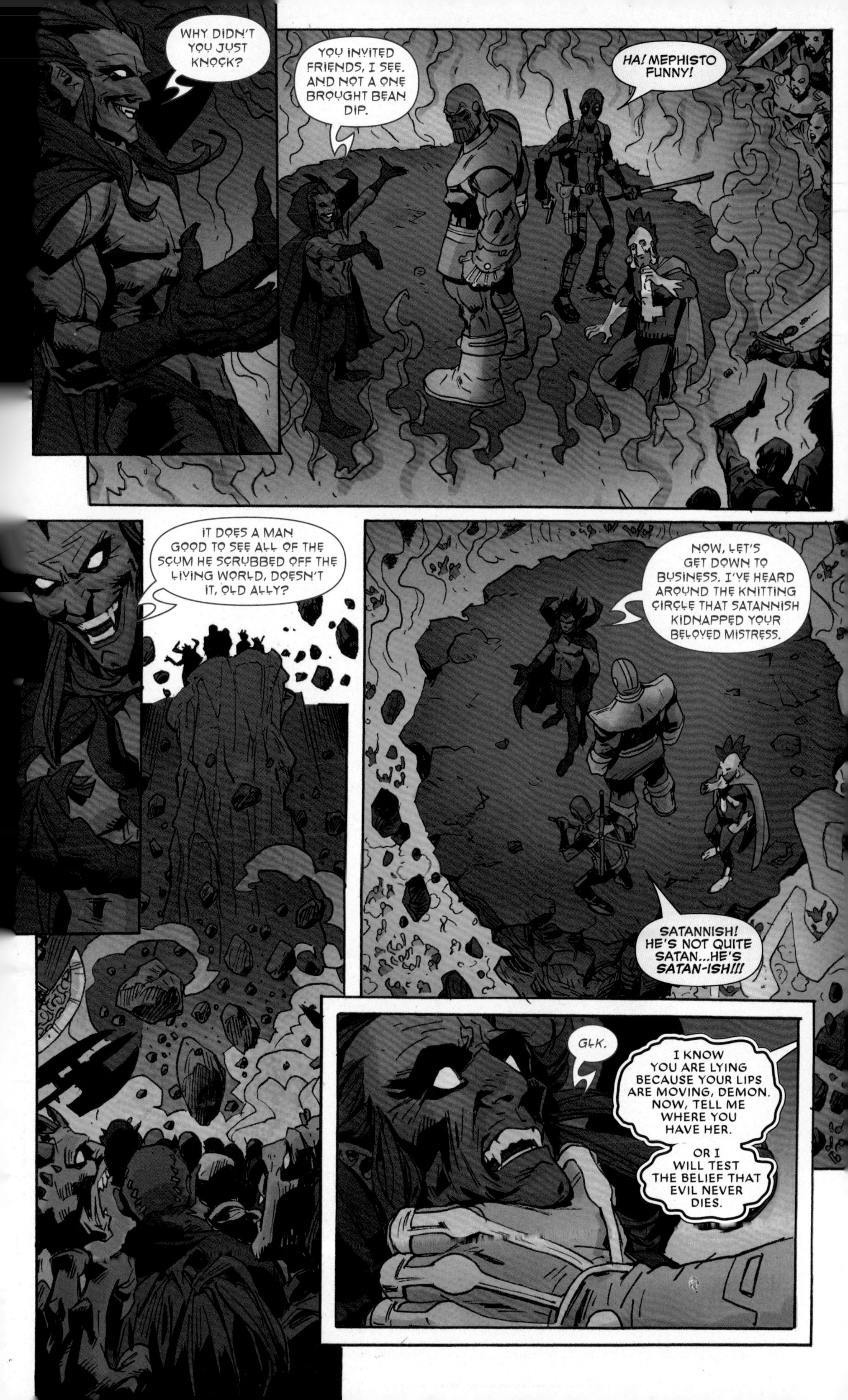
WHY DIDN'T YOU JUST KNOCK?
YOU INVITED FRIENDS, I SEE. AND NOT A ONE BROUGHT BEAN DIP.
HA! MEPHISTO FUNNY!
IT DOES A MAN GOOD TO SEE ALL OF THE SCUM HE SCRUBBED OFF THE LIVING WORLD, DOESN'T IT, OLD ALLY?
NOW, LET'S GET DOWN TO BUSINESS. I'VE HEARD AROUND THE KNITTING CIRCLE THAT SATANNISH KIDNAPPED YOUR BELOVED MISTRESS.
SATANNISH! HE'S NOT QUITE SATAN...HE'S SATAN-ISH!!!
GLK.
I KNOW YOU ARE LYING BECAUSE YOUR LIPS ARE MOVING, DEMON. NOW, TELL ME WHERE YOU HAVE HER.
OR I WILL TEST THE BELIEF THAT EVIL NEVER DIES.

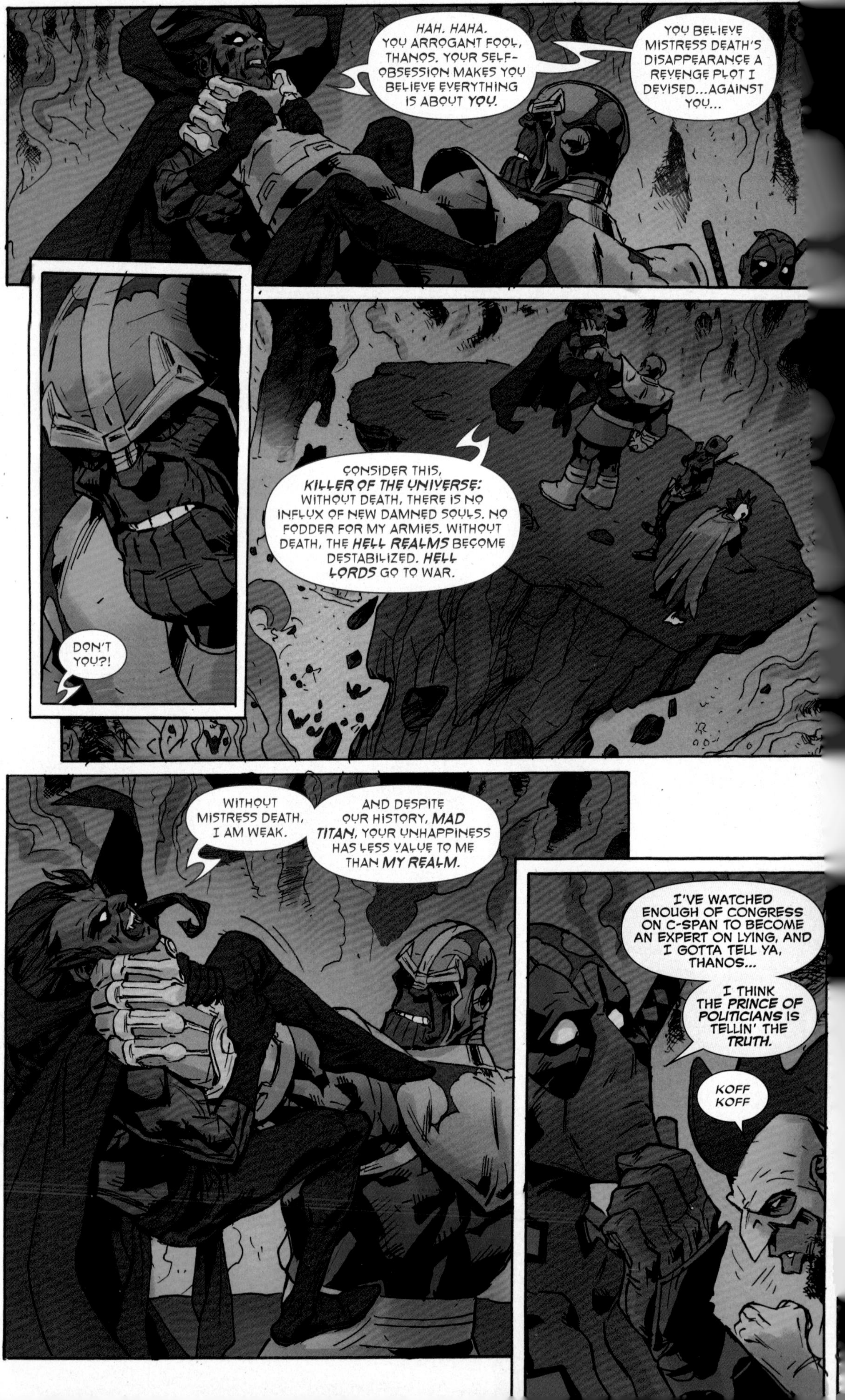
HAH. HAHA. YOU ARROGANT FOOL, THANOS. YOUR SELF-OBSESSION MAKES YOU BELIEVE EVERYTHING IS ABOUT YOU.
YOU BELIEVE MISTRESS DEATH'S DISAPPEARANCE A REVENGE PLOT I DEVISED...AGAINST YOU...
DON'T YOU?!
CONSIDER THIS, KILLER OF THE UNIVERSE: WITHOUT DEATH, THERE IS NO INFLUX OF NEW DAMNED SOULS. NO FODDER FOR MY ARMIES. WITHOUT DEATH, THE HELL REALMS BECOME DESTABILIZED. HELL LORDS GO TO WAR.
WITHOUT MISTRESS DEATH, I AM WEAK.
AND DESPITE OUR HISTORY, MAD TITAN, YOUR UNHAPPINESS HAS LESS VALUE TO ME THAN MY REALM.
I'VE WATCHED ENOUGH OF CONGRESS ON C-SPAN TO BECOME AN EXPERT ON LYING, AND I GOTTA TELL YA, THANOS...
I THINK THE PRINCE OF POLITICIANS IS TELLIN' THE TRUTH.
KOFF KOFF

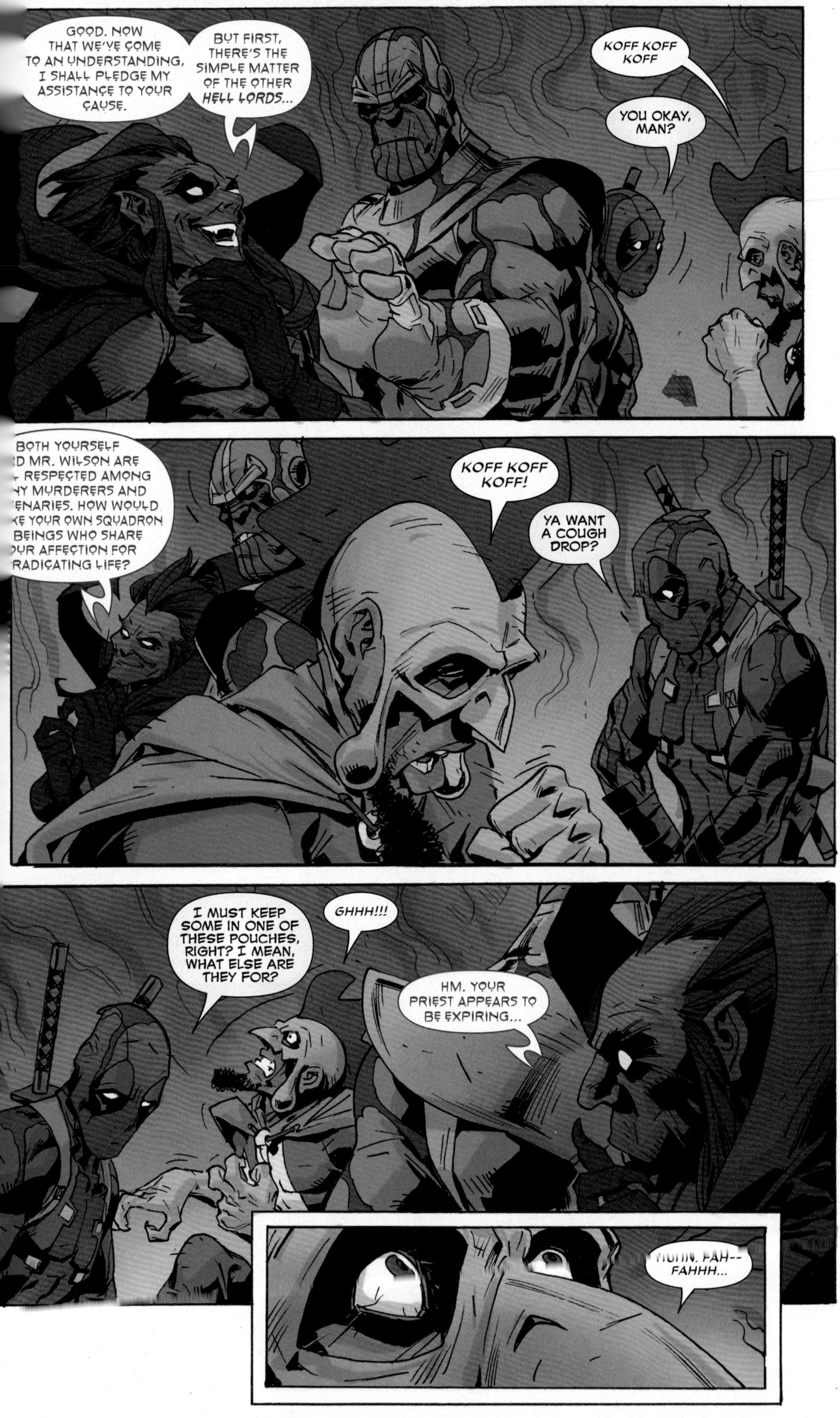
GOOD. NOW THAT WE'VE COME TO AN UNDERSTANDING, I SHALL PLEDGE MY ASSISTANCE TO YOUR CAUSE.
BUT FIRST, THERE'S THE SIMPLE MATTER OF THE OTHER HELL LORDS...
KOFF KOFF KOFF
YOU OKAY, MAN?
BOTH YOURSELF D MR. WILSON ARE RESPECTED AMONG NY MURDERERS AND ENARIES. HOW WOULD KE YOUR OWN SQUADRON BEINGS WHO SHARE UR AFFECTION FOR RADICATING LIFE?
KOFF KOFF KOFF!
YA WANT A COUGH DROP?
I MUST KEEP SOME IN ONE OF THESE POUCHES, RIGHT? I MEAN, WHAT ELSE ARE THEY FOR?
GHHH!!!
HM. YOUR PRIEST APPEARS TO BE EXPIRING...
FAH-- FAHHH...

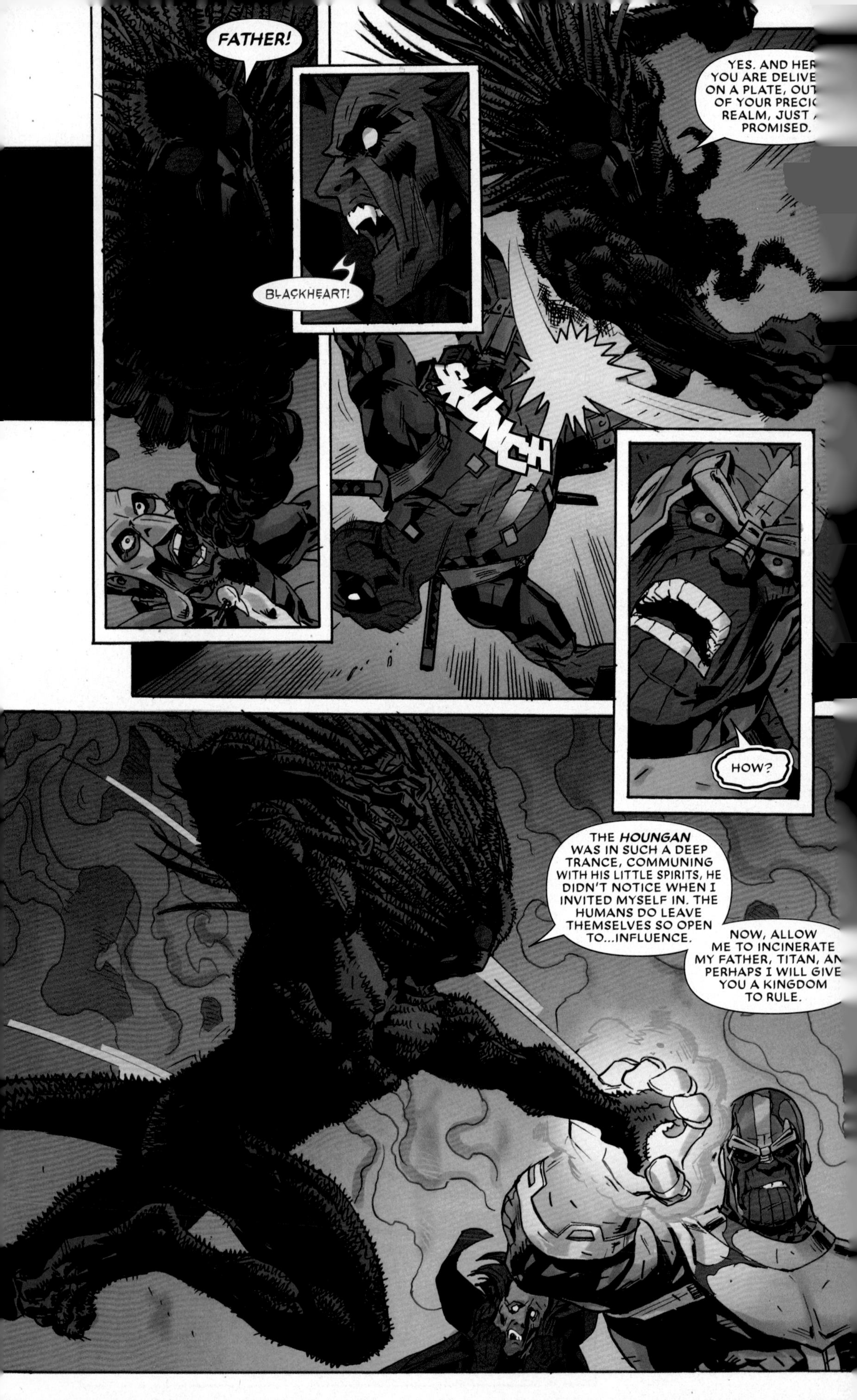
FATHER!
BLACKHEART!
SKUNCH
YES. AND HER
YOU ARE DELIVE
ON A PLATE, OUT
OF YOUR PRECI
REALM, JUST A
PROMISED.
HOW?
THE HOUNGAN WAS IN SUCH A DEEP TRANCE, COMMUNING WITH HIS LITTLE SPIRITS, HE DIDN'T NOTICE WHEN I INVITED MYSELF IN. THE HUMANS DO LEAVE THEMSELVES SO OPEN TO...INFLUENCE.
NOW, ALLOW ME TO INCINERATE MY FATHER, TITAN, AN
PERHAPS I WILL GIVE YOU A KINGDOM TO RULE.

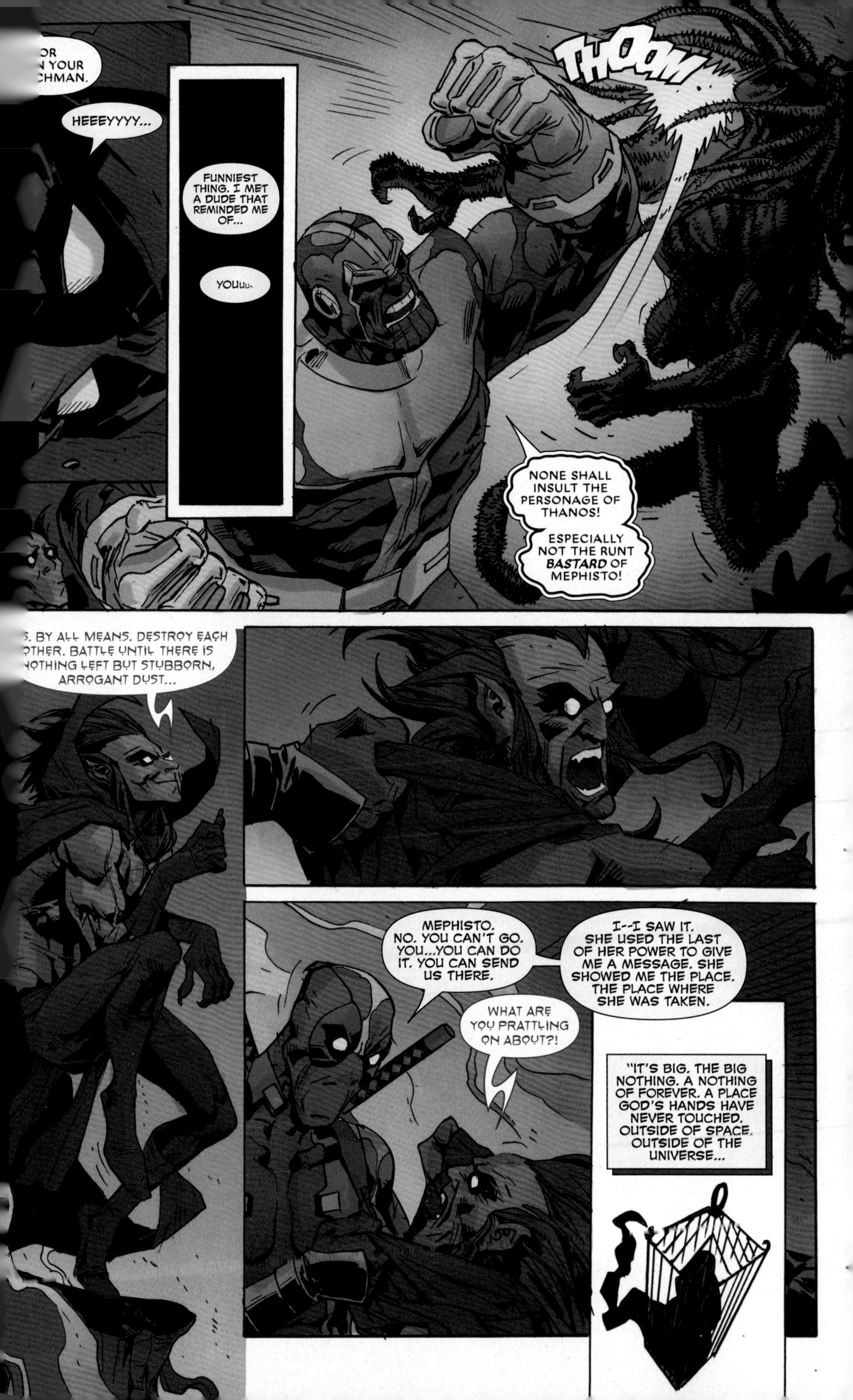
OR
N YOUR
CHMAN.
HEEEYYYY...
FUNNIEST THING. I MET A DUDE THAT REMINDED ME OF...
YOUuu..
THOOM
NONE SHALL INSULT THE PERSONAGE OF THANOS!
ESPECIALLY NOT THE RUNT BASTARD OF MEPHISTO!
S. BY ALL MEANS. DESTROY EACH OTHER. BATTLE UNTIL THERE IS NOTHING LEFT BUT STUBBORN, ARROGANT DUST...
MEPHISTO. NO. YOU CAN'T GO. YOU...YOU CAN DO IT. YOU CAN SEND US THERE.
I--I SAW IT. SHE USED THE LAST OF HER POWER TO GIVE ME A MESSAGE. SHE SHOWED ME THE PLACE. THE PLACE WHERE SHE WAS TAKEN.
WHAT ARE YOU PRATTLING ON ABOUT?!
"IT'S BIG. THE BIG NOTHING. A NOTHING OF FOREVER. A PLACE GOD'S HANDS HAVE NEVER TOUCHED. OUTSIDE OF SPACE. OUTSIDE OF THE UNIVERSE...

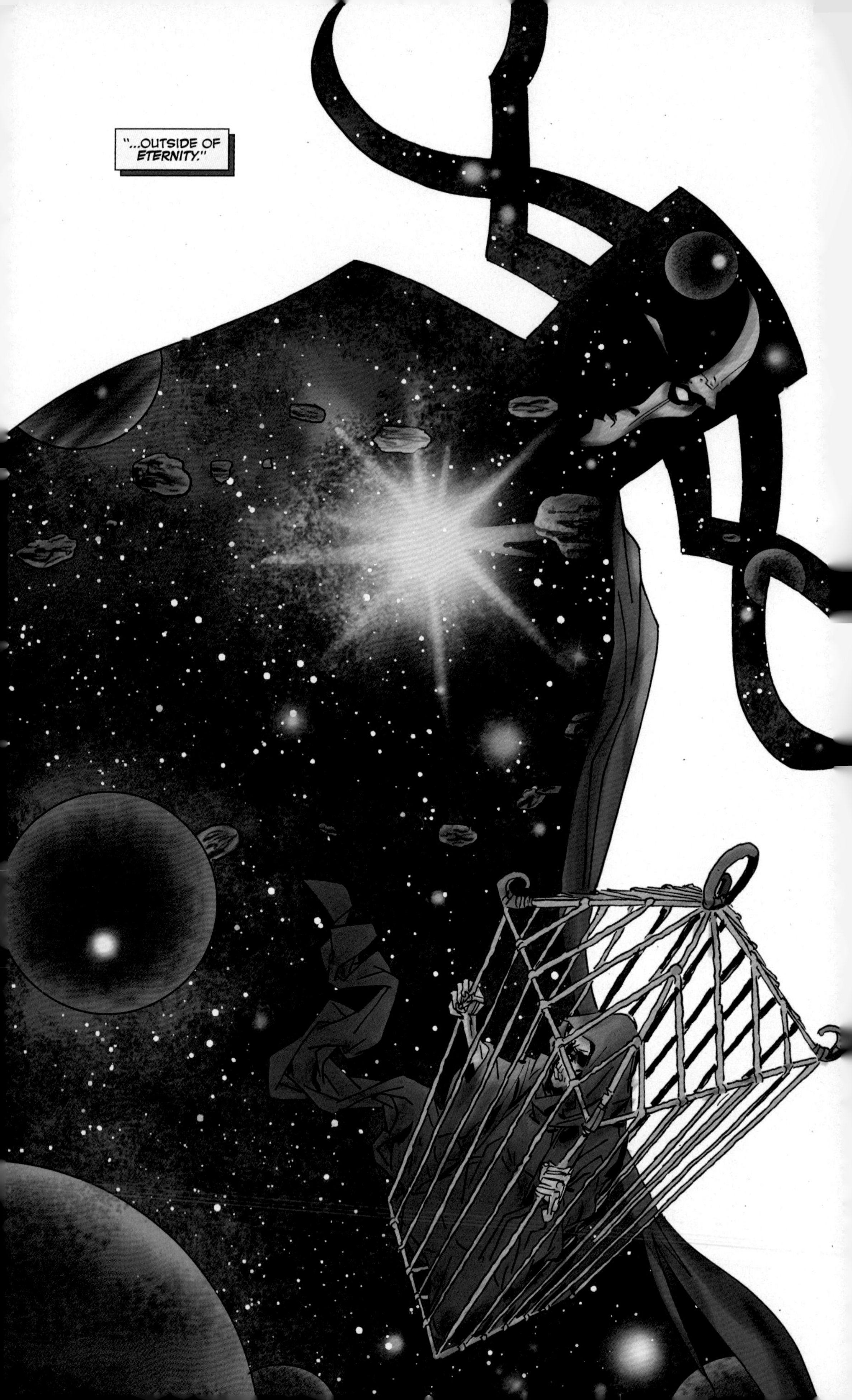
"...OUTSIDE OF ETERNITY."

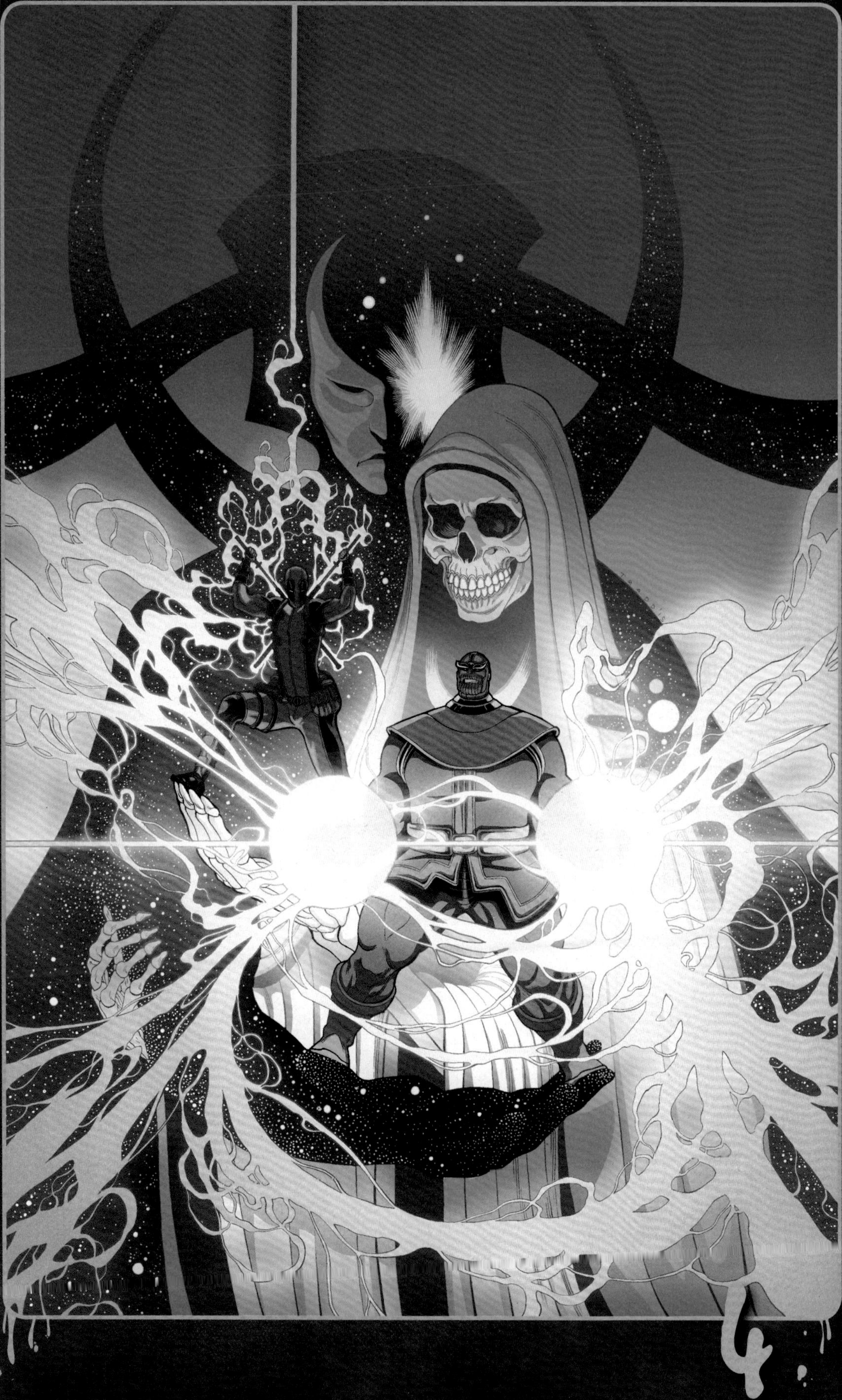
4

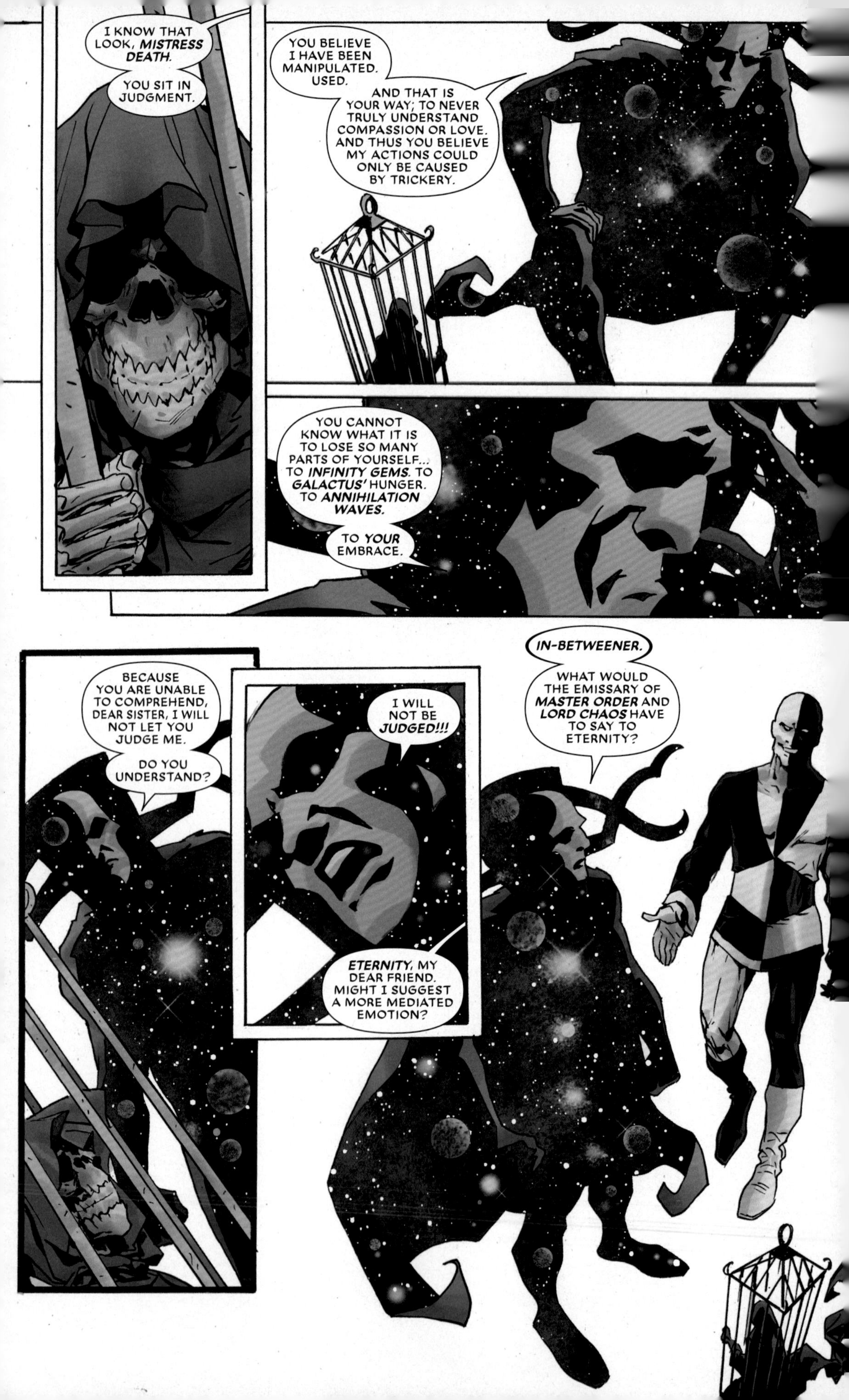

I KNOW THAT LOOK, MISTRESS DEATH.
YOU SIT IN JUDGMENT.
YOU BELIEVE I HAVE BEEN MANIPULATED. USED.
AND THAT IS YOUR WAY; TO NEVER TRULY UNDERSTAND COMPASSION OR LOVE. AND THUS YOU BELIEVE MY ACTIONS COULD ONLY BE CAUSED BY TRICKERY.
YOU CANNOT KNOW WHAT IT IS TO LOSE SO MANY PARTS OF YOURSELF... TO INFINITY GEMS. TO GALACTUS' HUNGER. TO ANNIHILATION WAVES.
TO YOUR EMBRACE.
BECAUSE YOU ARE UNABLE TO COMPREHEND, DEAR SISTER, I WILL NOT LET YOU JUDGE ME.
DO YOU UNDERSTAND?
I WILL NOT BE JUDGED!!!
ETERNITY, MY DEAR FRIEND. MIGHT I SUGGEST A MORE MEDIATED EMOTION?
IN-BETWEENER.
WHAT WOULD THE EMISSARY OF MASTER ORDER AND LORD CHAOS HAVE TO SAY TO ETERNITY?

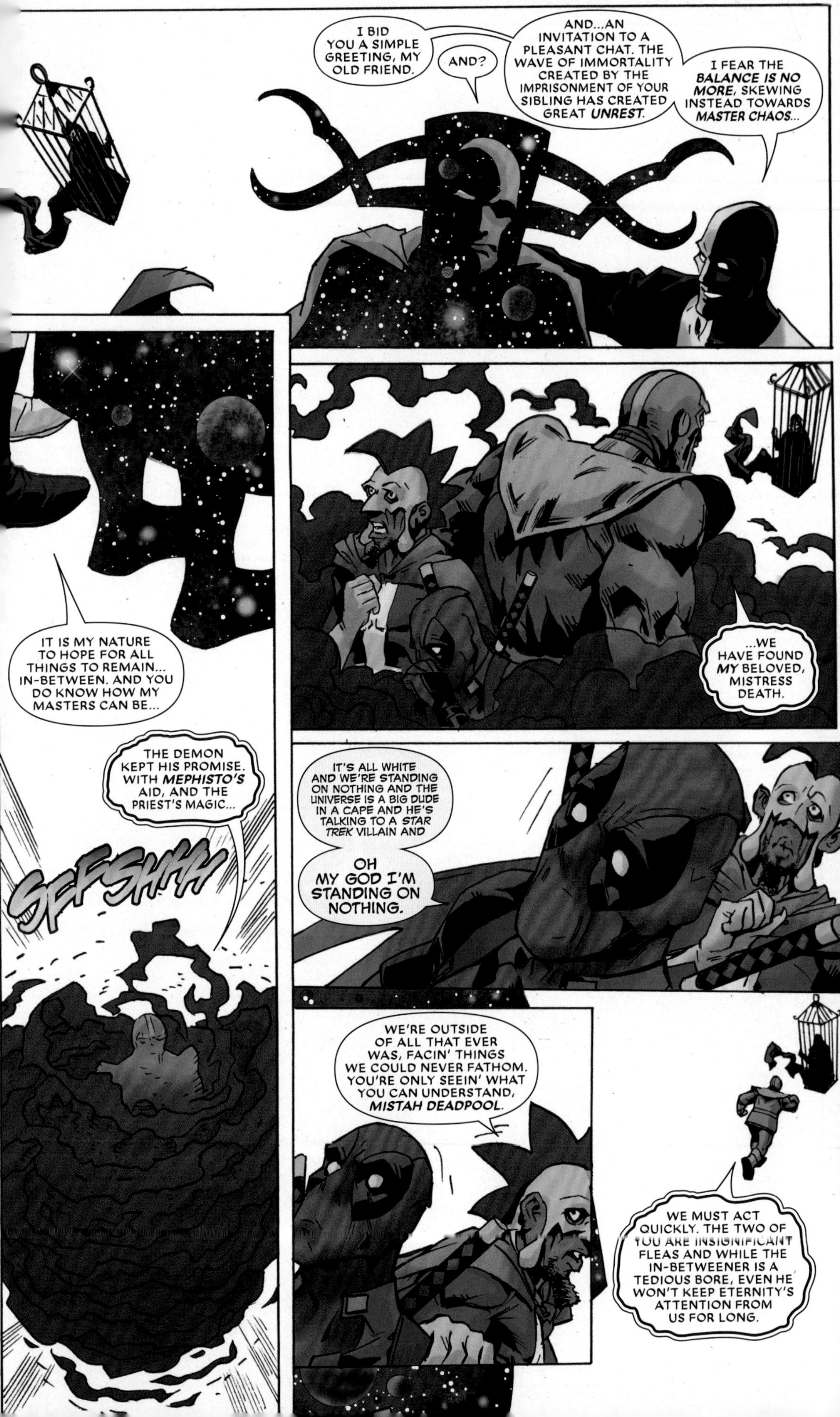
I BID YOU A SIMPLE GREETING, MY OLD FRIEND.
AND?
AND...AN INVITATION TO A PLEASANT CHAT. THE WAVE OF IMMORTALITY CREATED BY THE IMPRISONMENT OF YOUR SIBLING HAS CREATED GREAT UNREST.
I FEAR THE BALANCE IS NO MORE, SKEWING INSTEAD TOWARDS MASTER CHAOS...
IT IS MY NATURE TO HOPE FOR ALL THINGS TO REMAIN... IN-BETWEEN. AND YOU DO KNOW HOW MY MASTERS CAN BE...
...WE HAVE FOUND MY BELOVED, MISTRESS DEATH.
THE DEMON KEPT HIS PROMISE. WITH MEPHISTO'S AID, AND THE PRIEST'S MAGIC...
SFFSHHH
IT'S ALL WHITE AND WE'RE STANDING ON NOTHING AND THE UNIVERSE IS A BIG DUDE IN A CAPE AND HE'S TALKING TO A STAR TREK VILLAIN AND
OH MY GOD I'M STANDING ON NOTHING.
WE'RE OUTSIDE OF ALL THAT EVER WAS, FACIN' THINGS WE COULD NEVER FATHOM. YOU'RE ONLY SEEIN' WHAT YOU CAN UNDERSTAND, MISTAH DEADPOOL.
WE MUST ACT QUICKLY. THE TWO OF YOU ARE INSIGNIFICANT FLEAS AND WHILE THE IN-BETWEENER IS A TEDIOUS BORE, EVEN HE WON'T KEEP ETERNITY'S ATTENTION FROM US FOR LONG.

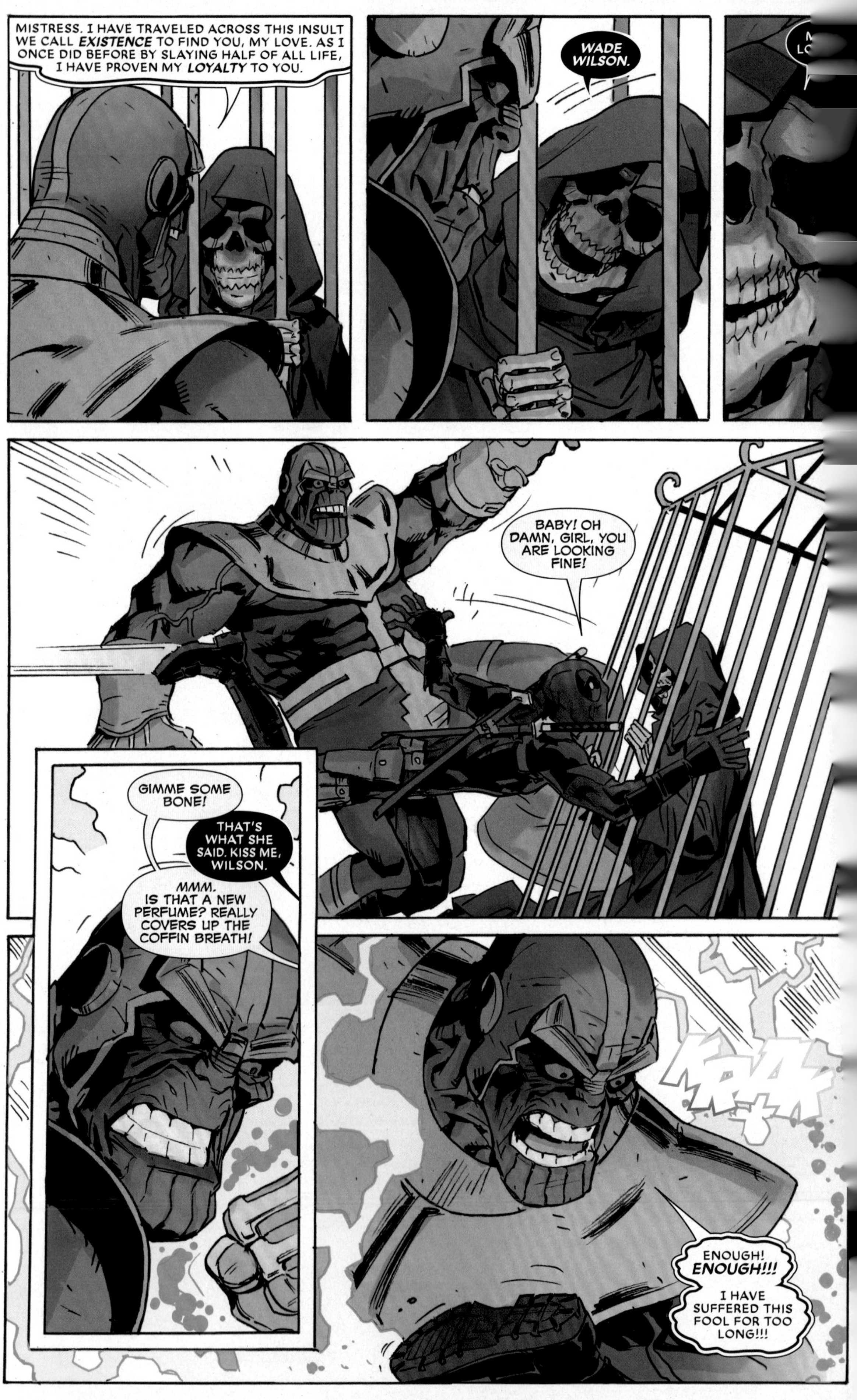
MISTRESS. I HAVE TRAVELED ACROSS THIS INSULT WE CALL EXISTENCE TO FIND YOU, MY LOVE. AS I ONCE DID BEFORE BY SLAYING HALF OF ALL LIFE, I HAVE PROVEN MY LOYALTY TO YOU.
WADE WILSON.
BABY! OH DAMN, GIRL, YOU ARE LOOKING FINE!
GIMME SOME BONE!
THAT'S WHAT SHE SAID. KISS ME, WILSON.
MMM. IS THAT A NEW PERFUME? REALLY COVERS UP THE COFFIN BREATH!
ENOUGH! ENOUGH!!!
I HAVE SUFFERED THIS FOOL FOR TOO LONG!!!

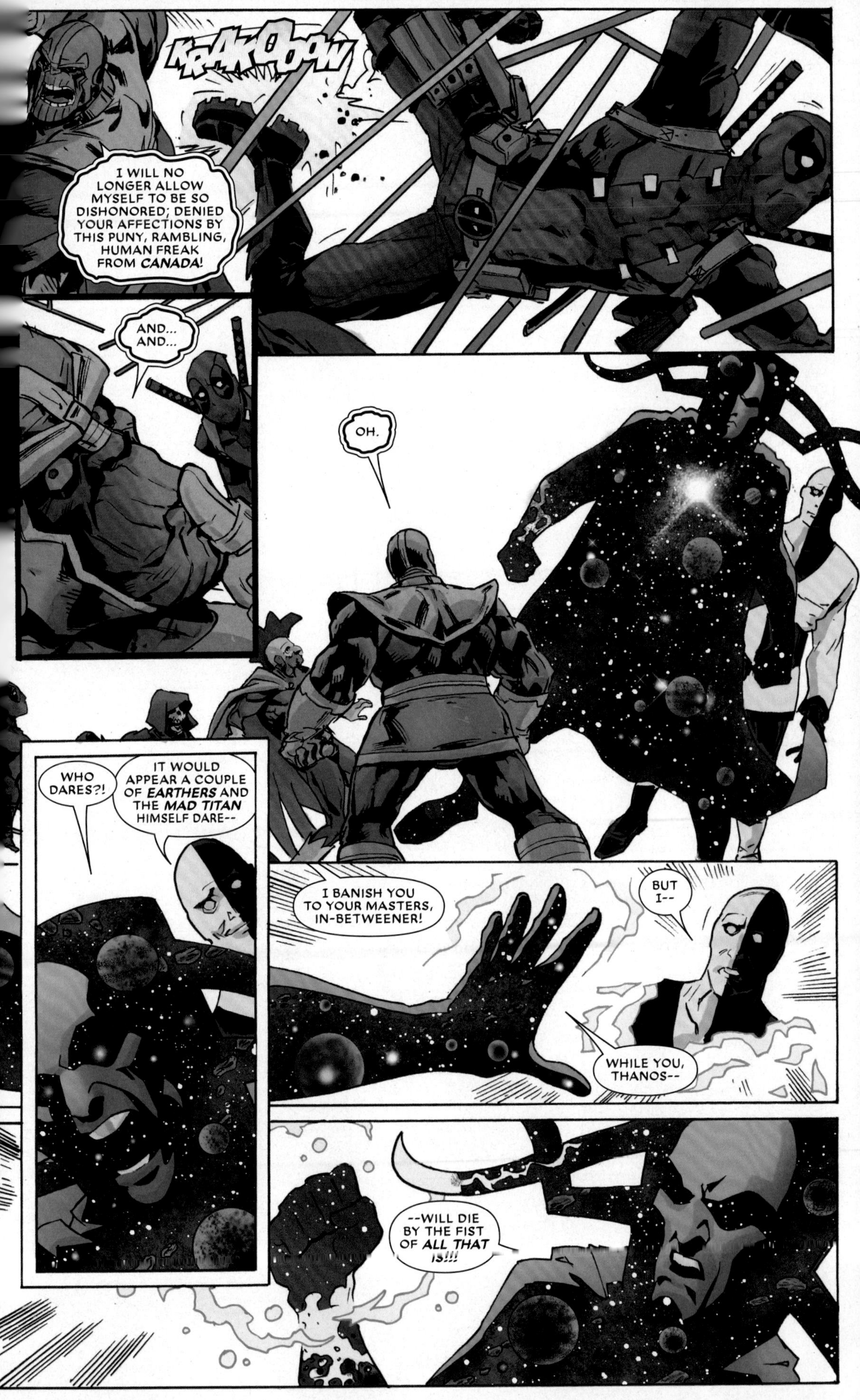
KRAKOOOW
I WILL NO LONGER ALLOW MYSELF TO BE SO DISHONORED; DENIED YOUR AFFECTIONS BY THIS PUNY, RAMBLING, HUMAN FREAK FROM CANADA!
AND... AND...
OH.
WHO DARES?!
IT WOULD APPEAR A COUPLE OF EARTHERS AND THE MAD TITAN HIMSELF DARE--
I BANISH YOU TO YOUR MASTERS, IN-BETWEENER!
BUT I--
WHILE YOU, THANOS--
--WILL DIE BY THE FIST OF ALL THAT IS!!!

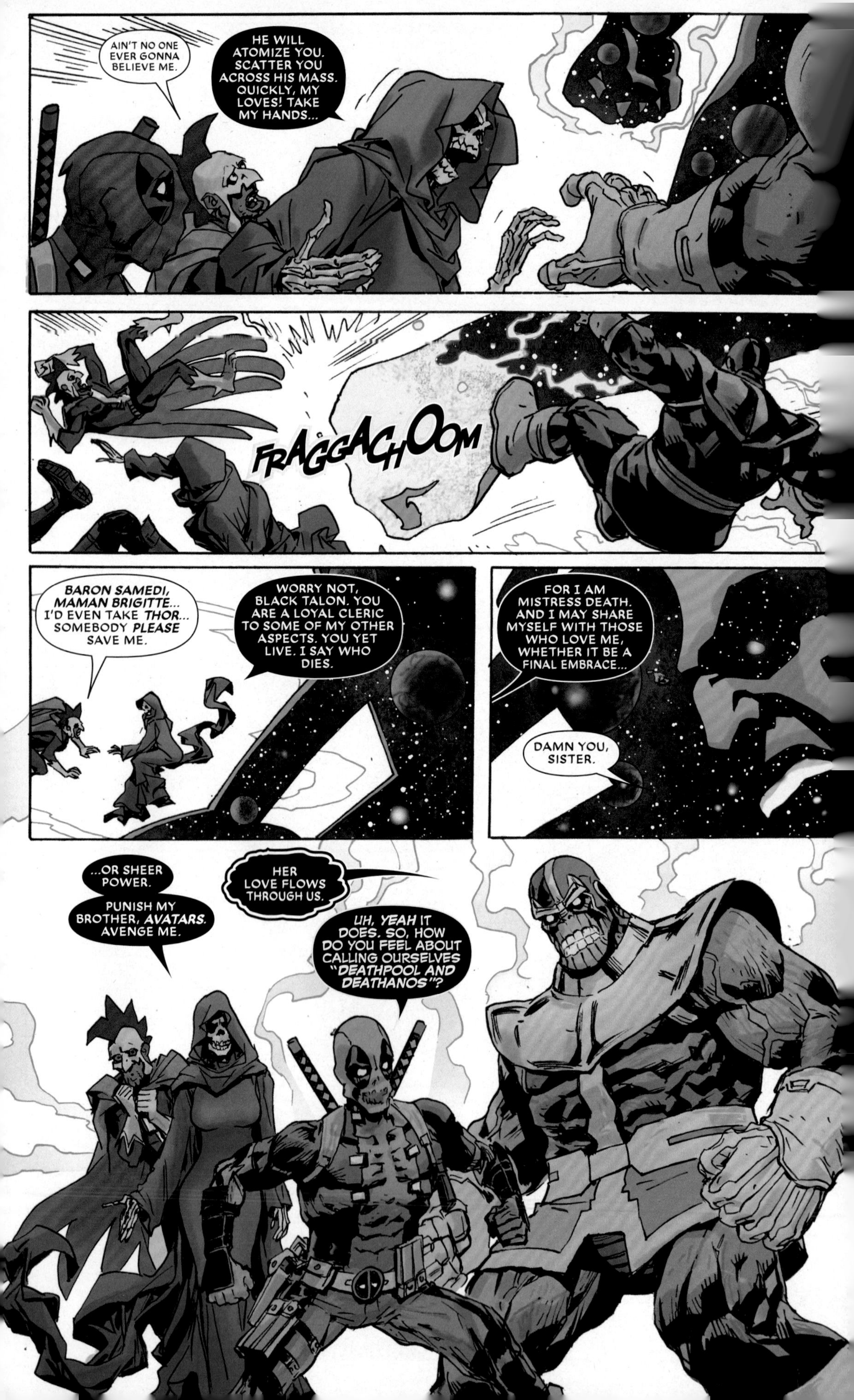
AIN'T NO ONE EVER GONNA BELIEVE ME.
HE WILL ATOMIZE YOU. SCATTER YOU ACROSS HIS MASS. QUICKLY, MY LOVES! TAKE MY HANDS...
FRAGGACHOOM
BARON SAMEDI, MAMAN BRIGITTE... I'D EVEN TAKE THOR... SOMEBODY PLEASE SAVE ME.
WORRY NOT, BLACK TALON. YOU ARE A LOYAL CLERIC TO SOME OF MY OTHER ASPECTS. YOU YET LIVE. I SAY WHO DIES.
FOR I AM MISTRESS DEATH. AND I MAY SHARE MYSELF WITH THOSE WHO LOVE ME, WHETHER IT BE A FINAL EMBRACE...
DAMN YOU, SISTER.
...OR SHEER POWER.
PUNISH MY BROTHER, AVATARS. AVENGE ME.
HER LOVE FLOWS THROUGH US.
UH, YEAH IT DOES. SO, HOW DO YOU FEEL ABOUT CALLING OURSELVES "DEATHPOOL AND DEATHANOS"?

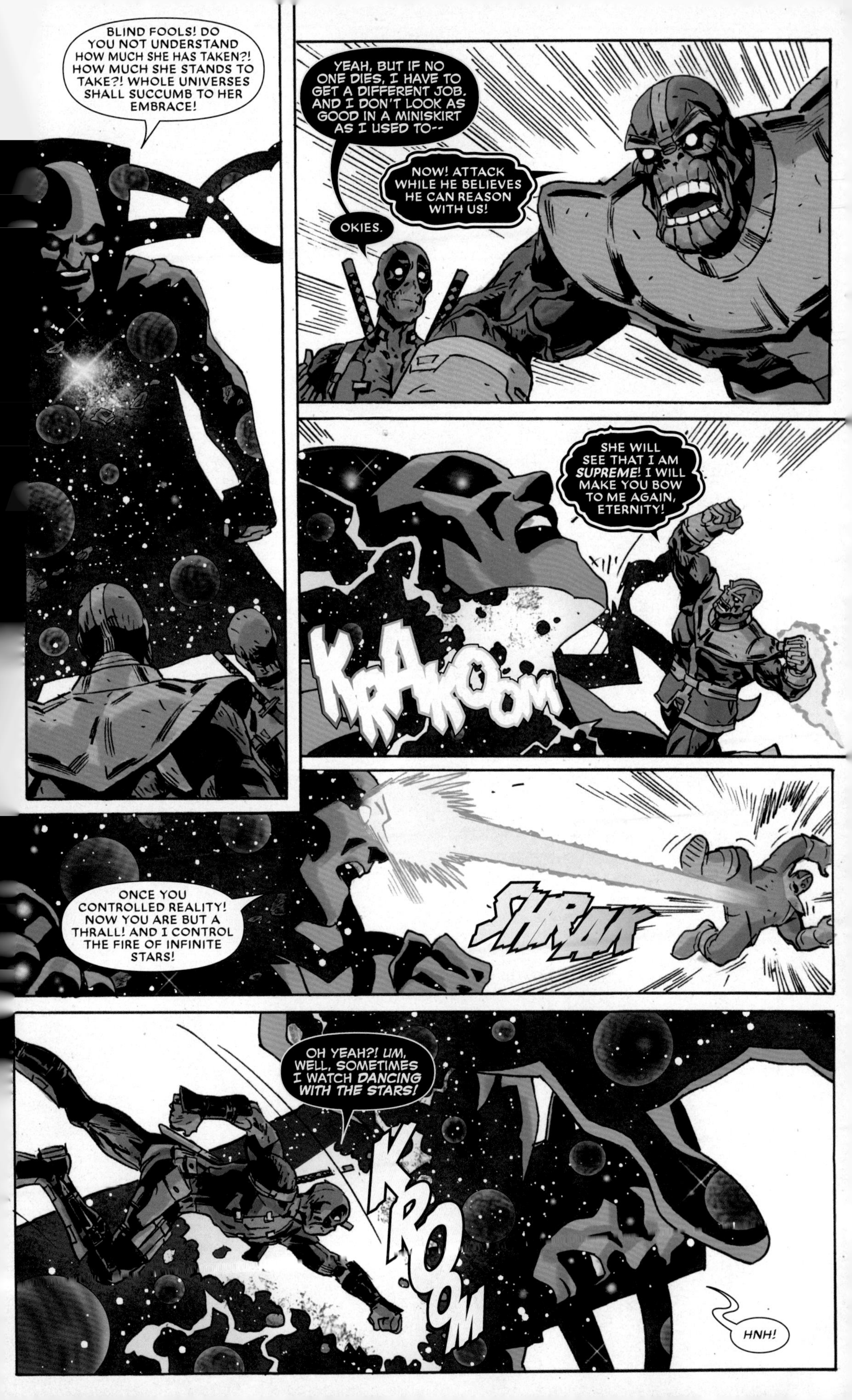
BLIND FOOLS! DO YOU NOT UNDERSTAND HOW MUCH SHE HAS TAKEN?! HOW MUCH SHE STANDS TO TAKE?! WHOLE UNIVERSES SHALL SUCCUMB TO HER EMBRACE!
YEAH, BUT IF NO ONE DIES, I HAVE TO GET A DIFFERENT JOB. AND I DON'T LOOK AS GOOD IN A MINISKIRT AS I USED TO--
NOW! ATTACK WHILE HE BELIEVES HE CAN REASON WITH US!
OKIES.
SHE WILL SEE THAT I AM *SUPREME*! I WILL MAKE YOU BOW TO ME AGAIN, ETERNITY!
KRAKOOM
ONCE YOU CONTROLLED REALITY! NOW YOU ARE BUT A THRALL! AND I CONTROL THE FIRE OF INFINITE STARS!
SHRAK
OH YEAH?! *UM,* WELL, SOMETIMES I WATCH *DANCING WITH THE STARS!*
KROOM
HNH!

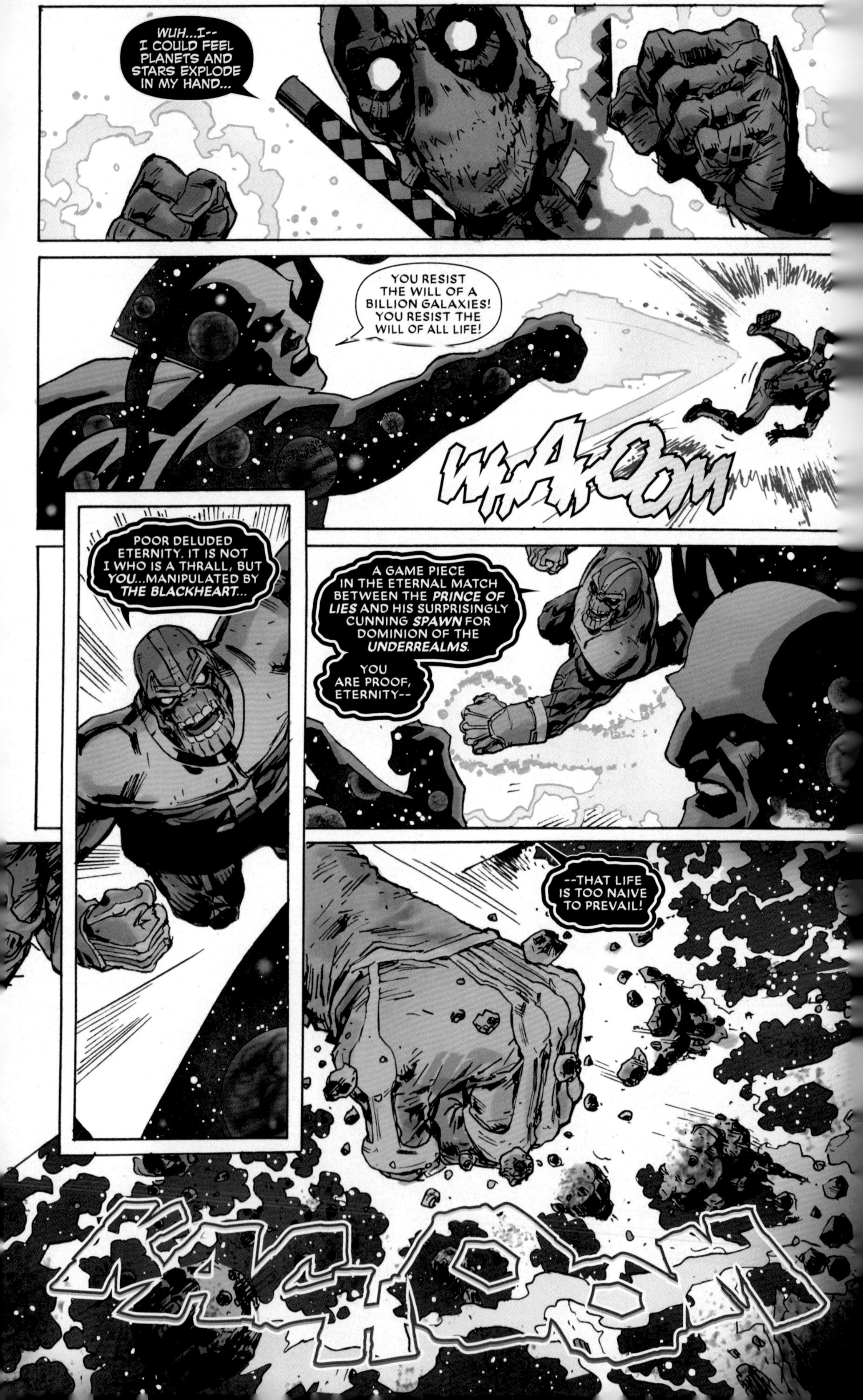
WUH...I-- I COULD FEEL PLANETS AND STARS EXPLODE IN MY HAND...
YOU RESIST THE WILL OF A BILLION GALAXIES! YOU RESIST THE WILL OF ALL LIFE!
WHAOOM
POOR DELUDED ETERNITY. IT IS NOT I WHO IS A THRALL, BUT YOU...MANIPULATED BY THE BLACKHEART...
A GAME PIECE IN THE ETERNAL MATCH BETWEEN THE PRINCE OF LIES AND HIS SURPRISINGLY CUNNING SPAWN FOR DOMINION OF THE UNDERREALMS.
YOU ARE PROOF, ETERNITY--
--THAT LIFE IS TOO NAIVE TO PREVAIL!

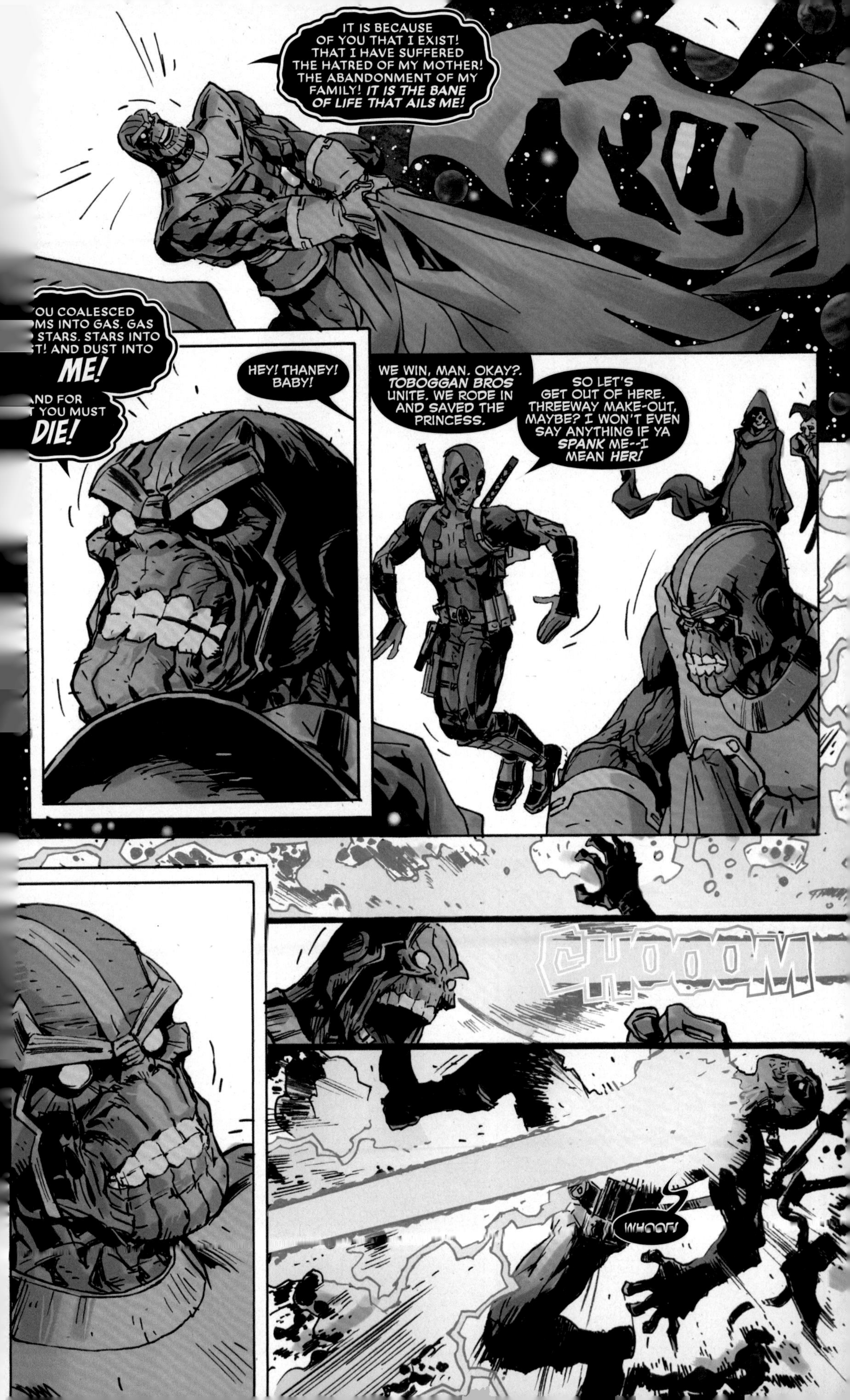
IT IS BECAUSE OF YOU THAT I EXIST! THAT I HAVE SUFFERED THE HATRED OF MY MOTHER! THE ABANDONMENT OF MY FAMILY! *IT IS THE BANE OF LIFE THAT AILS ME!*
YOU COALESCED
MS INTO GAS. GAS
STARS. STARS INTO
ST! AND DUST INTO
ME!
AND FOR
YOU MUST
DIE!
HEY! THANEY! BABY!
WE WIN, MAN. OKAY?. *TOBOGGAN BROS* UNITE. WE RODE IN AND SAVED THE PRINCESS.
SO LET'S GET OUT OF HERE. THREEWAY MAKE-OUT, MAYBE? I WON'T EVEN SAY ANYTHING IF YA *SPANK* ME--I MEAN *HER!*
CHOOOM
WHOOF!

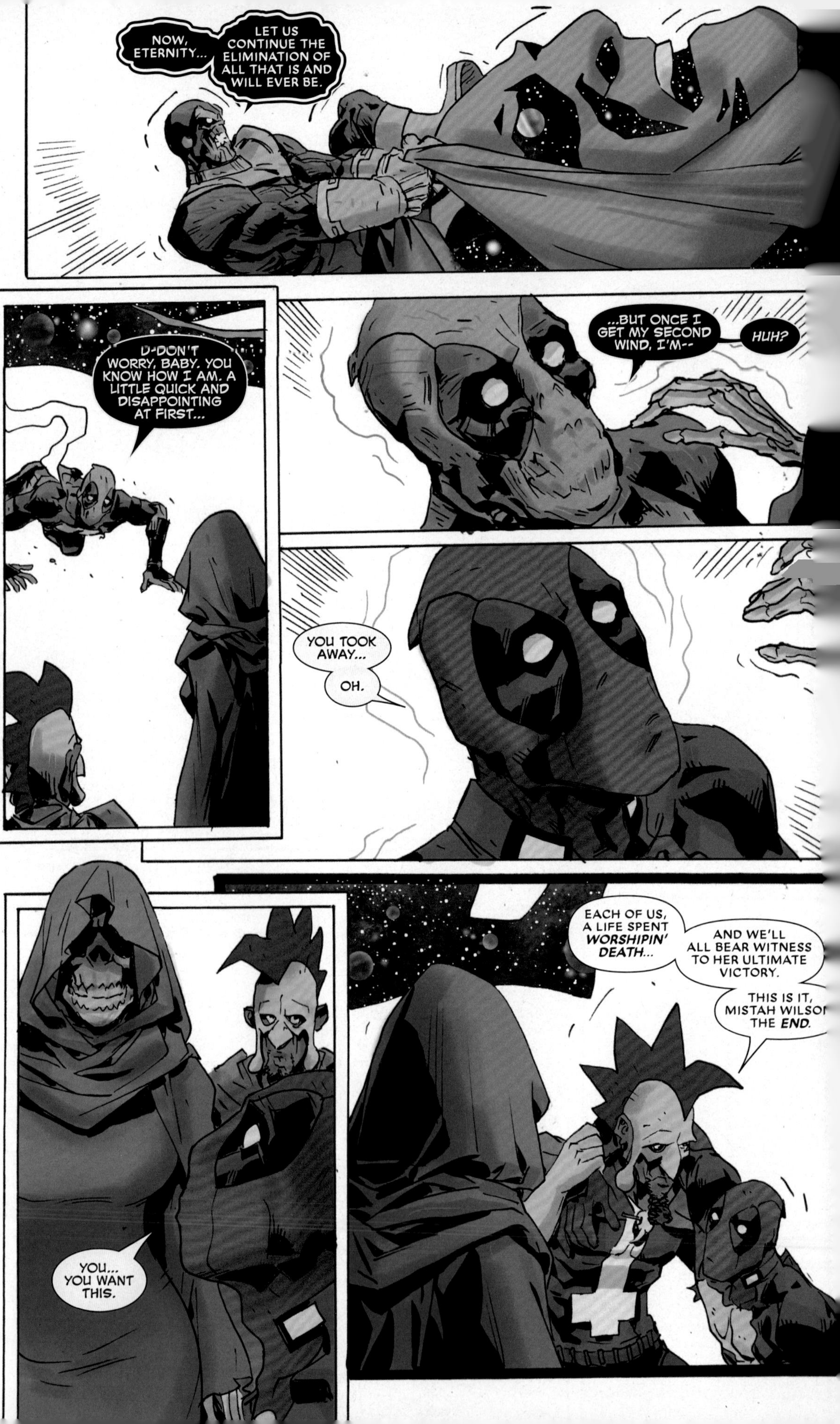
NOW, ETERNITY...
LET US CONTINUE THE ELIMINATION OF ALL THAT IS AND WILL EVER BE.
D-DON'T WORRY, BABY. YOU KNOW HOW I AM. A LITTLE QUICK AND DISAPPOINTING AT FIRST...
...BUT ONCE I GET MY SECOND WIND, I'M--
HUH?
YOU TOOK AWAY...
OH.
YOU... YOU WANT THIS.
EACH OF US, A LIFE SPENT WORSHIPIN' DEATH...
AND WE'LL ALL BEAR WITNESS TO HER ULTIMATE VICTORY.
THIS IS IT, MISTAH WILSON THE END.

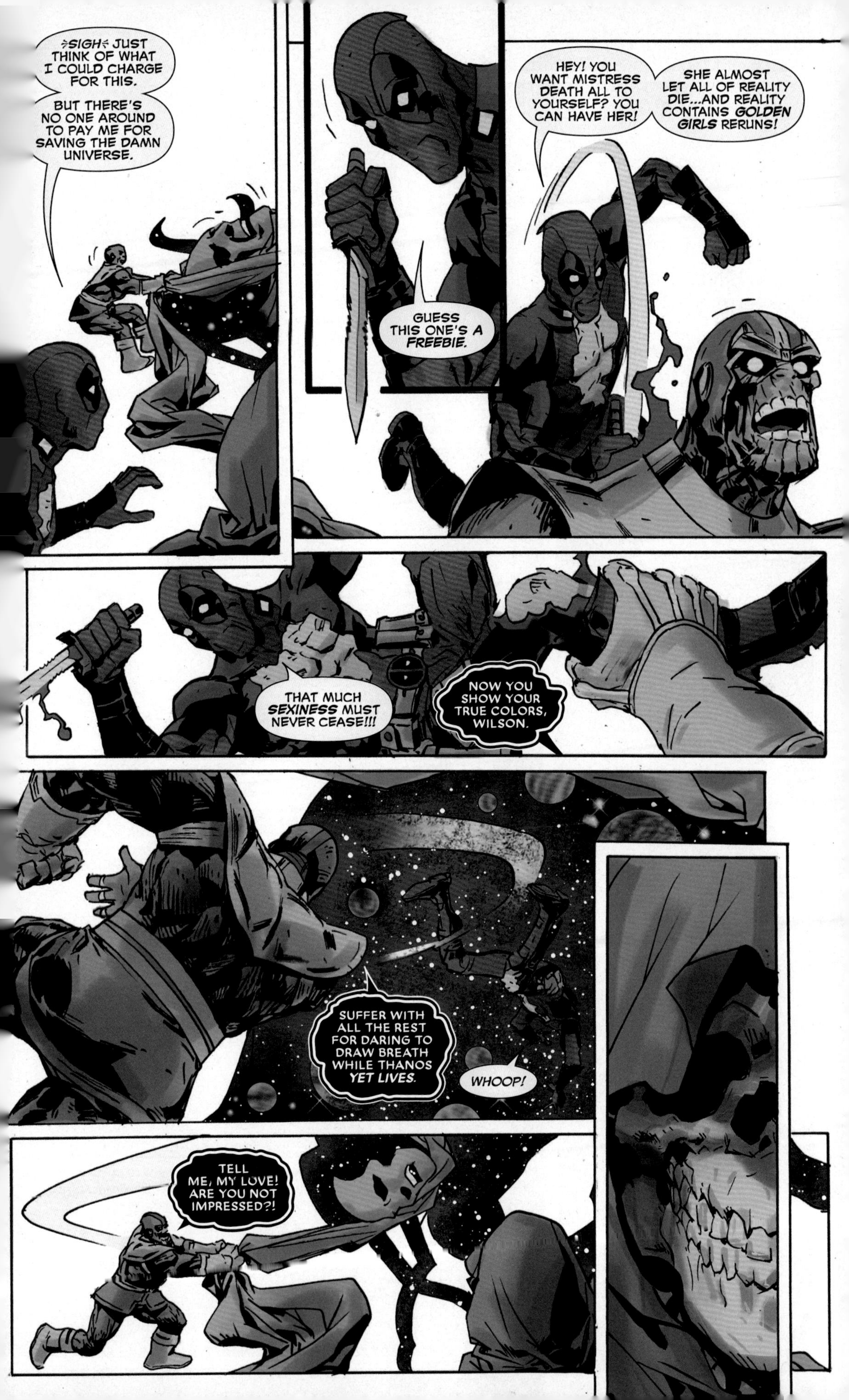

≶SIGH≷ JUST THINK OF WHAT I COULD CHARGE FOR THIS.
BUT THERE'S NO ONE AROUND TO PAY ME FOR SAVING THE DAMN UNIVERSE.
GUESS THIS ONE'S A FREEBIE.
HEY! YOU WANT MISTRESS DEATH ALL TO YOURSELF? YOU CAN HAVE HER!
SHE ALMOST LET ALL OF REALITY DIE...AND REALITY CONTAINS GOLDEN GIRLS RERUNS!
THAT MUCH SEXINESS MUST NEVER CEASE!!!
NOW YOU SHOW YOUR TRUE COLORS, WILSON.
SUFFER WITH ALL THE REST FOR DARING TO DRAW BREATH WHILE THANOS YET LIVES.
WHOOP!
TELL ME, MY LOVE! ARE YOU NOT IMPRESSED?!

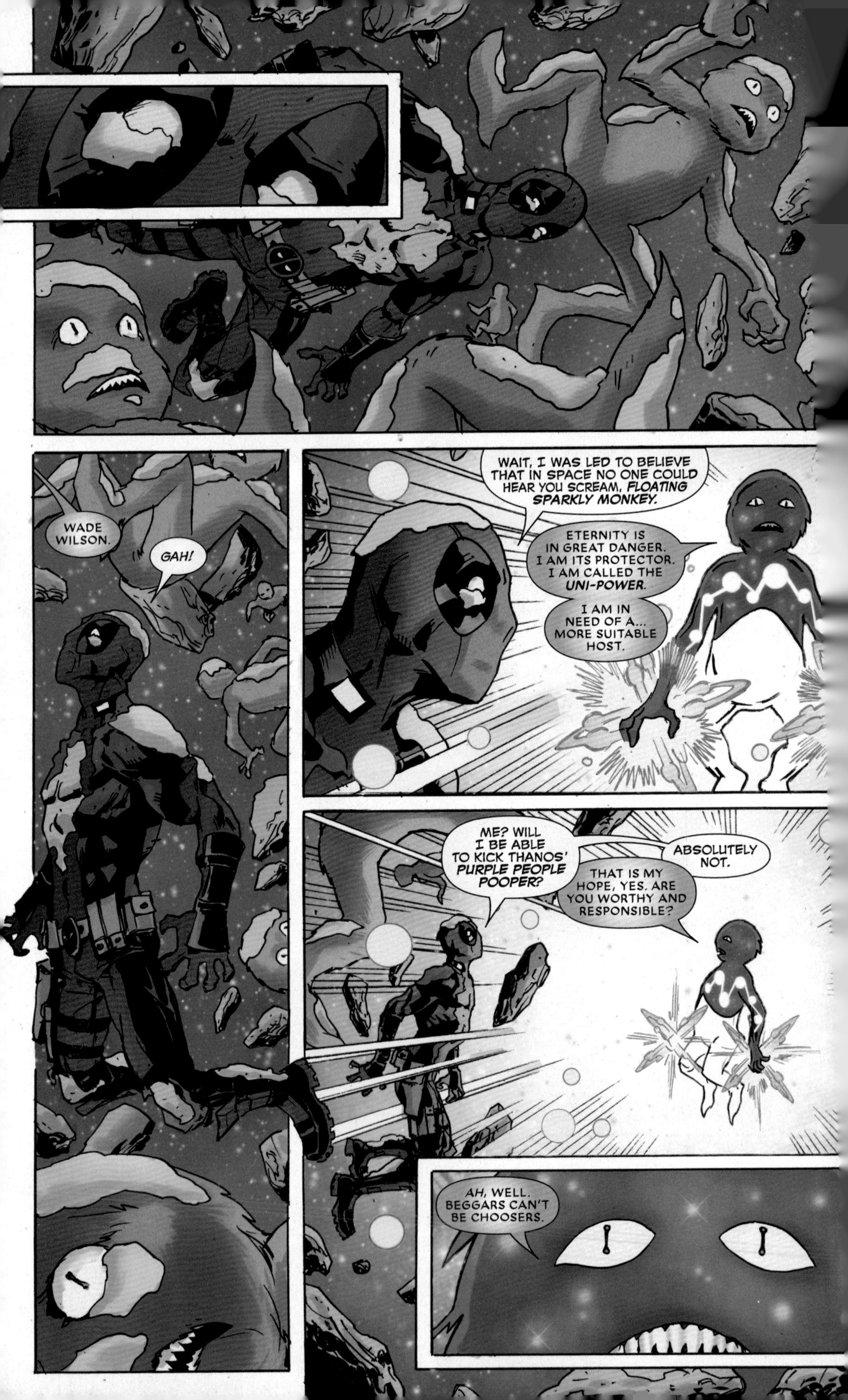

WADE WILSON.
GAH!
WAIT, I WAS LED TO BELIEVE THAT IN SPACE NO ONE COULD HEAR YOU SCREAM, FLOATING SPARKLY MONKEY.
ETERNITY IS IN GREAT DANGER. I AM ITS PROTECTOR. I AM CALLED THE UNI-POWER.
I AM IN NEED OF A... MORE SUITABLE HOST.
ME? WILL I BE ABLE TO KICK THANOS' PURPLE PEOPLE POOPER?
ABSOLUTELY NOT.
THAT IS MY HOPE, YES. ARE YOU WORTHY AND RESPONSIBLE?
AH, WELL. BEGGARS CAN'T BE CHOOSERS.

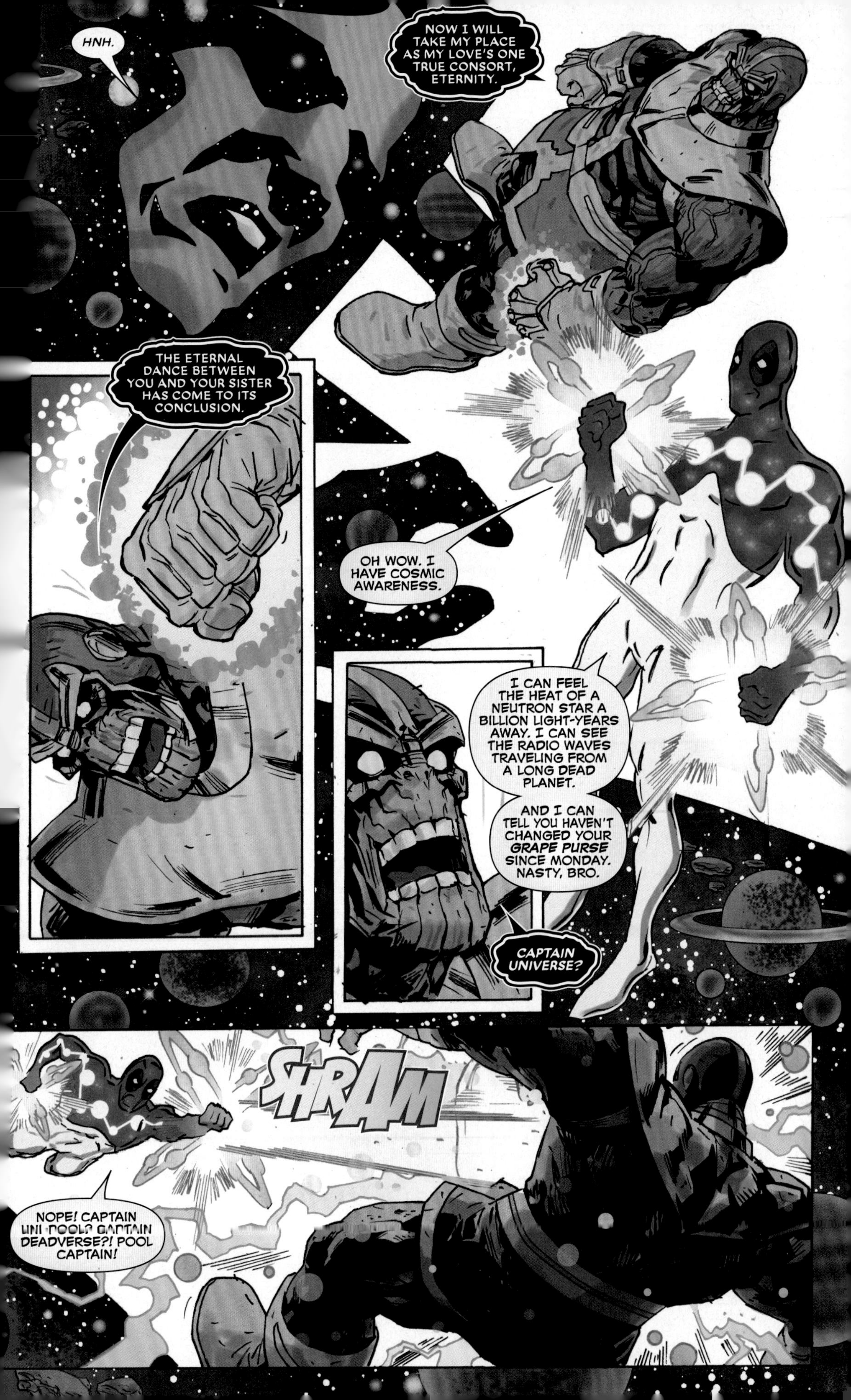
HNH.
NOW I WILL TAKE MY PLACE AS MY LOVE'S ONE TRUE CONSORT, ETERNITY.
THE ETERNAL DANCE BETWEEN YOU AND YOUR SISTER HAS COME TO ITS CONCLUSION.
OH WOW. I HAVE COSMIC AWARENESS.
I CAN FEEL THE HEAT OF A NEUTRON STAR A BILLION LIGHT-YEARS AWAY. I CAN SEE THE RADIO WAVES TRAVELING FROM A LONG DEAD PLANET.
AND I CAN TELL YOU HAVEN'T CHANGED YOUR GRAPE PURSE SINCE MONDAY. NASTY, BRO.
CAPTAIN UNIVERSE?
SHRAAM
NOPE! CAPTAIN UNI-POOL? CAPTAIN DEADVERSE?! POOL CAPTAIN!

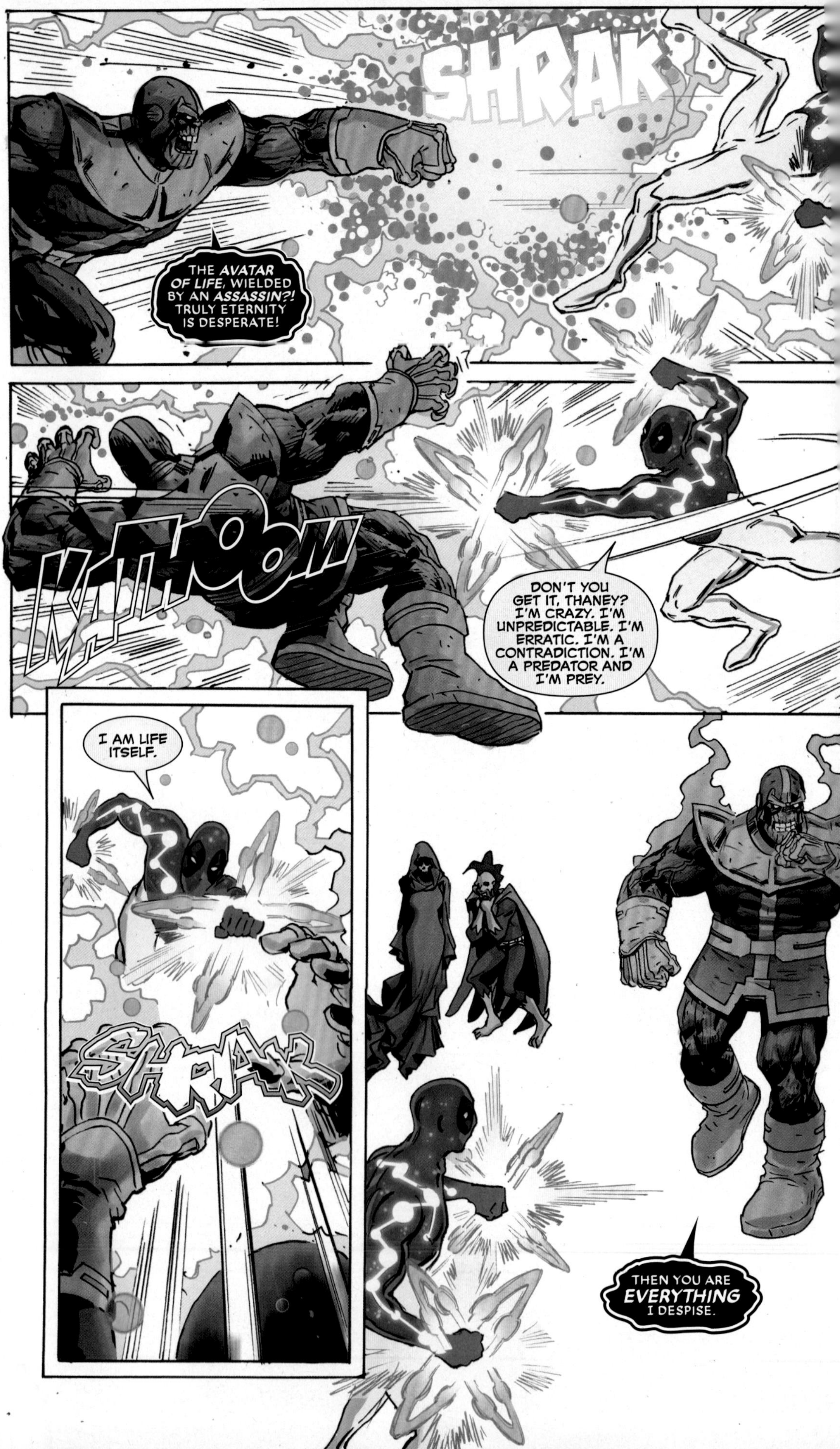
SHRAK!
THE AVATAR OF LIFE, WIELDED BY AN ASSASSIN?! TRULY ETERNITY IS DESPERATE!
KATHOOM
DON'T YOU GET IT, THANEY? I'M CRAZY. I'M UNPREDICTABLE. I'M ERRATIC. I'M A CONTRADICTION. I'M A PREDATOR AND I'M PREY.
I AM LIFE ITSELF.
SHRAK
THEN YOU ARE EVERYTHING I DESPISE.

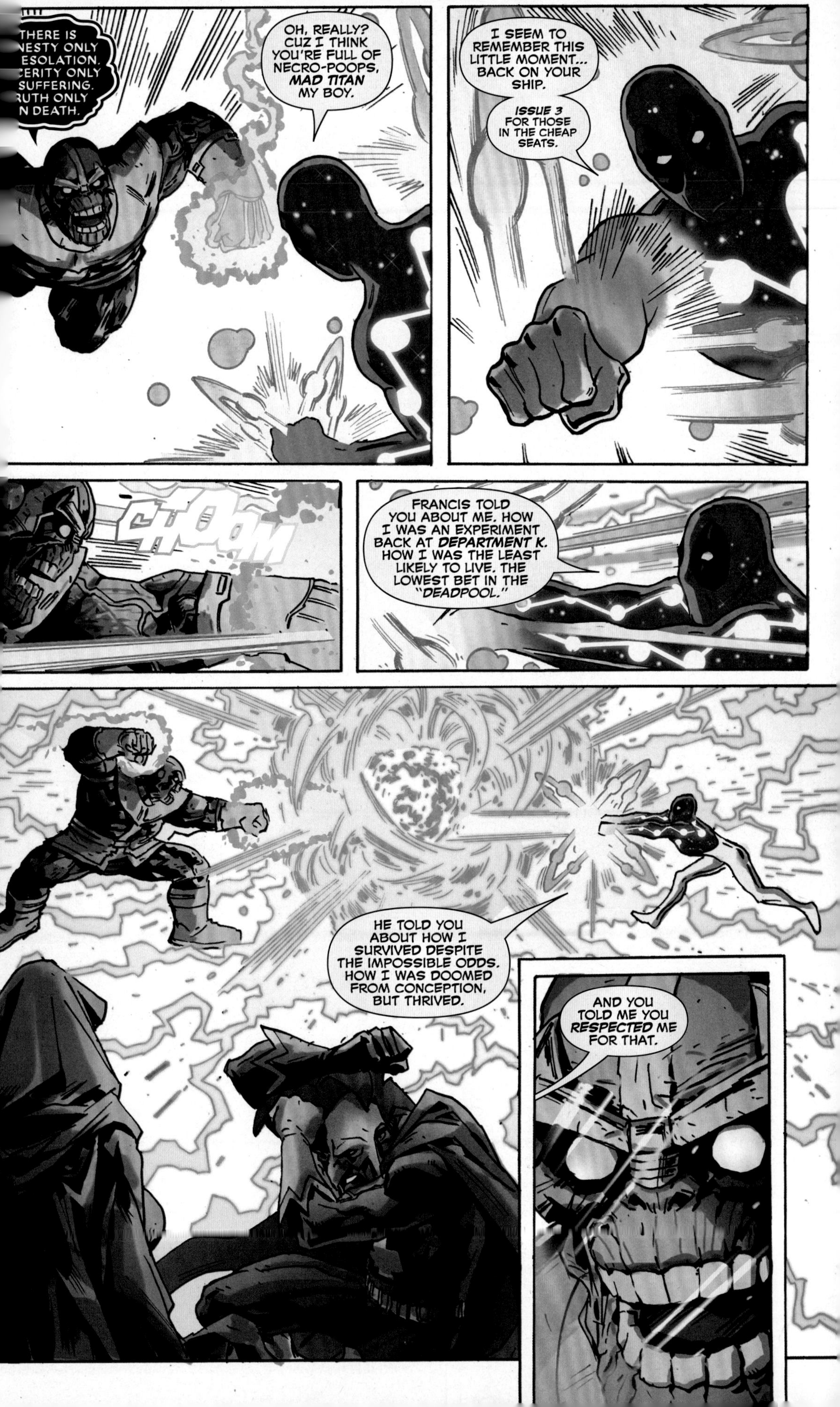

THERE IS NESTY ONLY ESOLATION. CERITY ONLY SUFFERING. RUTH ONLY N DEATH.
OH, REALLY? CUZ I THINK YOU'RE FULL OF NECRO-POOPS, *MAD TITAN* MY BOY.
I SEEM TO REMEMBER THIS LITTLE MOMENT... BACK ON YOUR SHIP.
ISSUE 3 FOR THOSE IN THE CHEAP SEATS.
CHOOM
FRANCIS TOLD YOU ABOUT ME. HOW I WAS AN EXPERIMENT BACK AT *DEPARTMENT K*. HOW I WAS THE LEAST LIKELY TO LIVE. THE LOWEST BET IN THE "*DEADPOOL*."
HE TOLD YOU ABOUT HOW I SURVIVED DESPITE THE IMPOSSIBLE ODDS. HOW I WAS DOOMED FROM CONCEPTION, BUT THRIVED.
AND YOU TOLD ME YOU *RESPECTED* ME FOR THAT.

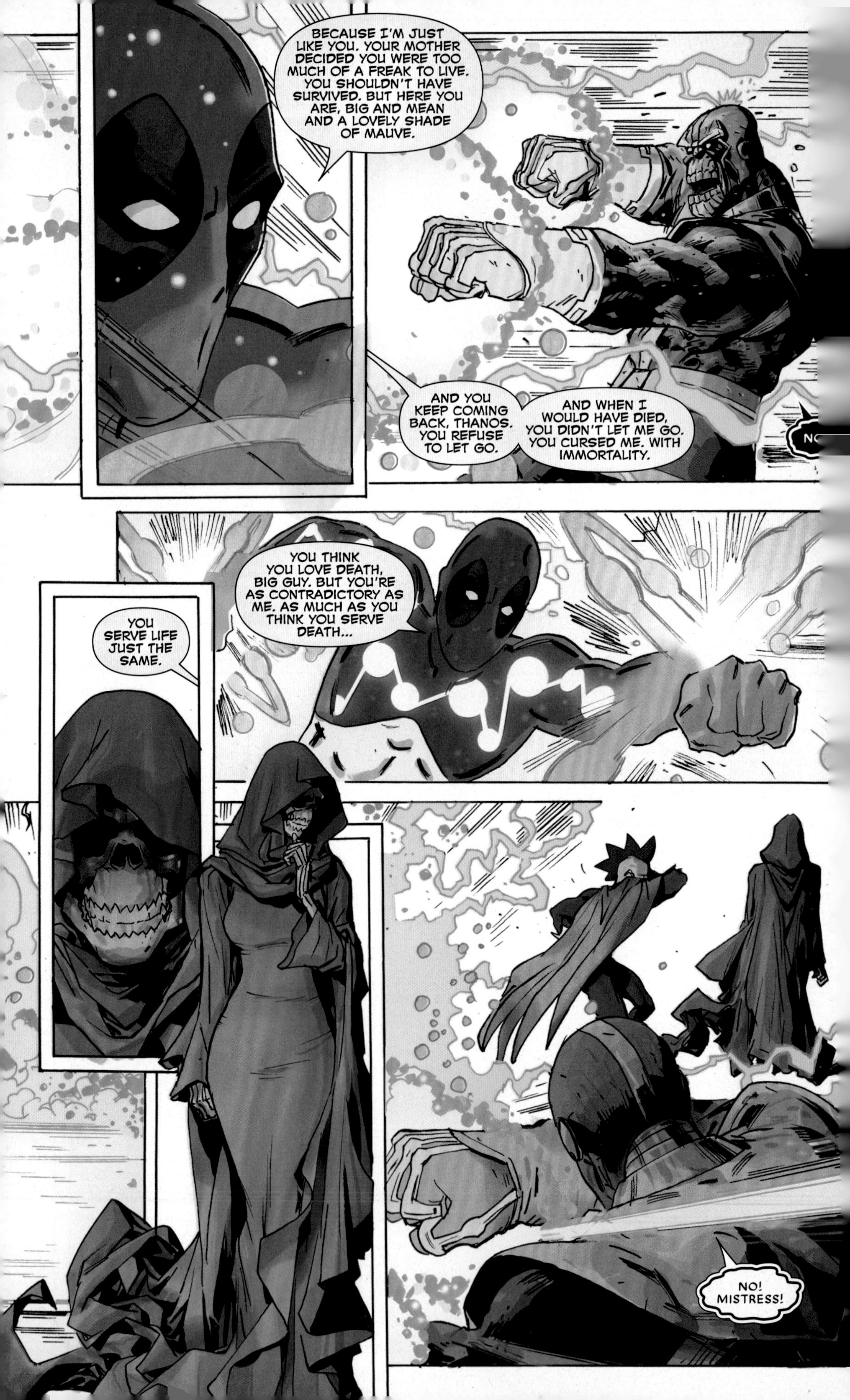
BECAUSE I'M JUST LIKE YOU. YOUR MOTHER DECIDED YOU WERE TOO MUCH OF A FREAK TO LIVE. YOU SHOULDN'T HAVE SURVIVED. BUT HERE YOU ARE, BIG AND MEAN AND A LOVELY SHADE OF MAUVE.
AND YOU KEEP COMING BACK, THANOS. YOU REFUSE TO LET GO.
AND WHEN I WOULD HAVE DIED, YOU DIDN'T LET ME GO. YOU CURSED ME. WITH IMMORTALITY.
YOU THINK YOU LOVE DEATH, BIG GUY. BUT YOU'RE AS CONTRADICTORY AS ME. AS MUCH AS YOU THINK YOU SERVE DEATH...
YOU SERVE LIFE JUST THE SAME.
NO! MISTRESS!

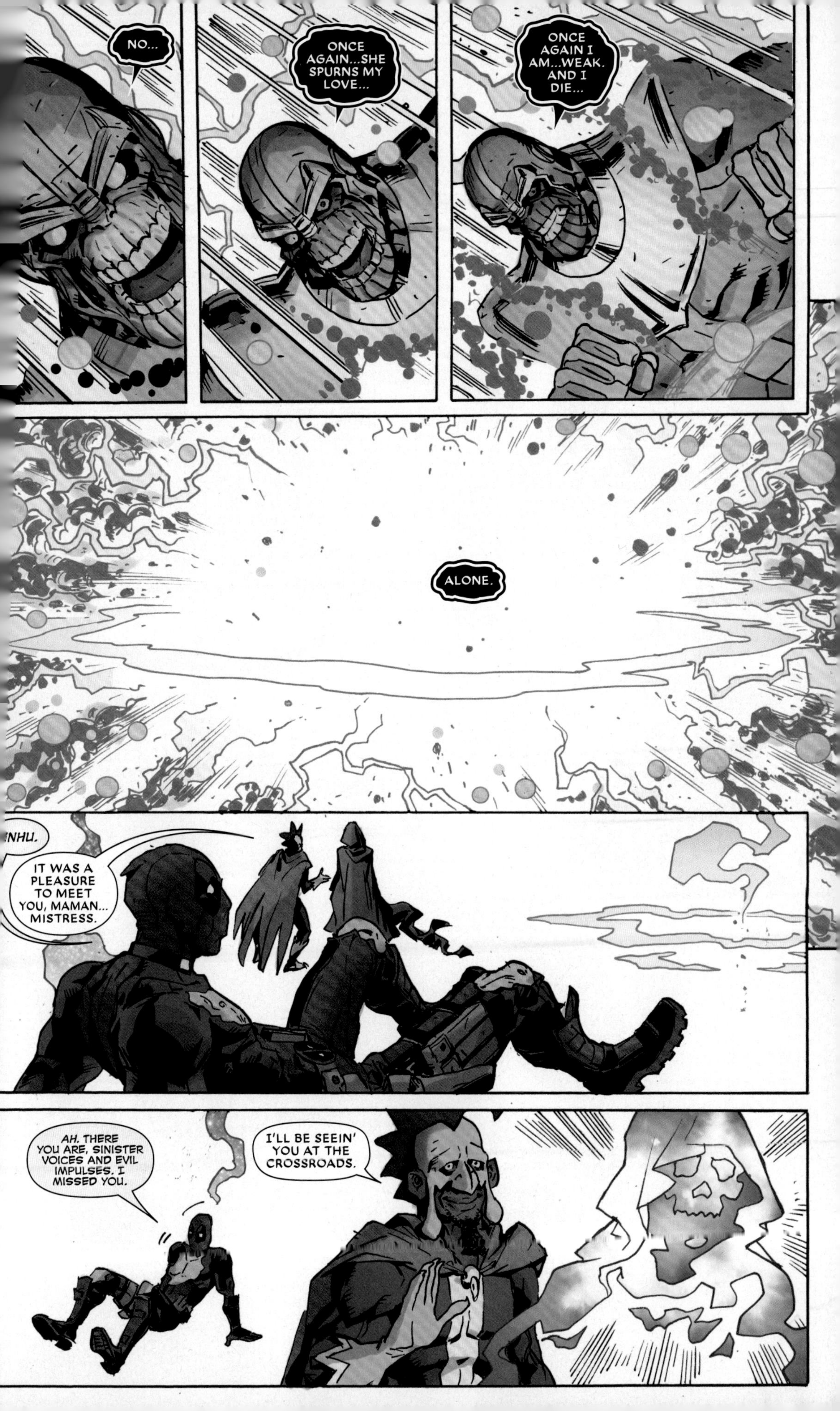
NO...
ONCE AGAIN...SHE SPURNS MY LOVE...
ONCE AGAIN I AM...WEAK. AND I DIE...
ALONE.
NHU.
IT WAS A PLEASURE TO MEET YOU, MAMAN... MISTRESS.
AH. THERE YOU ARE, SINISTER VOICES AND EVIL IMPULSES. I MISSED YOU.
I'LL BE SEEIN' YOU AT THE CROSSROADS.

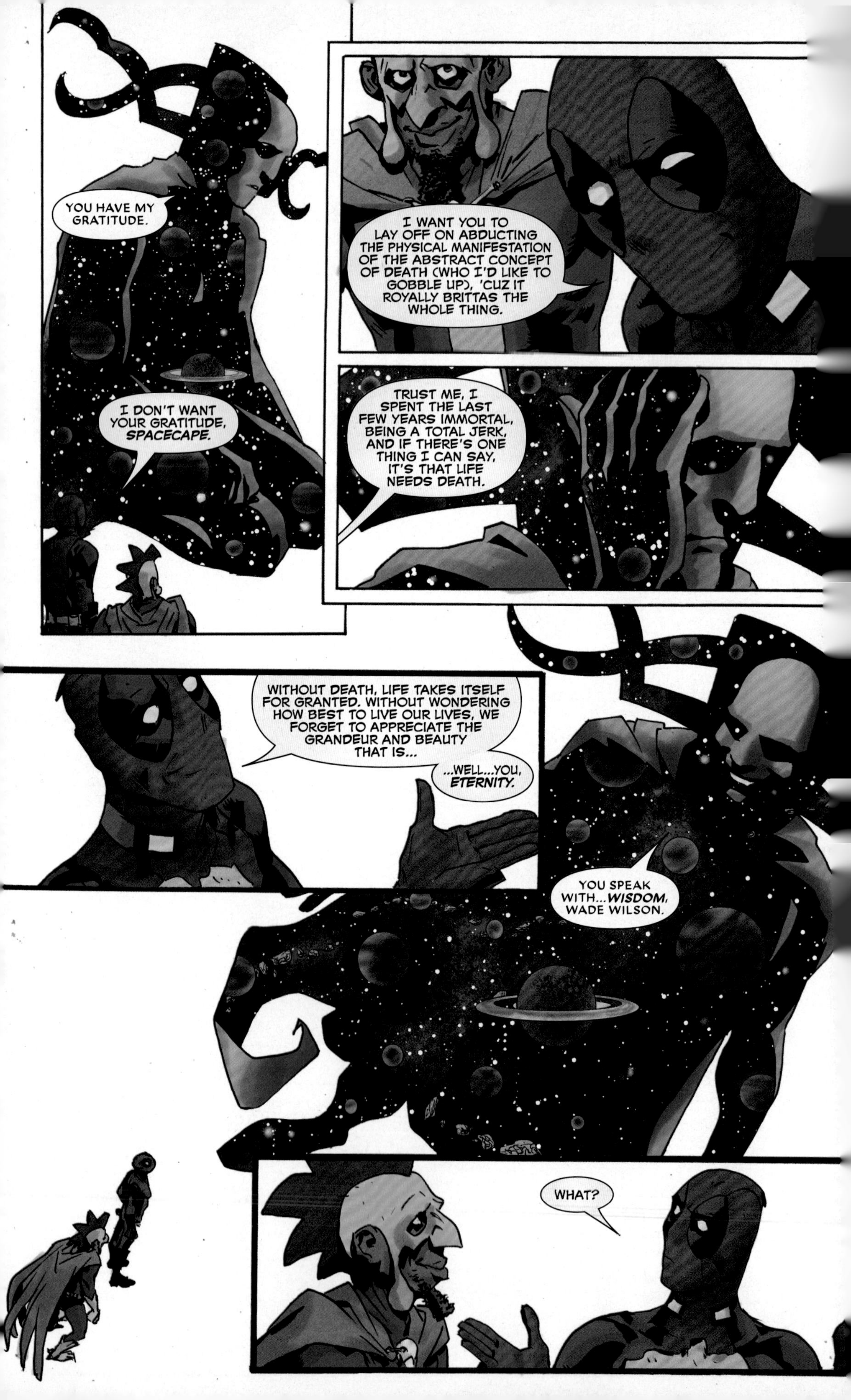
YOU HAVE MY GRATITUDE.
I WANT YOU TO LAY OFF ON ABDUCTING THE PHYSICAL MANIFESTATION OF THE ABSTRACT CONCEPT OF DEATH (WHO I'D LIKE TO GOBBLE UP), 'CUZ IT ROYALLY BRITTAS THE WHOLE THING.
I DON'T WANT YOUR GRATITUDE, *SPACECAPE.*
TRUST ME, I SPENT THE LAST FEW YEARS IMMORTAL, BEING A TOTAL JERK, AND IF THERE'S ONE THING I CAN SAY, IT'S THAT LIFE NEEDS DEATH.
WITHOUT DEATH, LIFE TAKES ITSELF FOR GRANTED. WITHOUT WONDERING HOW BEST TO LIVE OUR LIVES, WE FORGET TO APPRECIATE THE GRANDEUR AND BEAUTY THAT IS...
...WELL...YOU, *ETERNITY.*
YOU SPEAK WITH...*WISDOM,* WADE WILSON.
WHAT?

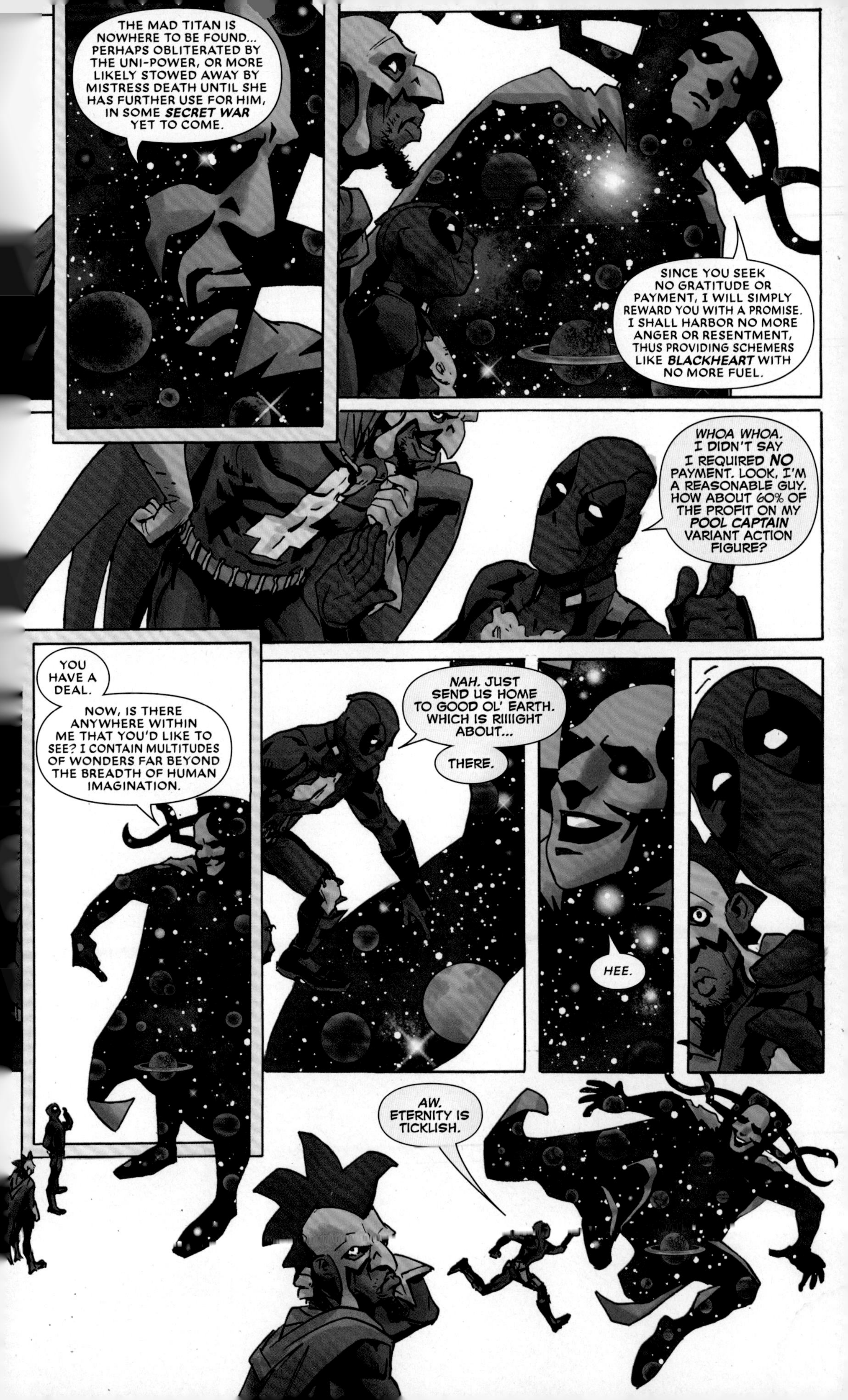
THE MAD TITAN IS NOWHERE TO BE FOUND... PERHAPS OBLITERATED BY THE UNI-POWER, OR MORE LIKELY STOWED AWAY BY MISTRESS DEATH UNTIL SHE HAS FURTHER USE FOR HIM, IN SOME SECRET WAR YET TO COME.
SINCE YOU SEEK NO GRATITUDE OR PAYMENT, I WILL SIMPLY REWARD YOU WITH A PROMISE. I SHALL HARBOR NO MORE ANGER OR RESENTMENT, THUS PROVIDING SCHEMERS LIKE BLACKHEART WITH NO MORE FUEL.
WHOA WHOA. I DIDN'T SAY I REQUIRED NO PAYMENT. LOOK, I'M A REASONABLE GUY. HOW ABOUT 60% OF THE PROFIT ON MY POOL CAPTAIN VARIANT ACTION FIGURE?
YOU HAVE A DEAL.
NOW, IS THERE ANYWHERE WITHIN ME THAT YOU'D LIKE TO SEE? I CONTAIN MULTITUDES OF WONDERS FAR BEYOND THE BREADTH OF HUMAN IMAGINATION.
NAH. JUST SEND US HOME TO GOOD OL' EARTH. WHICH IS RIIIIGHT ABOUT...
THERE.
HEE.
AW. ETERNITY IS TICKLISH.

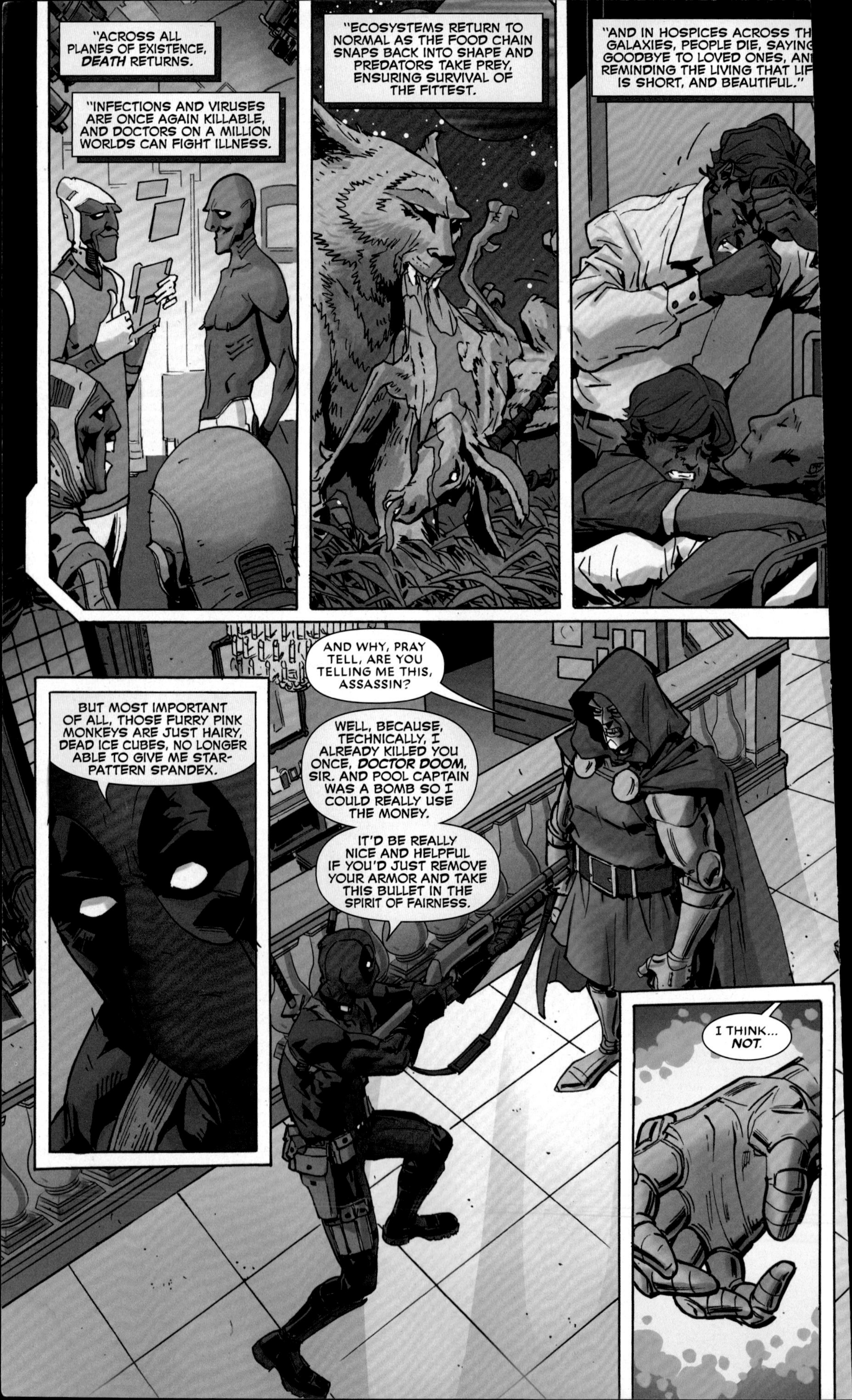
"ACROSS ALL PLANES OF EXISTENCE, DEATH RETURNS.
"INFECTIONS AND VIRUSES ARE ONCE AGAIN KILLABLE, AND DOCTORS ON A MILLION WORLDS CAN FIGHT ILLNESS.
"ECOSYSTEMS RETURN TO NORMAL AS THE FOOD CHAIN SNAPS BACK INTO SHAPE AND PREDATORS TAKE PREY, ENSURING SURVIVAL OF THE FITTEST.
"AND IN HOSPICES ACROSS TH GALAXIES, PEOPLE DIE, SAYING GOODBYE TO LOVED ONES, AN REMINDING THE LIVING THAT LIF IS SHORT, AND BEAUTIFUL."
BUT MOST IMPORTANT OF ALL, THOSE FURRY PINK MONKEYS ARE JUST HAIRY, DEAD ICE CUBES, NO LONGER ABLE TO GIVE ME STAR-PATTERN SPANDEX.
AND WHY, PRAY TELL, ARE YOU TELLING ME THIS, ASSASSIN?
WELL, BECAUSE, TECHNICALLY, I ALREADY KILLED YOU ONCE, DOCTOR DOOM, SIR. AND POOL CAPTAIN WAS A BOMB SO I COULD REALLY USE THE MONEY.
IT'D BE REALLY NICE AND HELPFUL IF YOU'D JUST REMOVE YOUR ARMOR AND TAKE THIS BULLET IN THE SPIRIT OF FAIRNESS.
I THINK... NOT.

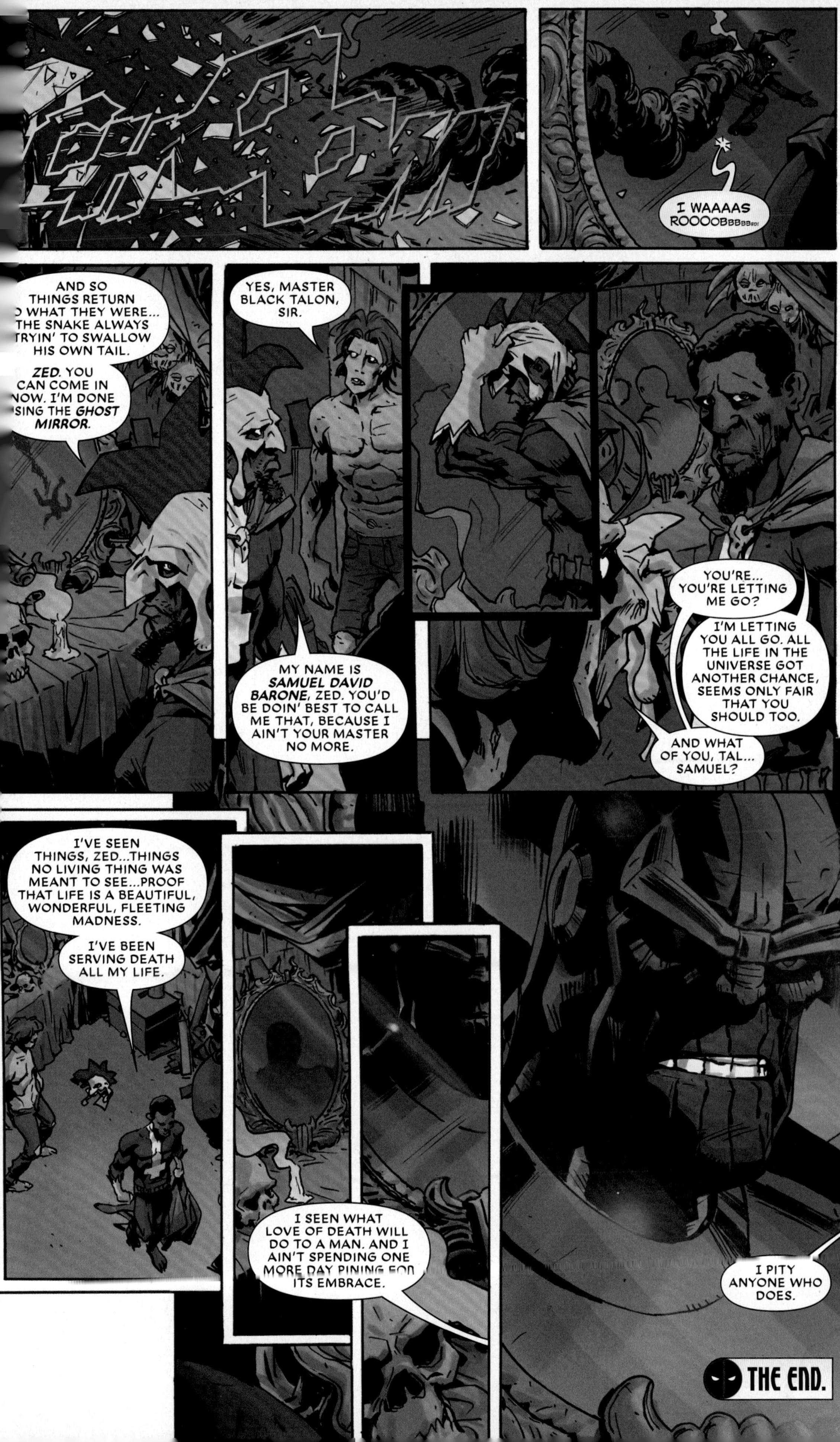
I WAAAAS ROOOOBBBBBED!
AND SO THINGS RETURN
O WHAT THEY WERE... THE SNAKE ALWAYS
TRYIN' TO SWALLOW HIS OWN TAIL.
ZED. YOU CAN COME IN
NOW. I'M DONE
SING THE GHOST MIRROR.
YES, MASTER BLACK TALON, SIR.
MY NAME IS SAMUEL DAVID BARONE, ZED. YOU'D BE DOIN' BEST TO CALL ME THAT, BECAUSE I AIN'T YOUR MASTER NO MORE.
YOU'RE... YOU'RE LETTING ME GO?
I'M LETTING YOU ALL GO. ALL THE LIFE IN THE UNIVERSE GOT ANOTHER CHANCE, SEEMS ONLY FAIR THAT YOU SHOULD TOO.
AND WHAT OF YOU, TAL... SAMUEL?
I'VE SEEN THINGS, ZED...THINGS NO LIVING THING WAS MEANT TO SEE...PROOF THAT LIFE IS A BEAUTIFUL, WONDERFUL, FLEETING MADNESS.
I'VE BEEN SERVING DEATH ALL MY LIFE.
I SEEN WHAT LOVE OF DEATH WILL DO TO A MAN. AND I AIN'T SPENDING ONE MORE DAY PINING FOR ITS EMBRACE.
I PITY ANYONE WHO DOES.
THE END.

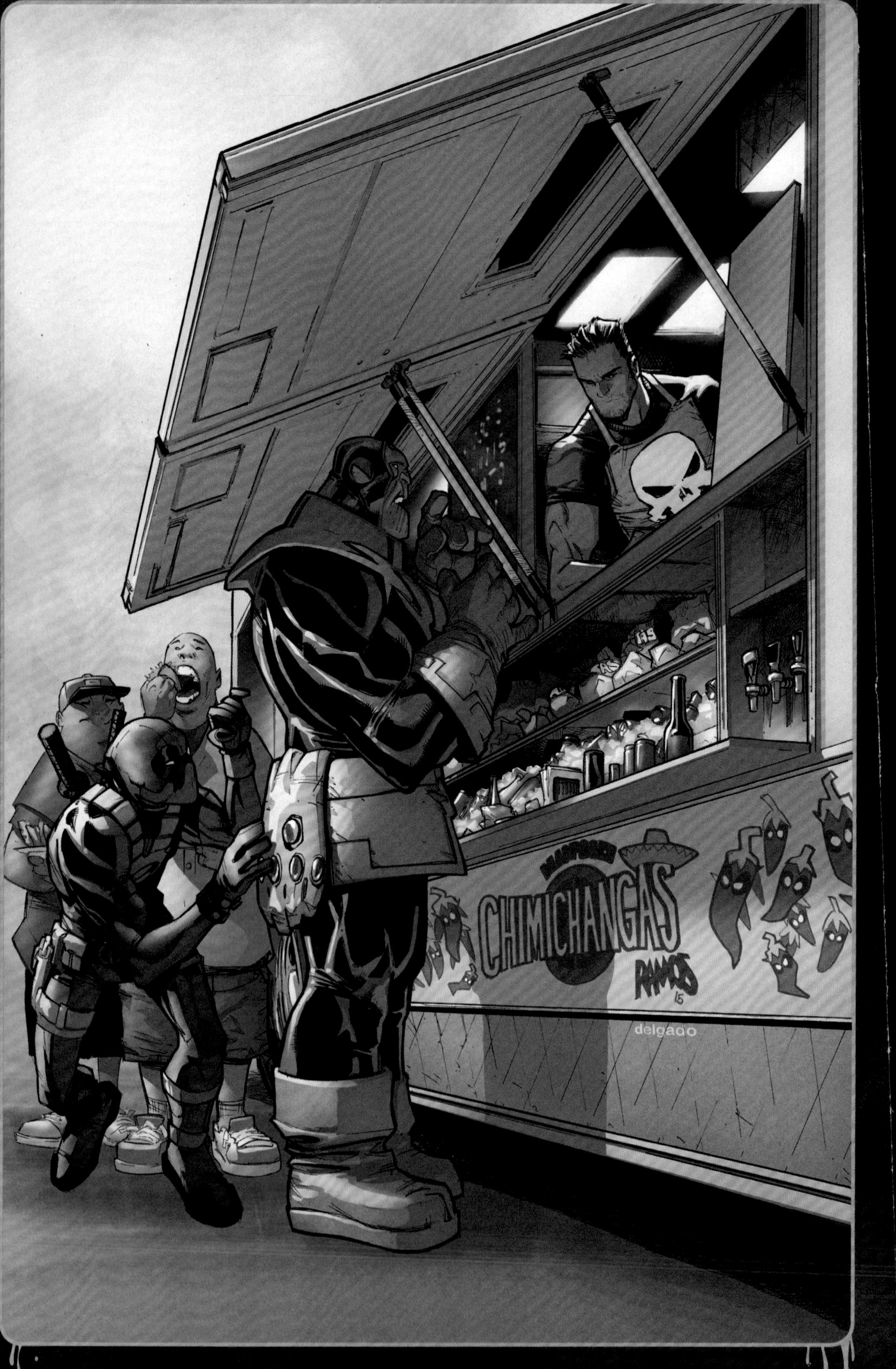
CHIMICHANGAS
RAMOS
15
delgado

#1 Variant by Humberto Ramos & Edgar Delgado

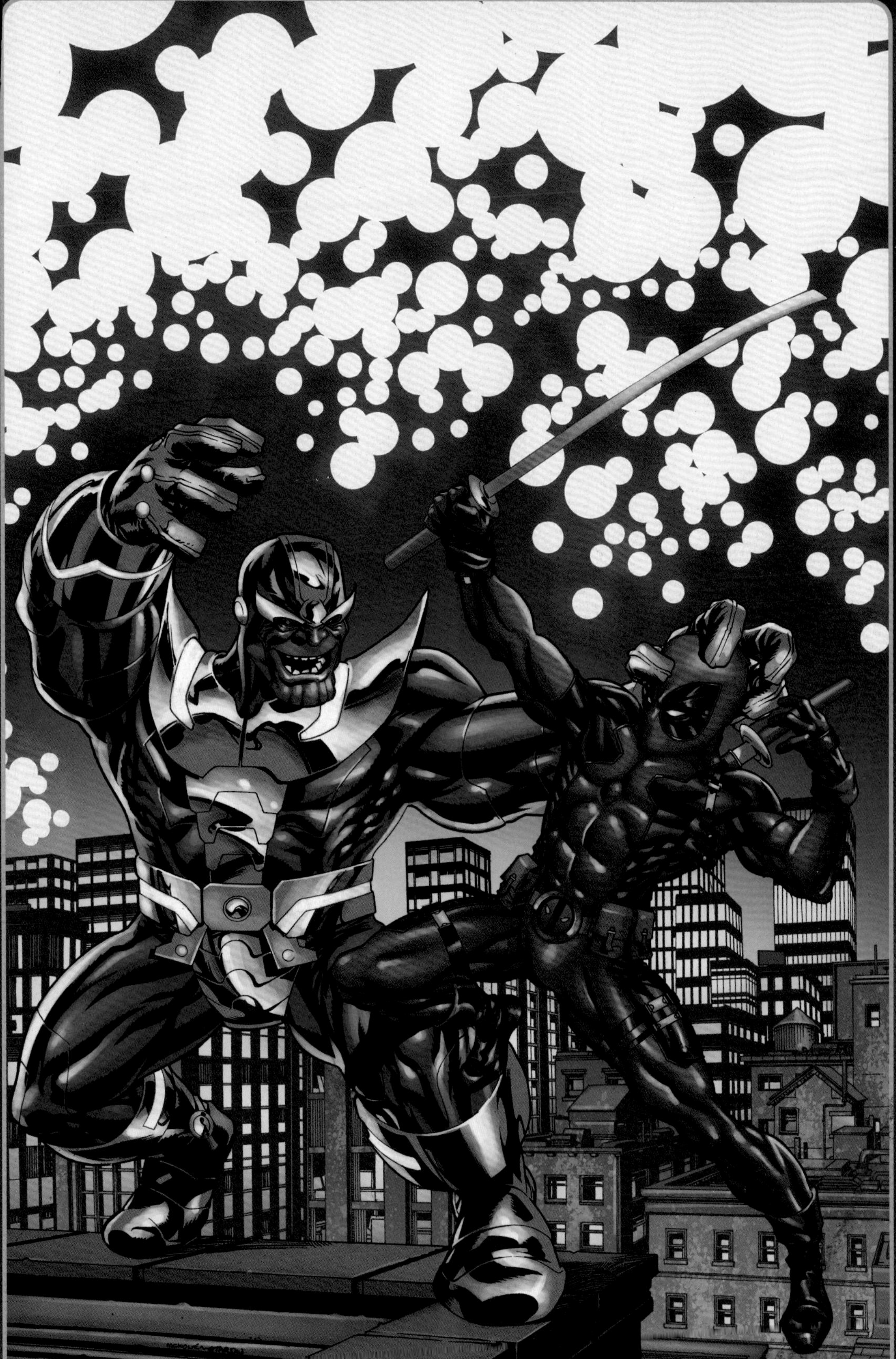

#1 Variant by Mike McKone & Chris Sotomayor

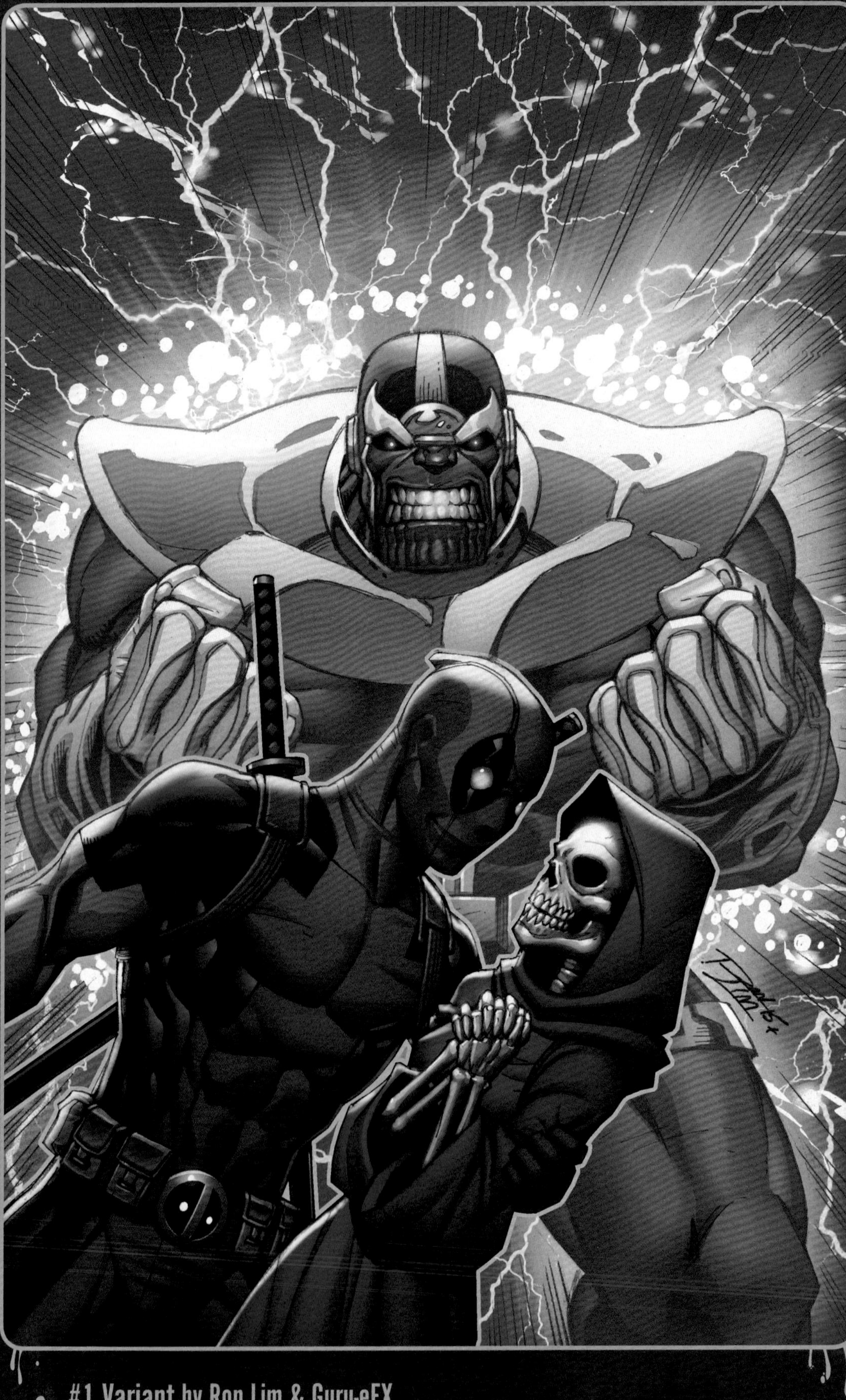

#1 Variant by Ron Lim & Guru-eFX

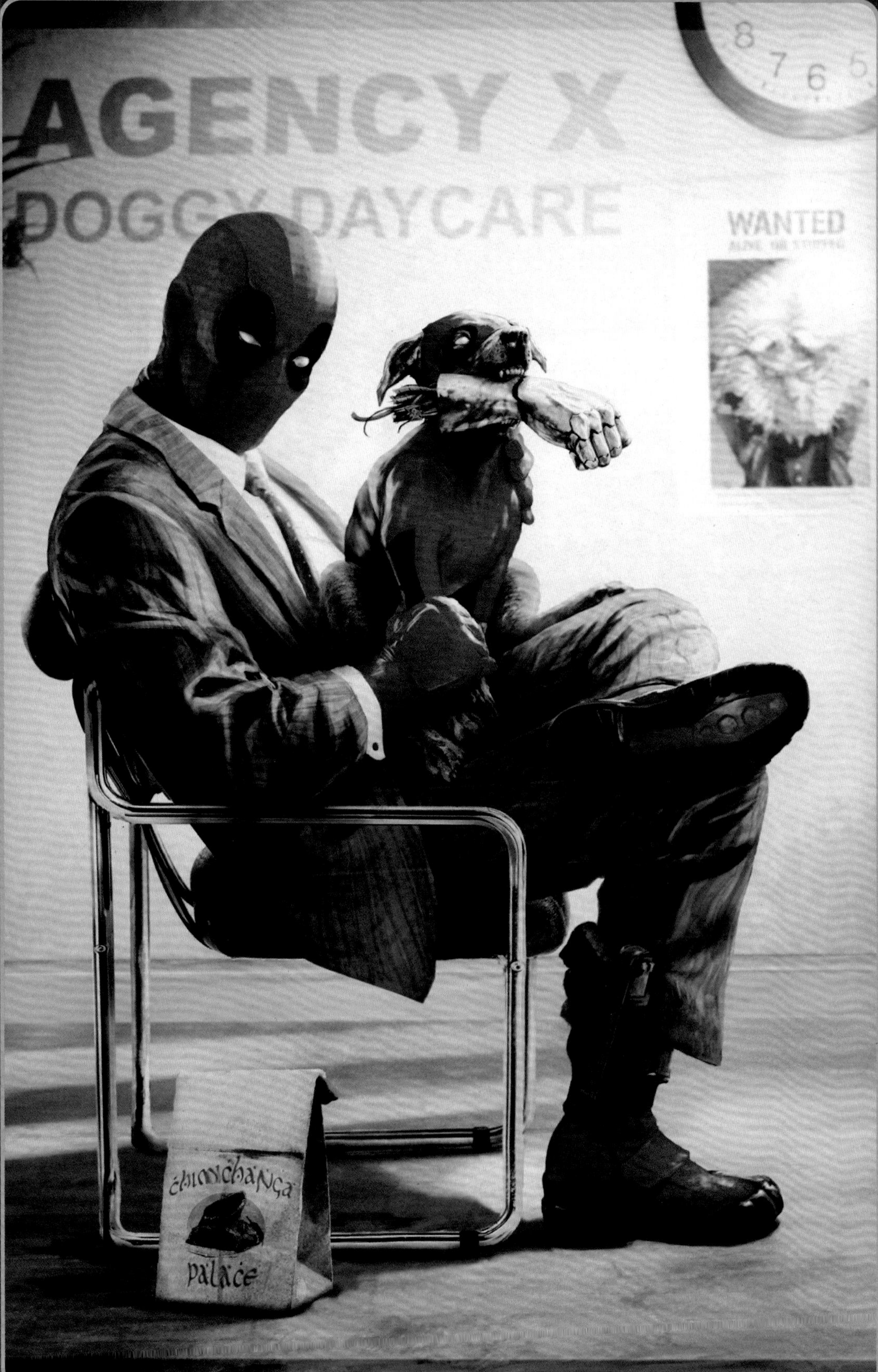
AGENCY X
DOGGY DAYCARE
WANTED
chimichanga
palace

#1 Variant by Aleksi Briclot

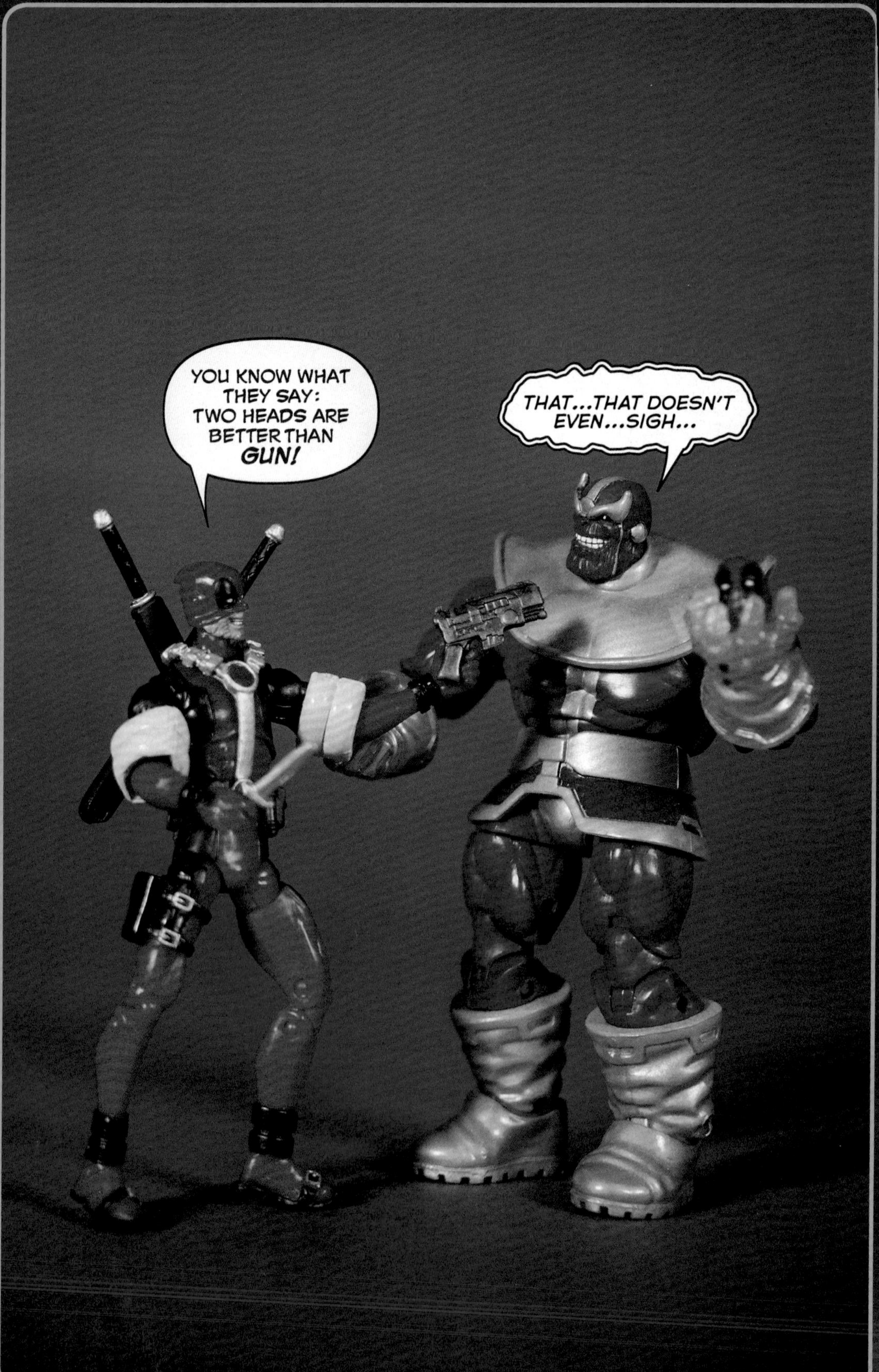
YOU KNOW WHAT THEY SAY: TWO HEADS ARE BETTER THAN GUN!
THAT...THAT DOESN'T EVEN...SIGH...

#1 Action Figure Variant

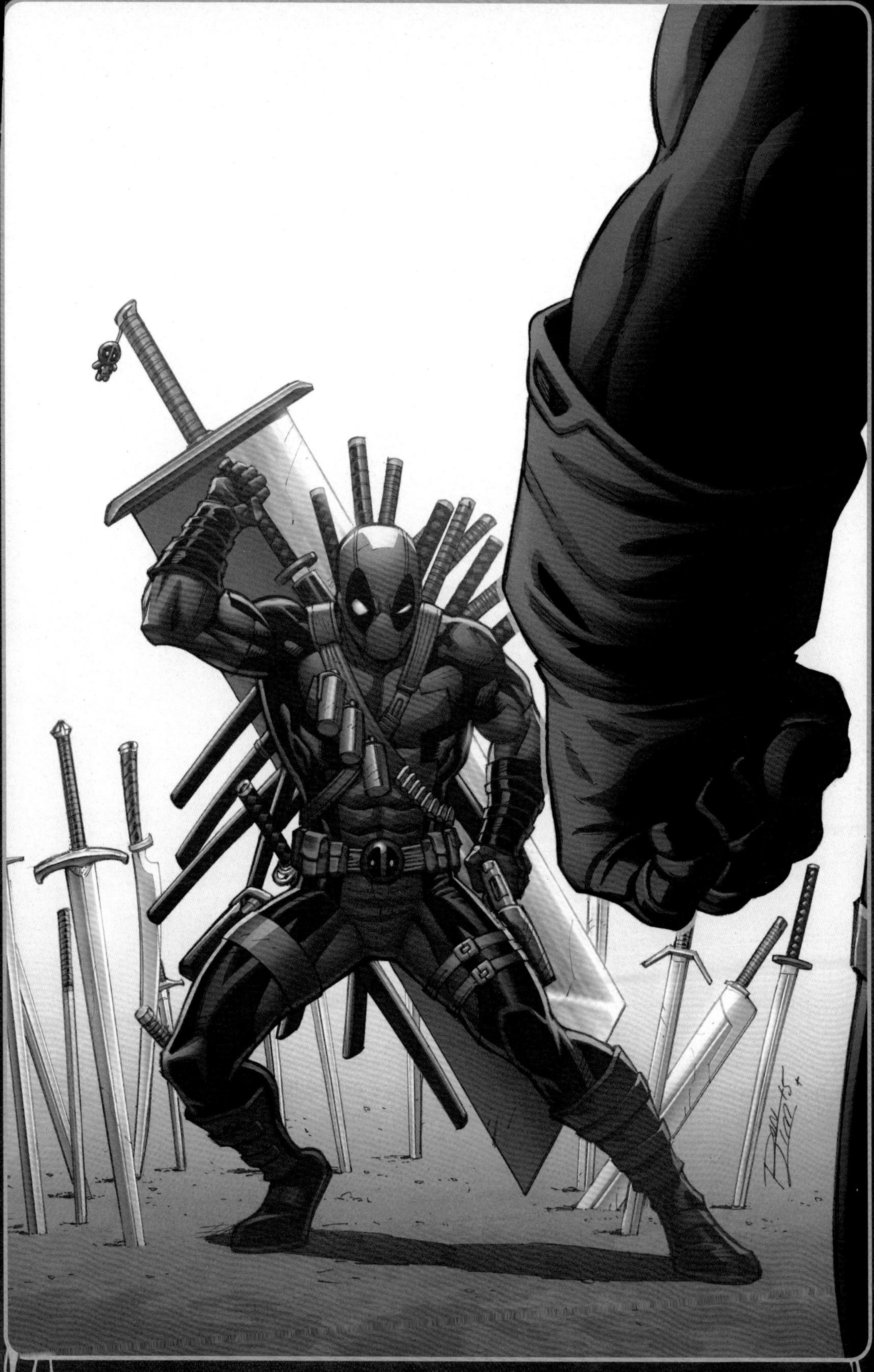

#2 Variant by Ron Lim & Guru-eFX

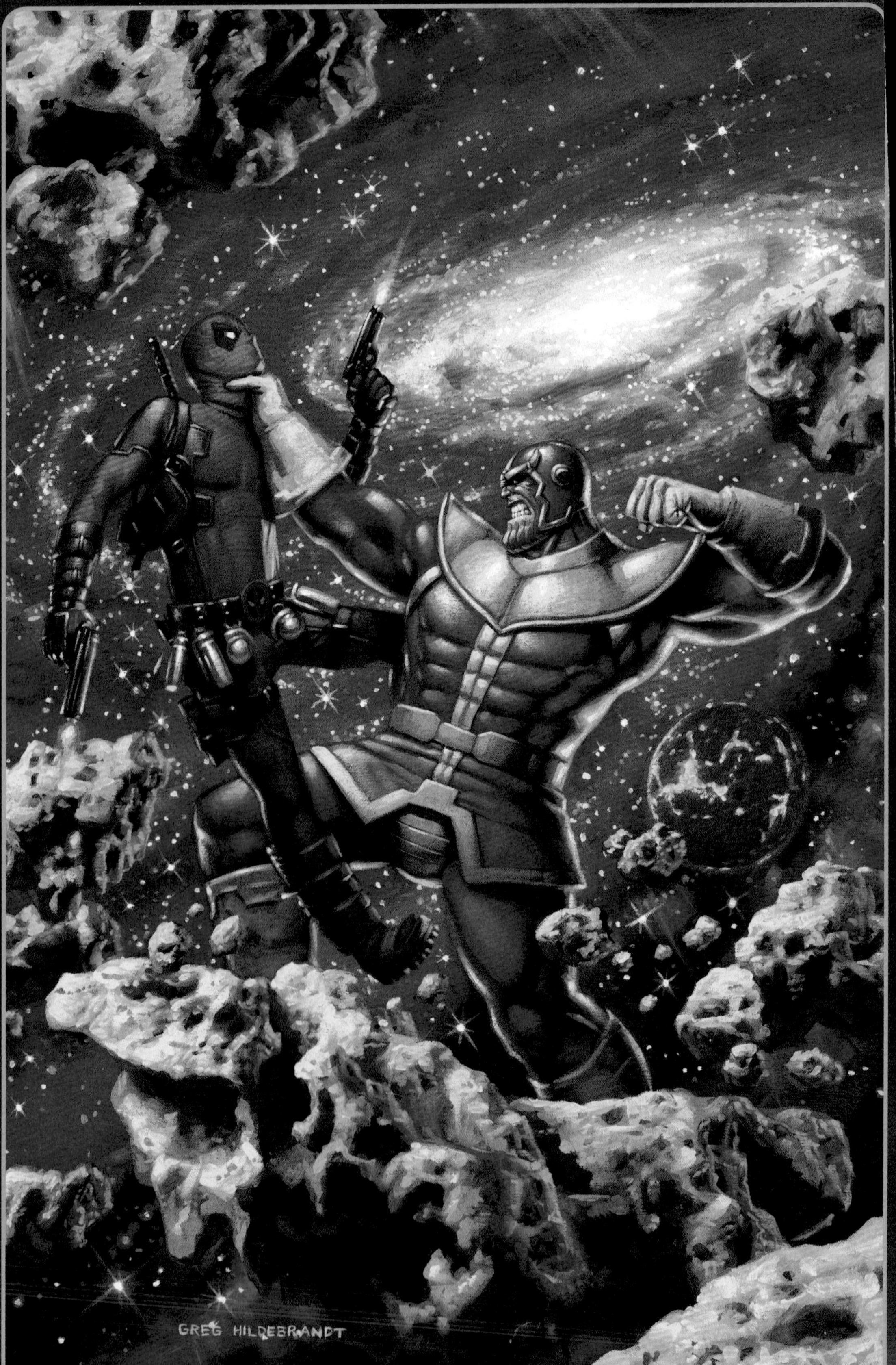
GREG HILDEBRANDT

#2 Variant by Greg Hildebrandt

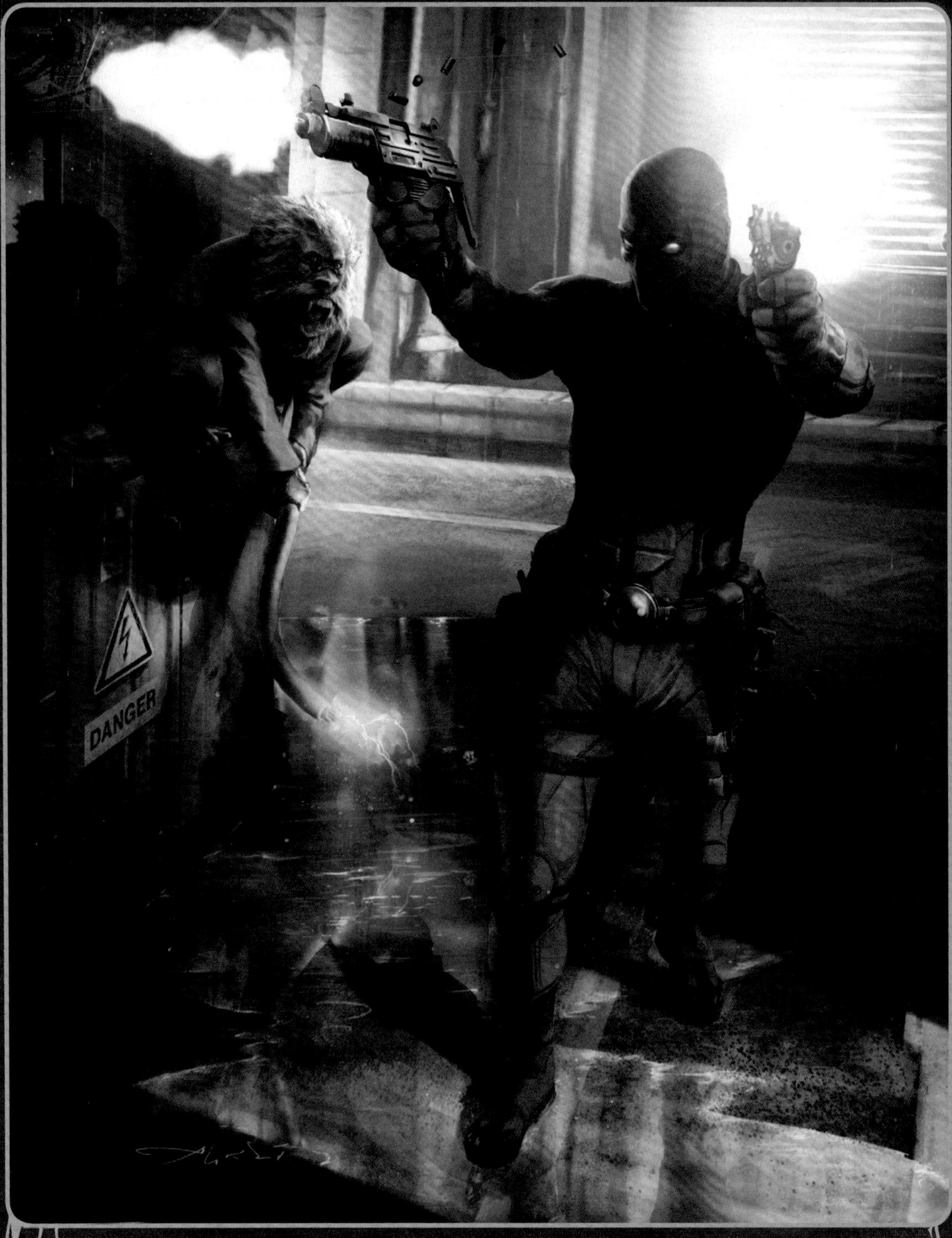
DANGER

#2 Variant by Aleksi Briclot

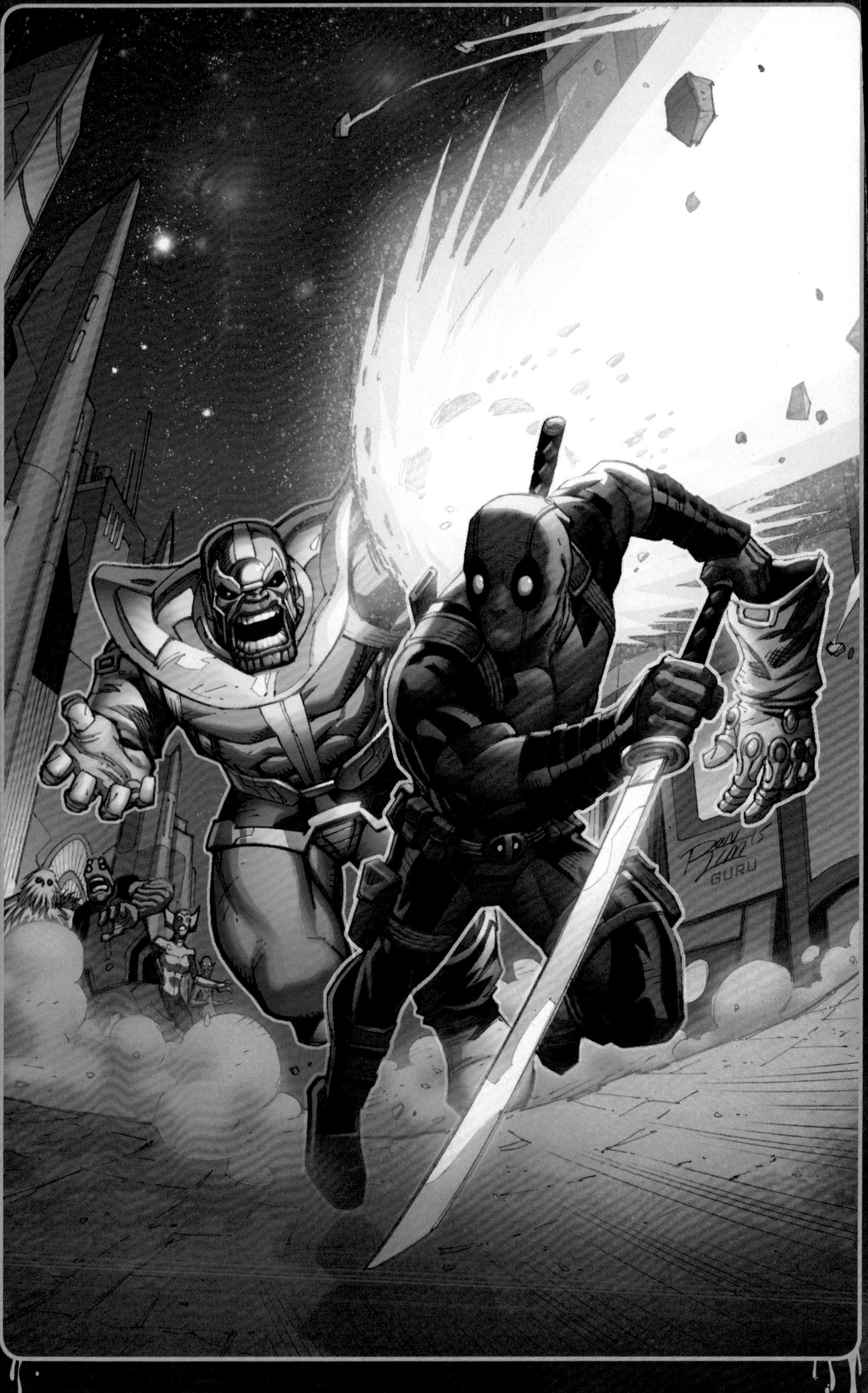
GURU

#3 Variant by Ron Lim & Guru-eFX

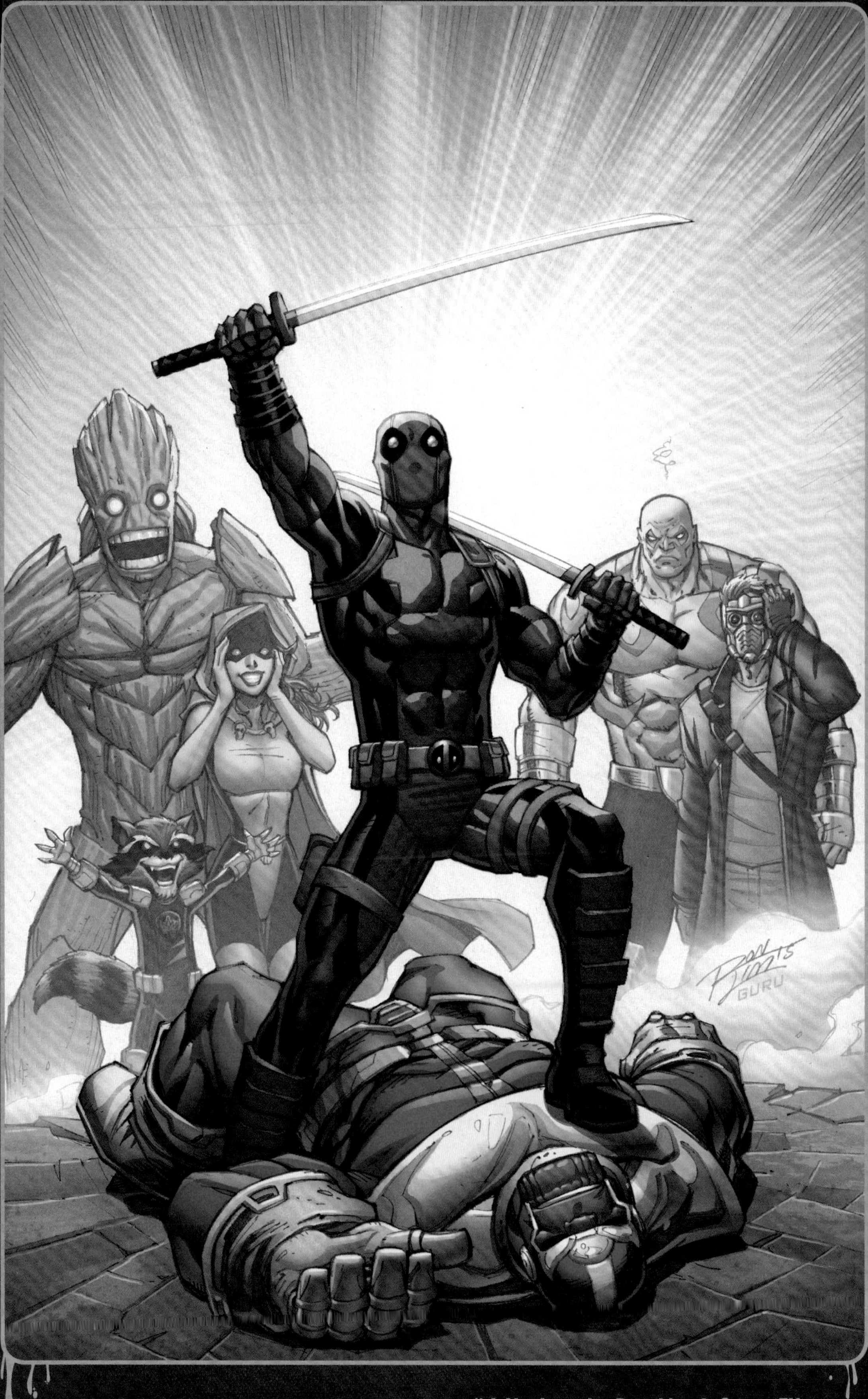

#4 Variant by Ron Lim & Guru-eFX

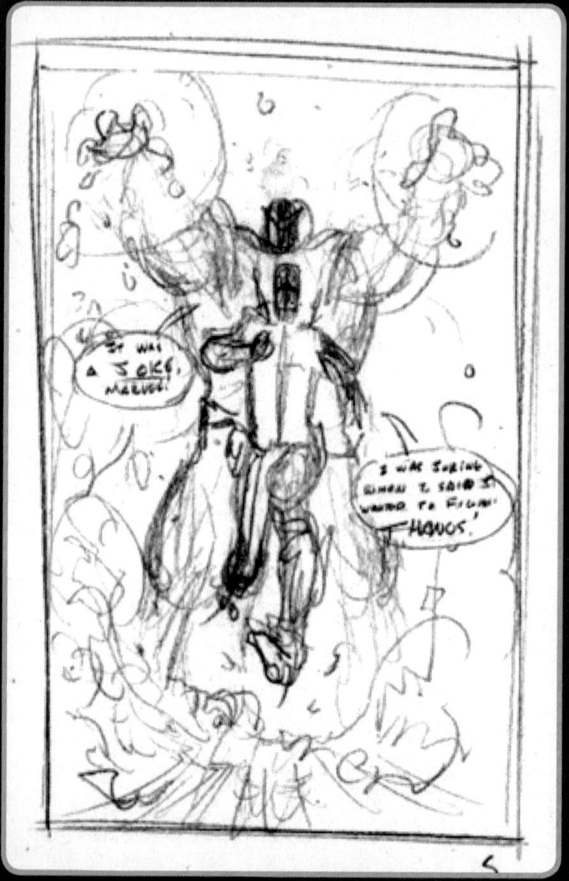

#1

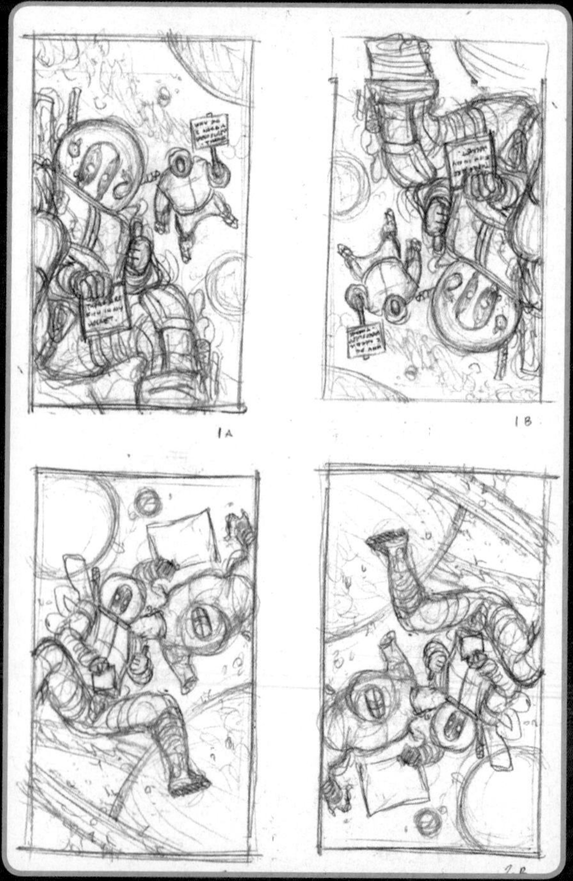

#2

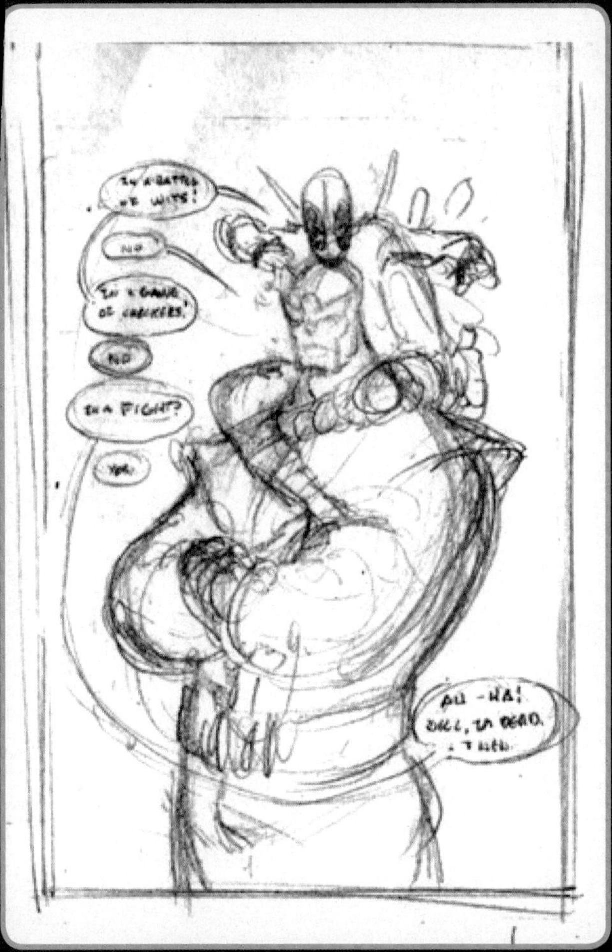
IN A FIGHT?

#3

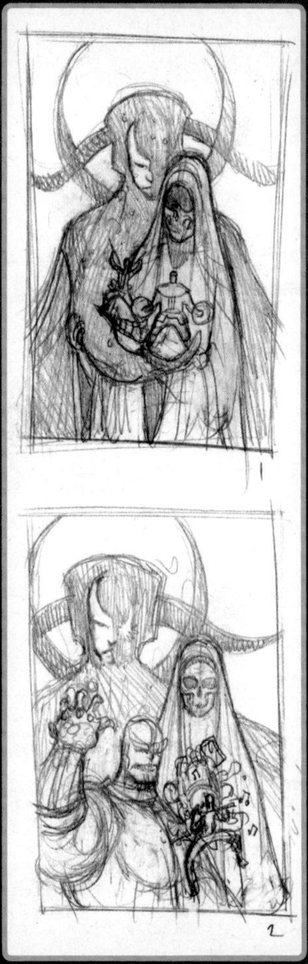

#4

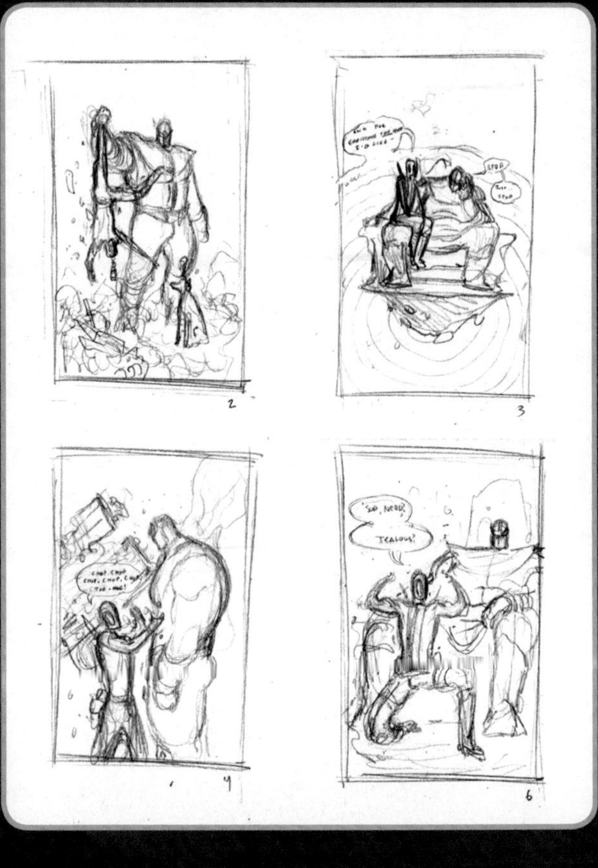

Unused Sketches

Variant Cover Sketches by RON LIM

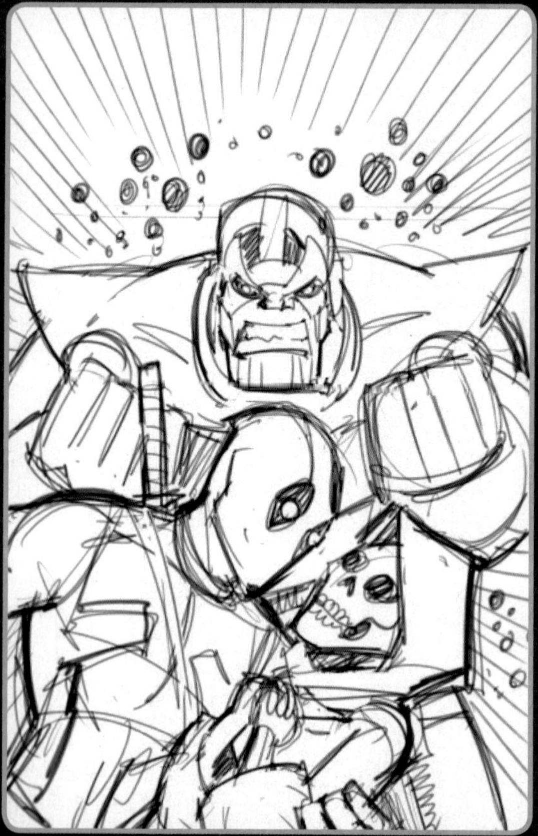

#1

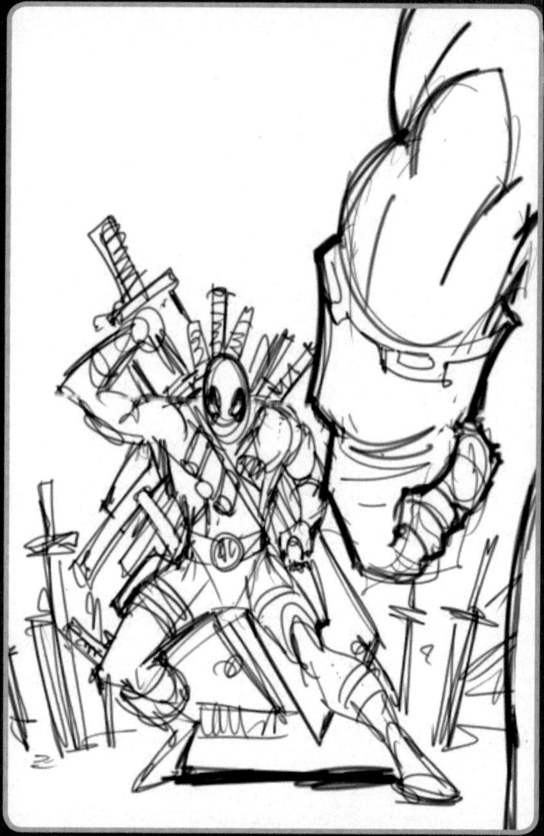

#2

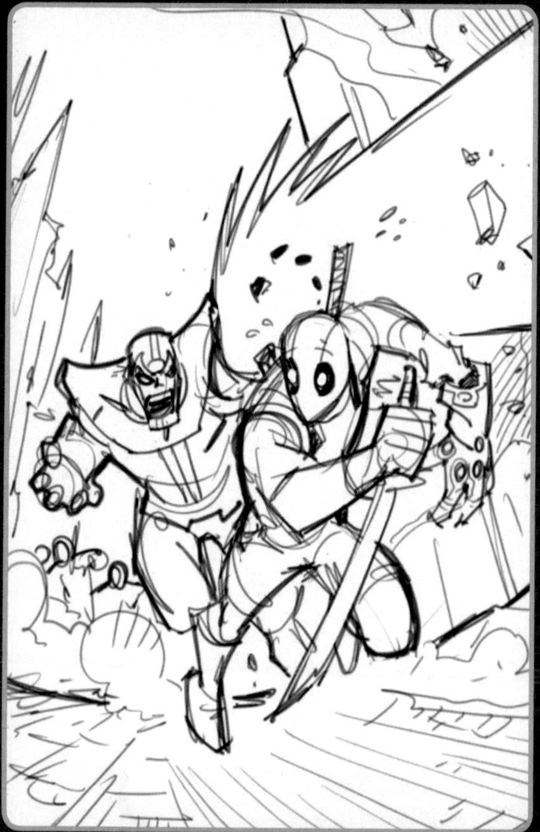

#3

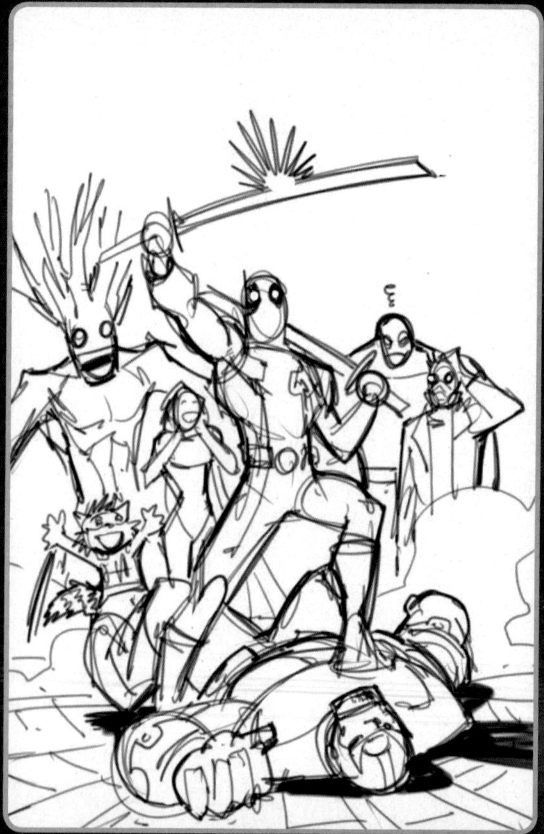

#4

Unused Variant Cover Sketches by RON LIM

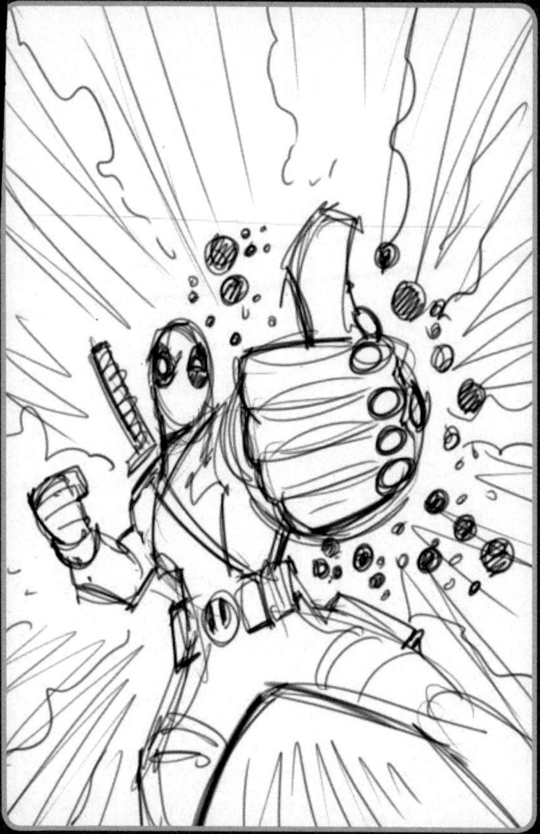

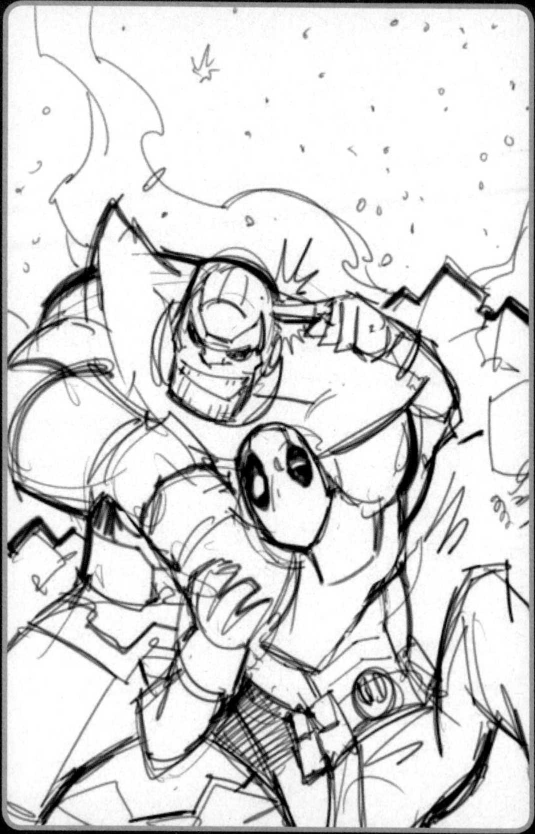

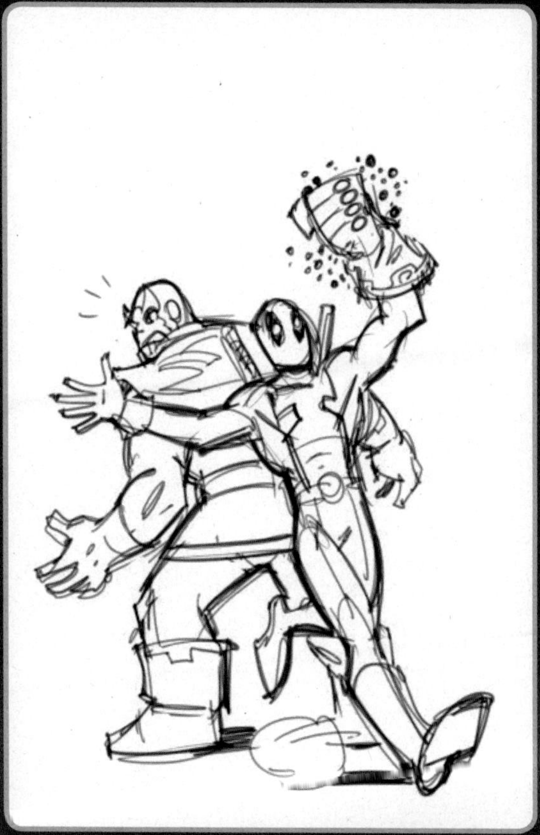

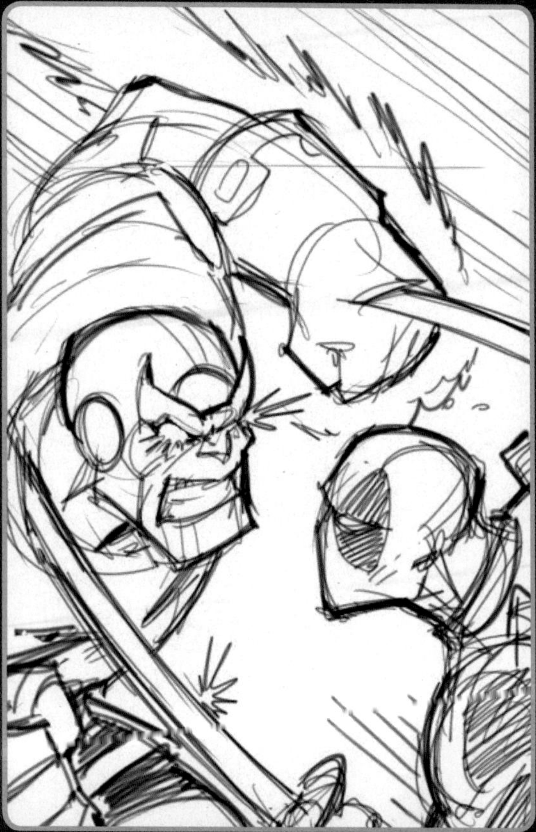

PAGE 1

We'll open with a series of shots that establish the tone...little vignettes. They can be the same size, making a 6-panel grid, to set up a rhythm that we'll then break with page 2.

Panel 1: We open on the Sanctuary II ship hanging in space.

> THANOS (from ship): You pathetic, feeble-minded fool.

Panel 2: Inside the ship we see a beautiful statue of "Mistress Death" in elegant marble, spattered with blood.

> THANOS (free floating): Why is it that your planet eternally begs for eradication?

Panel 3: Now, we focus on the powerful arms of Thanos, cut and bleeding, as he plucks a katana from the spot it was embedded in his tricep.

> THANOS (free floating): What is it about your entire species that believes it is so central to the workings of the universe that you need fear nothing?

Panel 4: Now we see Deadpool scooting along the floor of the ship. His legs are broken. His back is broken. His costume is torn. He looks rough. But he's still making jokes.

> THANOS (free floating): What makes you believe you can take it upon yourself... to challenge a god?
>
> DEADPOOL (small): Cojones, my chin-ribbed friend. Spanish for...wooden box I think?

Panel 5: We see Thanos' massive hand grip Deadpool's ankle/foot.

> THANOS (free floating): Once, I cast a spell of darkest necromancy and cursed you to undeath, Wade Wilson of Earth. I gave you eternal life.
>
> DEADPOOL (small): And here I thought it was a health benefit from a steady diet of quesaritos and ham water.

Panel 6: And we focus on Deadpool's face, eyes wide with "fear."

THANOS (free floating): But for your effrontery here today, in my very own Sanctuary...

DEADPOOL (small): "A-front-tree?" Thaney, honey, I'm more of a back-tree man.

PAGE 2

Panel 1: SPLASH!

Pull back. Setting...the interior throne room of Sanctuary II, a large window off in the background overlooking the universe.

The Mad Titan Thanos, full of seething hate and disgust, punches Deadpool's head and torso right into the ground, literally, with his glowing right fist. It looks like the kind of hit no one could survive, even our tumor-ridden merc. Energy radiates from the point of impact as does a lovely arc of blood and bits.

THANOS: I take back my gift.

SFX: THROOM!

PAGE 3

We want to drop the reader right into the middle of an existing action scene!

Panel 1: An establishing shot of a tropical island.

    CAPTION: Saint Cynthia Island.

    CAPTION: Privately owned.

    CAPTION: Yesterday.

    BUSBOY (free floating): Yes, everything is ready for our most esteemed guest.

Panel 2: We see a "bus boy" standing outside a particularly fancy cabin. He looks sort of like an "igor" type...a hand-wringing, slovenly, butt-kissing sycophant to all bad guys. He's talking to someone else via a communications device. Near him is a bushy, leafy tropical tree.

    BUSBOY: Of all of his holdings, Saint Cynthia is his favorite, second only to our beloved homeland.

    BUSBOY: Indeed. He shall have a full view of the pool, the volleyball courts, and the live torture chambers.

Panel 3: Close in on the busboy a bit as we see a pair of arms coming down from the canopy. Red suited arms with gloves holding a garrote.

    BUSBOY: We live to serve the will of our Lord of Latveria, Victor Von Doo–

Panel 4: Suddenly the garrote loops around the busboy's throat lifting him off the ground as he chokes.

    BUSBOY: Oogk!

Panel 5: The evil busboy jerks a couple of times as he chokes.

    BUSBOY: ughk.

    DEADPOOL (from canopy): Aw yeah!

Panel 6: Deadpool jumps to the ground near the body, smiling excitedly through his mask. He's got a shotgun and a sword at his back.

> DEADPOOL: Aw yeah! Got him right in the middle of exposition. Figure out the plot now, Wednesday Warriors!

PAGE 4

Panel 1: And now we cut to a hotel room. We focus in on the chest area of Dr. Doom. We don't see his face yet, just the familiar gauntlets, and gold cape clasps as Dr. Doom undoes the clasps...

> NO DIALOGUE

Panel 2: And pulls off the gauntlets...

> NO DIALOGUE

Panel 3: And pulls off the boots.

> NO DIALOGUE

Panel 4: We see Dr. Doom, wearing his helmet and an extravagant green silk robe, from behind on the resort below. His cape and armor are on the bed next to him. He's smelling a beautiful flower, pulled from a vase on the nightstand.

> DR. DOOM: I named this island for you, dear mother. Beautiful, singular and resilient, just as you once were.

Panel 5: Small shot. Doom looks back at the sound of a knock on his door.

SFX: NOK NOK

DOOM: Who dares?

DEADPOOL (from off panel): Just your friendly welcoming committee, sir!

PAGE 5

Panel 1: Doom goes to open the door.

DR. DOOM: What do you want?

DEADPOOL (from off panel): I've got a complimentary shot to celebrate your arrival, sir!

Panel 2: And suddenly he gets blown away by a huge gun blast!! WOAH!!

SFX: KACHOOM!

DOOM: Agh!

Panel 3: BIG SHOT. And we see Deadpool walking in with a smoking shotgun. Doom lies dead on the ground.

DEADPOOL: Complimentary shot. I hope you like 'buck.'

PAGE 6

Panel 1: Deadpool nonchalantly gets his phone out of his pocket. He's singing. The dead body of Doom is behind him. Very clearly dead.

DEADPOOL: "Workin' nine to five..."

DEADPOOL: Hello? Is this Tony Stark's office?

Panel 2: Deadpool on the phone. He's sort of entertaining himself as he talks, looking through the snacks in the refrigerator.

DEADPOOL: I missed him? Is he out being Iron Man? Is Thor there maybe? No? Well, you sound nice.

Panel 3: Same basic shot. Now he's checking out the television listings.

DEADPOOL: Oh, well, nothing too important. I just wanted to tell Tone (he lets me call him that) that I totally did what he and his unusually handsome god friend could never do.

Panel 4: Same basic shot. DP scratches his ass. Still oblivious to dead Doom...who begins to stir behind him.

DEADPOOL: See, I took some of SHIELD's dirty Fury money, infiltrated a top-secret private island, fought off a whole skein of doombots...

DEADPOOL: And then totally killed the hell out of Doctor Doom.

Panel 5: Same basic shot, as Deadpool walks into the bathroom. Doom is standing, almost zombie-like.

DEADPOOL: No no...DOOM. Like the movie starring the Rock. D. O. O– yeah, that guy.

Panel 6: Deadpool is in the bathroom, as Doom puts on one of his gauntlets.

DEADPOOL: Yeah, just tell Tony I did his job, and if he wants to take me for drinks he can pick me up in the Bugatti.

PAGE 7

Panel 1: Deadpool comes out of the bathroom...totally Pulp Fiction "Vincent Vega and Butch style," to see Doom standing there, glowing gauntlet out, pointed at DP.

DEADPOOL: And you know what, tell him he should bring you along too. Wear something in animal print. Zebra–Oh.

DEADPOOL: Whyfore aren't thou dead, Doomeo?

Panel 2: On Doom. He looks confused, and surely not dead.

DOOM: I—I felt pain. Such pain. And then darkness. There was a light. I was in my childhood home. I saw my mother. And then—

DOOM: I was back. Alive. A small mercy, perhaps?

Panel 3: And he unleashes a blast from his gauntlet, which strikes Deadpool.

DOOM: Nonetheless, a mercy I shall not share with you.

SFX: SHRAKOOM!

Panel 4: Deadpool sails through the air, right out of the hotel. His body is smoking, like a comet across the sky.

DEADPOOL: At least I get to see my baeeeee—

Panel 5: And lands in the ocean.

SFX: SPLSH!

Panel 6: And we close in on Deadpool's face. He's underwater...blood coming from his mouth, yelling up a storm, bubbles coming from his mouth.

DEADPOOL (underwater): Pllbbt plrrb pbrnn!

Panel 7: Same shot. But as he dies, the bubbles are disappearing.

DEADPOOL: Plbt.

DEADPOOL: plp.